MARKET GUIDE
for
YOUNG
WRITERS

ABOUT THE AUTHOR

Kathy Henderson, originally from Detroit, divides her time between writing, speaking, and helping on the family's dairy farm near the tip of the "thumb" of Michigan. Her interest in helping young writers began in 1984 when her daughter's eleven-year-old Oklahoma pen pal wanted advice on marketing the two hundred short stories and three science fiction novels he had already written. In addition to the *Market Guide for Young Writers*, first published in 1986, Mrs. Henderson has written a dozen other books for young people. She is an active member of several national writer's organizations, and enjoys the many visits she makes to schools, libraries and conferences around the country.

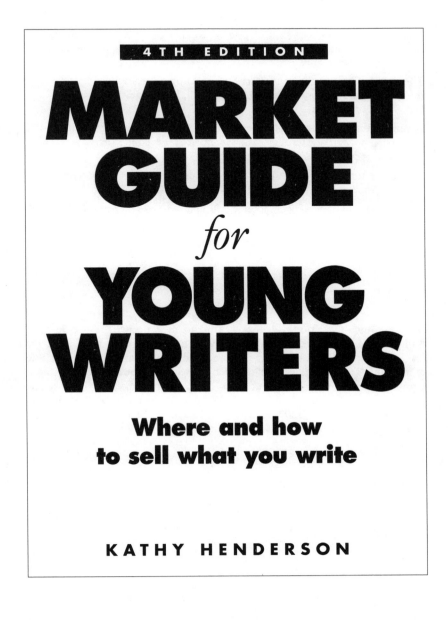

4TH EDITION

MARKET GUIDE
for
YOUNG WRITERS

Where and how to sell what you write

KATHY HENDERSON

WRITER'S DIGEST BOOKS
Cincinnati, Ohio

The poem, *Unwritten*, appearing on page 52 is copyright © 1990 by Amity Gaige, from the published book, *We Are a Thunderstorm*. Reprinted by permission of Landmark Editions, Inc.

The sample film and audio/video scripts appearing on pages 56 and 57 are reprinted by permission of Richard L. Rockwell, WOAK Station Manager, Royal Oak Schools (Missouri).

Excerpts from "The Nagua Hunters" on pages 47 and 49 are reprinted by permission of Matthew Cheney. The story first appeared in *Merlyn's Pen: The National Magazine of Student Writing*.

The illustration appearing on page 118 was prepared by Linda Montgomery for "Gulububble," a short story written by Natalka Roshak.

The illustrations appearing on pages 1, 102 and 166 were prepared by Jennifer Bolten.

Photos of Beth Lewis (page 124) and Jill Bond (page 146) are copyright © Glamour Shots.

97 96 95 94   5 4 3 2

Library of Congress Cataloging in Publication Data

Henderson, Kathy
  Market guide for young writers / by Kathy Henderson. — 4th ed.
        p.   cm.
  Includes index.
  ISBN 0-89879-606-7 (pbk.)
    1. Children as authors. 2. Authorship—Handbooks, manuals, etc.
  3. Authorship—Competitions. [1. Authorship—Handbooks, manuals, etc.
  2. Authorship—Competitions.] I. Title.
PN171.C5H4   1993
808.06'8'0835—dc20   93-28818
                                                              CIP

Edited by Jack Heffron
Designed by Sandy Conopeotis

To Carol Fenner for her help in

finding hidden treasure

and

in memory of

Hilda Stahl

ACKNOWLEDGMENTS

I would like to express my appreciation to author Stephen King for generously allowing me to reprint a short story written in his youth; to Amity Gaige for her inspiration; to David Melton and Nan Thatch for their dedication to young writers and artists; to Kent Brown for his vote of confidence; to Liz Levindowski and Kate Leach for the extra efforts they made; to Dick Rockwell for sharing his Focal Point Tools and scriptwriting assistance; to Sandy Asher for sharing her playwriting expertise; to Emilio the bartender, who keeps me informed, and his good friend Jack Smith, head SYSOP of GEnie's Writers.Ink RoundTable; to CompuServe's Student Forum Associate SYSOP Tom Pinkerton for inviting me behind the boards; to my husband for his willingness to cook meals and tend chores while I struggled to meet deadlines; to Cindy Marks for her clerical help; to my editor Jack Heffron for his patience, prodding and editorial skill; and to the many editors, contest sponsors, teachers, young people and fellow writers who have contributed information and ideas for this edition.

With special thanks to:

Tim and Ryan Jessop	Arun Toké
Vicki May Larkin	Carole Trapani
Kate Hackett	Margaret Larkin
Duncan MacKay	Jill Bond
Natalka Roshak	Maxine Pinson
Matthew Cheney	Vaughn Larson
Beth Lewis	Jim Stahl
Amy Wu	Lucy LaGrassa
Tanya Beaty	Jeff Church

TABLE OF CONTENTS

PART ONE

Chapter One
THE STARTING GATE 2

Chapter Two
THE BASICS OF GETTING PUBLISHED 18

PART TWO

Chapter Six
YOUNG WRITERS IN PRINT..103

Chapter Seven
EDITORS ARE REAL PEOPLE, TOO..133

PART THREE

Chapter Eight
THE MARKET LIST

Chapter Nine
CONTEST LIST

FROM THE AUTHOR

Dear Reader,

Have you ever watched racehorses as they're standing in the starting gate? They're full of energy, chomping at the bit, ready to burst out full speed the moment the gate swings open.

They remind me of the eager young writers I meet through the letters they write or at the schools I visit. They, like you I imagine, are full of energy and excitement, eager to burst out onto the track that leads to publishing success. If you rush out unprepared, however, the race to the finish line could be a sad, disappointing one.

This book was written as a training guide to help prepare you for the publishing tracks that excite you. Even if you are familiar with past editions, please take the time to read through this edition before racing to the sections where markets and contests are listed. While the basic advice remains the same, a lot of new information has been added, information many of you have asked for. Plus, a whole new batch of successful young writers and dedicated editors and contest sponsors share their experiences and advice.

Don't miss the special material from two of today's hottest authors — Stephen King and Michael Crichton.

Happy Writing!
Kathy Henderson

FOREWORD

Once when I was in the fourth grade, our class was getting ready for Thanksgiving. I'm sure we heard stories about the Pilgrims and the Wampanoag Indians who befriended them. I can't really remember. In fact, even when I search my memory, I can't remember the name of a single classmate. I can only remember one thing about the entire fourth grade.

That one thing is a picture I drew of a turkey. The teacher hung it up high over the chalkboard. In front of the whole class she said, "Look how good Kent's turkey is."

I felt very proud at the time. Somehow that sense of accomplishment has stayed with me for almost forty years. The good feeling I had in being recognized for my creative work has been a lasting influence on me, and on my career.

I think there must be no better feeling than one that comes from the sense of creating something yourself. It may be a picture of a turkey, a rabbit made from clay, or a story or poem.

Writing gives me great joy. I believe it is so with you also.

Over the years I've had the fun of seeing poems and stories from thousands of young people. Some of these stories interested me as a reader more than others. A few we picked to publish in *Highlights*. I always remember one thing when I read these—the writer's sense of accomplishment; the pleasure he or she gained through the experience of writing.

Writing is more than just putting one word down after another. You cannot write without thinking. Good, clear writing is a sign of good, clear thought.

Writing helps you think. It helps you reflect on ideas and explore your thoughts. You can first try your ideas and words out on yourself. Then you can share them with others.

This book is about sharing your ideas and thoughts. It's about a good way to share a little bit of yourself with others. Your audience may at first be friends and family. After a while, you may want a larger audience for that bit of yourself.

The author of this book has been writing for a long time. She came to want a larger audience early on in her writing. She had felt the satisfaction and joy of writing, and she felt a strong wish to share with others.

We can imagine that Kathy Henderson found a number of ways to share her work.

Remembering the joy of sharing—as well as the difficulty of finding out how to share—prompted Kathy to write this book.

This edition is the result of a desire to refine and improve the information given in earlier volumes. By helping countless young writers, Kathy has given back some of the joy writing has given her.

In this book you will meet a number of young writers. Notice how much they are like you. You will meet here, too, a number of editors. Notice they seem like people you could sit down and talk with.

There is sound advice in this book—lots of tips on getting started, helpful pointers about the writing process, and a host of ways to give yourself encouragement. Rejection, a part of every writer's life, is explored in a sensible way.

The up-to-date listing of where to send your writing is the best I've seen, by far. It gives you a broad choice of publications and a wide number of contests. The publications and contests listed here will allow you to find your audience. They allow you to share your thoughts and talents.

This is a book to be used. On its pages lie the hard-won wisdom of an author who has learned how to share the joy of writing with others.

Kathy Henderson is offering young writers like you valuable knowledge about writing. By using the information in this book you can increase that sense of personal accomplishment gained through writing.

Kent Brown, Editor
Highlights for Children

PART ONE

Chapter One

The Starting Gate

Each month the work of dozens of young writers appears in publications all across the country. To do what these young people have done, you don't need to be at the top of your class in reading or writing, or to be labeled "gifted" or "talented." You don't need to know "somebody in the business," have lots of money or years of experience. You don't need to live in an unusual place or lead an unusual life. And you don't need any fancy equipment. As many young writers have proven already, you don't even need to wait until you are older to try.

There are only two things you do need to know beforehand: *who* publishes the type of material you like to write, and *how* to prepare your finished story, poem, article, play or script before mailing it to an editor or contest. *Market Guide for Young Writers* has that special information plus a lot more to help you become a *published* young writer.

In this chapter you'll find advice for using this book to locate potential markets and contests for your work. You'll also find important information about the types of publishers and contests you should avoid. Chapter 2 explains the basics of getting published, and directions for formatting and mailing manuscripts are in Chapter 3. If you have prior marketing experience, these chapters will refresh your memory. "The Market List" (Chapter 8) and "The Contest List" (Chapter 9) will bring you up to date on who is publishing what.

WHAT'S NEW IN THIS EDITION
I encourage all readers, including those familiar with past editions, to take the time to read all of this edition. Besides the revised and

> **Author's Tip:**
> ....
> If you are serious about writing and plan to make it a career, I recommend that you read *The Young Person's Guide to Becoming a Writer*, by Janet E. Grant. This practical book will help you develop your talent, explore your options, find help, and chart a course for success.

updated lists of markets and contests, and profiles featuring a new group of young writers, editors and contest sponsors, this edition contains new and expanded information in many other areas. More important, from your standpoint, I've added a lot more about what it means to be a writer, why it's important to work to continually improve your writing skills, and how to research, study and evaluate opportunities. In particular look for:

- More detailed formatting directions (plus examples) for plays and scripts
- Special advice from author/playwright Sandy Asher
- Examples of properly formatted poems
- Information about query and cover letters
- A completely revised chapter focusing on electronic "online" communications to better reflect this growing field; you'll even get to eavesdrop on an online conference with author Michael Crichton
- More answers to the questions young writers ask most
- More detailed information on how to study markets and their guidelines
- Advice about markets and contests to avoid
- Expanded information and coverage of local and regional opportunities
- 98 new market and contest listings; 115 special starred opportunities for young writers; 156 total listings
- A special reprint of a young Stephen King short story
- Special *Author's tips*, like the one on this page, that will alert you to recommended resources, additional information, warnings and reminders

The market and contest lists in this book are the result of a special survey of editors and contest sponsors across the United States and Canada. Their enthusiastic responses helped me group together a promising list of publications and contests that are especially receptive to submissions from young writers. Many of the magazines have specific sections or whole issues written entirely by young people. Others, such as those whose readers are mainly adults, make a special effort to encourage young writers and are willing to consider their work, especially essays, opinions, profiles and personal experience pieces. Contests may be specifically for young writers or they may have separate categories for them. A few markets and contests have no preferences or restrictions regarding age at all; however, they recognize that some young writers are producing work as good as or better than many of the submissions they receive from adults. Remember, however, that only those markets and contests responding to my survey and agreeing to be listed are included. The main criteria is that they will seriously consider submissions made by young writers for awards and/or publication.

Why are so many editors interested in hearing from you? The answer is simple: Many of them were once young writers too! One editor wrote, "Your guide is a great idea. I only wish it had been available eight or ten years ago for me."

MORE ABOUT THE LISTINGS

Many of these markets not only publish material from young writers, but offer payment as well. Others offer free copies of issues containing your work instead of payment. Sometimes they offer both. As you search through the listings, pay special attention to entries marked with a star, or asterisk (*). Markets and contests bearing this symbol represent especially good opportunities for young people. They are the ones that have special issues, columns or departments featuring work from young writers and, therefore, are likely to accept more material from them than will other markets. If you are a very young writer (12 and under) or are especially anxious to get published, these are the opportunities to stick with.

Writers 13 and up, especially those with little writing or marketing experience, should also concentrate on starred markets and contests. Consider other listings only after carefully studying the requirements and objectively evaluating the quality and maturity of your own manuscript. Don't make the mistake of thinking these opportunities aren't challenging. Many are among the most highly respected in their fields. However, your work has the best chance of fitting in here. Submitting to other markets and contests now would be like trying to stuff Cinderella's stepsister's big foot into her tiny glass slipper. Highly unlikely!

A new sign, the double cross (‡) indicates markets and contests that should only be considered by more mature young writers (14 and up) or very determined and experienced younger ones. Watch also for a special "Author's note" that appears at the bottom of some of these opportunities. They are often highly specialized and sophisticated. Getting a manuscript accepted here can be difficult even for adult writers. Still, the editors and sponsors of these markets and contests have said they are willing to consider manuscripts by young writers. Consider your work carefully before trying these markets. Submitting material that has little chance of being accepted is a waste of time and energy for both you and the publication.

A few starred listings will also have the double cross symbol. This means that even though they offer young writers some special opportunities, competition is exceptionally tough. Sometimes this is due to the high number of submissions a market receives compared to the space it has reserved to print them. An editor who receives one thousand submissions every month but only has space to print ten during an entire year will have to reject most of them. Thus, often well-written and correctly submitted manuscripts get rejected.

A checkmark (✔) indicates that a listing is new to this edition. It may not be a new publication or contest in the sense that it has recently been established.

DOLLARS AND SENSE

Be aware that a few markets insist that writers become subscribers before they will consider their work for publication. In addition, many contests require an entry fee. A dollar sign ($) will alert you to these listings. Entry fees for most contests are minimal and are normally used to help defray the costs of the contest, including payment for prizes and/or publication of winning entries. Many of these contests are also marked with a star, meaning that despite the entry cost they are still good places for young writers to consider. A few contests require more substantial entry fees, often $5 or more.

You should not disqualify a market or contest just because it has an entry fee or insists that only subscribers or club members may submit material. Take into account other factors as well. For instance:

- Who is sponsoring this contest?
- Is the entry fee reasonable?
- How are the fees used?
- How much competition will my entry or submission face?
- Will I be competing with others my own age or with similar experience?
- Do I need to subscribe first, or will the price of a subscription or membership be deducted from my payment if my work is accepted for publication?
- Would I enjoy being a member of this writer's organization?
- Have I studied the contest's rules or the market's guidelines carefully to determine if my planned submission would be appropriate?
- Are there any extra benefits which make the entry fee worthwhile? For example, does the contest or market offer writers professional critiques of their entries for no or little additional cost?
- Do I know other people who have entered this contest? What was their experience?
- Can I afford the fee?
- Are there other markets or contests that would be better for me to try first?

Remember that there is always some cost involved in submitting to markets and contests, even if it's just paper, envelopes and postage — one to send your manuscript and another (known as an SASE or self-addressed stamped envelope) to have it sent back if not accepted. Entry and subscription fees add to that. No matter how minor the cost, make sure your material is not only good

---

Author's Note: Warning!

Beware of publishers and contests that ask you to pay to see your work in print or in order to collect your prize. Read all acceptances, evaluations and award notices *carefully*. You should *never* have to pay to have accepted manuscripts published, or to collect awards from contests.

---

enough but also appropriate, to make the cost of submitting a worthwhile risk.

DON'T BE FOOLED BY OPPORTUNITIES THAT SEEM TOO GOOD

If you enjoy writing, the prospect of getting published or winning an award can be very exciting. Unfortunately, some publishers and contests attract amateur writers with promises of publication and large cash awards, trophies, or other prizes for a fee. You may receive information from such publishers and contests through the mail or see ads for them in magazines and newspapers. Often, you will not realize that a publication or contest expects *you* to pay to have your work published until *after* you have submitted your manuscript. This is similar to subsidy or vanity publishing, which is discussed below.

Be aware also that some literary consultants or agents—working independently or in conjunction with a publisher or contest—offer "free" evaluations and publishing advice in exchange for what's called a "reading fee." A reading fee may be one price, such as $150 for a book manuscript, or charged on a per-page basis.

If you want advice or help with a manuscript, I suggest you look for less expensive, and often more productive, solutions. Find out if a writer's group meets in your school or neighborhood. Ask for references from teachers, librarians or bookstore clerks. They can recommend books to read, or they may know of an experienced writer willing to work with you. Chapter 4, "Opportunities Online," explains how to get help from experienced writers and become involved with manuscript critique sessions, workshops and conferences, all conducted electronically using a personal com-

> **Author's Note:**
> ....
> Many authors enjoy receiving letters from people who have read their books. I know I do. However, due to our busy schedules, we can't always respond as quickly as we'd like. Oftentimes we are asked for information that would not be appropriate or possible for us to give.

puter and modem. Many organizations, such as the National Writer's Club, include manuscript help as part of the yearly dues or for a reasonable fee. Some writers exchange manuscripts with other writers through the mail, supplying envelopes and postage to have their manuscripts returned to them.

SUBSIDY PUBLISHERS AND VANITY PRESSES

Subsidy book publishers (also known as vanity presses) are publishers that invite you to submit your manuscript, accept it for publication, *then* tell you how much it will cost you. They often offer "free" information in the form of how-to-get-published booklets or other valuable-sounding gifts. Their ads may say that you can obtain a free, professional evaluation of your manuscript without obligation. Sometimes, they cite the names of now-famous authors whom they claim to have worked with in the past.

Subsidy publishers typically respond to submissions in one of two ways. First, they may praise you as a writer blessed with the talent to be a bestselling author. They can't wait to sign you up as a client and help you get your work published. It will all happen quickly, they promise. Second, they may claim your work has merit but it isn't quite good enough to publish—yet. They will go on, however, and say that with their expert editorial help and publishing guidance, they can help you produce a published book. Whatever the exact words of their pitch, the catch is the same: *You* must provide all or most of the funds to get your book published. In other words, when *you* send them enough money, they will make the arrangements to get your book printed.

Selling your new book to readers is another matter entirely. Despite the promises they may make, subsidy publishers have little incentive to market the books they publish. All of their costs, plus a handsome profit, have already been covered by the authors themselves. Likewise, it may not matter to them if the book is well-written or just a writer's ego on display. If their primary purpose is to get *you*, the writer, to pay to have your book published, how objective do you think they will be when discussing the merits of your manuscript?

If you're a fan of the *Little House on the Prairie* television series, you may remember the character Charles Ingalls falling into this trap when he submitted his father's autobiography to a publisher. Grandpa Ingalls wanted so much to have his book published. And Charles, after reading the publisher's praise and not wanting to disappoint his father, sent the money he had saved for a badly needed new plow. At first everyone celebrated the publishing success of Grandpa Ingalls. But before long, everyone realized that it was a hollow victory. Grandpa Ingalls, in particular, was embarrassed and disillusioned, especially after bragging so much about his writing ability and publishing success.

WATCH OUT FOR CONTESTS WITH HIDDEN COSTS

Similar tactics are used by some contests. The initial entry fee may seem quite reasonable, perhaps only a dollar or two. Or no entry fee is required at all. Sometimes, an entry fee will be referred to as "nominal" or "modest," even though they expect you to pay $25, $30, $50 or even more to enter your work. Like subsidy book publishers, they may offer free information. Typically, their ads boast of awarding thousands of dollars in prizes annually plus publication of winning entries in anthologies.

You will be delighted when an official-looking letter arrives proclaiming you one of the winners. But your heart will sink to your shoes when you realize that in order to *see* your masterpiece in print you must first buy a copy of the anthology in which it will appear. It's not uncommon for a single copy to cost $60 or more. I've also seen letters from contests that only awarded prizes (cash and/or trophies) to "winning" contestants who paid to attend the awards banquet. Others may offer to send a certificate verifying your winning entry, then offer to mount it "free" on a beautiful

> **Author's Tip:**
>
> *Webster's New World Dictionary* defines honorarium as "a payment as to a professional person for services on which no fee is set or legally obtainable."
>
> Honorariums (gifts or money) are often given to speakers as a token of appreciation from the sponsoring organization. Reputable contests *do not* require winners to pay *anything* in order to collect their awards.

plaque that will only cost you $50 to have engraved and shipped to your home.

Here is a portion of an actual award letter sent to an unsuspecting friend of mine. (For legal reasons, references to the organization's identity have been omitted.)

> Dear _____ Entrant:
> CONGRATULATIONS! The judging has been completed in your category/categories, and one or more of your entries has been selected for a _____ award.
> The entries this year were exceptional in all categories, and yours was/were among the best.
> The honorarium for each category award is $110. Your total *contribution* [italics mine] is $220. Each category winner is (sic) the beautiful Gold, Silver, or Bronze ____ statuette.
> **PLEASE REMIT YOUR HONORARIUM ALONG WITH THE PROPER FORM/FORMS BY DECEMBER 31, 1992.**
> Again, congratulations for being a _____ winner!

Accompanying this "awards" letter was a sheet claiming: "Most recipients of the _____ award wish to order additional duplicate statuettes and certificates for other individuals who have contributed to the creative and productive aspects of the winning entry." The price for each duplicate statuette was even *higher* than the first one. Plus, they wanted $15 for a duplicate certificate!

"What turnip truck did they fall off of?" asked my friend incredulously. While she did not bother to collect her award, I doubt the contest sponsors really cared. Before declaring her a winner, they had already collected $60 in fees for the two essays she had entered.

Such publication and contest offers, before their true nature is exposed, are particularly enticing to beginning writers anxious to see their names in print or writers frustrated by a continual stream of rejection slips. (Even experienced adults get fooled occasionally. The friend mentioned above is an editor.) There is nothing illegal about such offers. But, to me, they take unfair advantage of writers' dreams of success by getting them to believe that this is how the publishing business works. Worse, they usually charge writers a lot more than it would cost them to take their manuscripts to a local print shop and have them typeset, printed, and bound into book form. *That* is known as "self-publishing."

THE SELF-PUBLISHING DIFFERENCE

Many poets, writing clubs or other community groups self-publish collections of their work, primarily to share with family and friends. This is similar to students publishing a yearbook, school magazine or classroom anthology. They may sell a few copies; some even make a profit. The difference is that when people self-publish their work, they understand from the beginning what they are responsible for and have control over how much it will cost. For instance, they can choose the number of copies to print, what type of paper to use, how it will be bound. No one is making exaggerated claims of fame and fortune. (I hope!)

EGO ALERT!

The worst thing about subsidy publishers and vanity presses is that they often puff up writers' egos with flattery that has no connection to the truth. Like Grandpa Ingalls, some writers think it's an honest appraisal of their talent or potential as a writer. And, like him, they declare themselves failures when they learn the truth about the circumstances. What they don't realize is that they haven't learned *anything* objective about their talent or potential at all! After such an experience, some good writers will give up writing entirely thinking they can't ever succeed, while others

---

Author's Tip:

....

Books that many elementary students write, illustrate and help bind in conjunction with Young Authors Day are an excellent example of worthwhile self-publishing projects.

Draw & Write Your Own Picture Book, by Emily Hearn and Mark Thurman, is an excellent reference book that even younger students can read and follow themselves. Teachers and older students will find more detailed advice in David Melton's book, *Written & Illustrated by . . . .*

The Complete Guide to Self-Publishing, by Tom and Marilyn Ross, is for older teens and adults who want to know everything about writing, publishing, promoting and selling their own books.

---

charge blindly ahead, believing they are great writers producing work which could never be improved.

Don't become victims of such misguided assumptions and sales tactics. This is not how reputable publishers and contests operate. Beware of any publisher or contest that asks you to pay to see your work in print or in order to collect your prize. Read all acceptances, evaluations and award notices *carefully*. When in doubt, check it out with someone more experienced.

In compiling this guide, I have taken great care to avoid listing such questionable opportunities. Please write to me immediately if you receive a request for money to collect an award or to guarantee your work will be published from any of the listings included in this book, or any others you might become aware of. Send a detailed letter and include photocopies, if possible, of any correspondence you have received to:

Kathy Henderson, MGYW
% Writer's Digest Books
1507 Dana Avenue
Cincinnati OH 45207

ADVICE TO THOSE WHO SELF-PUBLISH

As pointed out earlier, self-publishing can be a fun, inexpensive and worthwhile experience, especially for students or community groups. Unfortunately, too many writers waste time and money self-publishing their work as a way to avoid or ignore the editing process, assuming that it would destroy the quality or creativity of their work. As can happen when you work with subsidy publishing and vanity presses, this may lead to questions about the credibility, integrity and quality of your work or your writing ability later on.

If you insist on self-publishing larger works, such as books or newsletters, at least do so responsibly. You may be able to do all the necessary editing on your own by following advice found in many excellent reference books. However, it is much wiser to enlist the help of someone with professional editing and publishing experience. Find someone whose judgment you respect but who can also be counted on to bring objectivity and perspective to the task. Rewriting, revising and polishing are key steps to producing quality work. Producing a quality product should be the goal of any publisher.

GAINING A COMPETITIVE EDGE

Unfortunately, no one can guarantee that all writers will find a willing, reputable market for their work. There are, however, several things you can do to give your material an edge against the competition. These key steps (covered in Chapter 2) are the same ones followed by professional writers. Bear in mind that while other people may be available to help you, you alone are responsible for the final content and condition of the manuscripts you submit.

If all this is beginning to sound like work, you're right! But marketing can be fun and challenging, too. The individual steps are easy to understand. How often and thoroughly you apply them is up to you. Concentrate on submitting to markets and contests that require only minimum effort, if you like. Or dive deep to explore the wide range and variety of opportunities that exist.

GETTING DOWN TO BUSINESS

If your parents have ever paid out good money to give you music lessons, you've heard them say a million times, "Go practice." And off you trot to your piano, tuba, drum or violin, and try to hammer

Author's Tip:

Have trouble thinking up new ideas? Can't tell a good idea from a bad one? Then check out *Where Do You Get Your Ideas?* by Sandy Asher.

or blow or rap or stroke out the notes of the scale. All the while, your mom's taken refuge in the garage, gratefully out of earshot, and your dad is in the kitchen trying in vain to tap his foot to your beat.

But hand your mom or dad a little story or poem you just wrote from the top of your head and out come the "Ohs" and "Ahs" and "Neanderthal is sooooo talented. He's a natural-born writer." No one ever tells you, "Go practice your writing."

Until now.

I'm telling you, "Go practice your writing." Give that budding talent a chance to bloom and grow. You'll be amazed at what a little daily stretching of the mind and fingers will do for the quality of your writing. Quality writing gets published. Practice will also help keep the idea mill churning.

FOR YOUR EYES ONLY

Try keeping a notebook handy for writing down special thoughts or feelings. Jot down descriptions of places you visit. What makes them different from other places you've seen? Why do some places, like McDonald's or Kmart, look the same wherever you go? Try to describe your home to someone who is blind or deaf.

Learn to exercise your senses. What does your living room sofa *feel* like? Is it rough or smooth? Can you smell the kind of stuffing it has? Go through each room recording how things feel, smell, sound, look and sometimes taste.

Study how people look. What do their expressions say about them? Have you ever been really close to very old people? Can you smell the different medicines and other odors than seem to seep from their bodies? What does a baby smell and look like while he's messing a diaper? Don't just wrinkle your nose, *show* what he looks and smells like using word pictures. What comparisons can you make?

Record how people talk. Do they use slang or proper English? Do their clothes reflect the way they talk? Do they slur their words, and if they do, why? Is it a speech impediment or just out of laziness? Are they bashful and shy, or boisterous and loud? If you could feel the voice of a big husky man, what would it feel like? Does he pound out his words like a jackhammer? Does his breath smell?

How does your teacher look when you first see her each morning? How does she look at the end of the day? Can you tell if the day has been good or bad?

Read, read, read. But avoid reading only what currently interests you. Read a variety of things — books, magazines, newspapers — even if you don't quite fully understand them. Sample topics and genres[1] you would normally skip.

While reading the work of favorite authors can be a great help in learning to write well, you should postpone it while drafting your own stories, especially if you tend to be too critical of your own work. Besides deflating your confidence it can hamper your originality, making it harder for you to finish the stories you start. Some writers deliberately read a few pages of what they would ordinarily consider boring material in order to motivate themselves to get back to their own work.

A SECRET WEAPON ONLY YOU CAN USE

If I asked one hundred people to write a story based on the same idea, do you know what I'd get? One hundred different stories. That's because each of us is unique, no two exactly the same.

Exercise your writing mind daily, and your writing will grow stronger and more creative. You'll gain the confidence needed to risk writing stories only you can tell. You will get a feel that is natural for you, for the way words can be woven together in interesting, inspiring and informative ways. With practice, your writing will take on a special cadence; a distinct rhythm that flows with

---

[1]Pronounced <u>zhan ra</u>, genre means kind or type. For instance, romances are one genre, westerns are another. Realistic fiction, science fiction, fantasy, historical fiction and how-to are other examples of genres.

> ### Author's Tip:
>
> To better understand how successful writers draw from their own interests and experiences, read biographies and other thought-provoking works by or about well-known writers. My favorite is *Gates of Excellence: On Reading and Writing Books for Children*, by Katherine Paterson, author of such wonderful books as *The Bridge to Terabithia*, *The Great Gilly Hopkins*, and *Jacob Have I Loved*.
>
> For help in developing your own writing style and habits, try *Writing from the Inside Out*, by Charlotte Edwards, and *Becoming a Writer*, by Dorothea Brande. Both these books include stimulating exercises. Brande's book is especially useful for writers who lack self-confidence, have trouble finishing what they start, or sit down to write and suddenly find they can't get started. Don't let some of the big or old-fashioned words and phrases discourage you. Look up or skip over words that confuse you, but read it from cover to cover!

your tone. This is part of what's known as a writer's *style*. It helps to make your writing different from all other writing. Your style may vary with each new manuscript you create. What's important is that your style develop from the inside out, as you draw on your own emotions, interests and experiences to create something brand new.

Style is what makes our writing special. And *your* style is the secret weapon only you can develop and use in becoming a successful writer.

THE POST POSITION

In horse racing, jockeys like to start from lane one, the post position, because it offers the shortest distance around the track to the finish line.

If there's a shortcut to getting published, it's taking time to first find out what editors and contest judges want. So before you burst out of the starting gate, set yourself up for the post position by reading Chapter 2, "The Basics of Getting Published," and

Chapter 3, "How to Prepare Your Manuscript." For inspiration and insight read about the races other young writers have won in Chapter 6 which begins on page 103, and get a behind-the-scenes look at several markets and contests in "Editors Are Real People, Too" (Chapter 7).

Chapter Two

The Basics of Getting Published

Have you ever played Pin the Tail on the Donkey?

It can be pretty hard to get that tail to stick in just the right place while you're wearing a blindfold.

A lot of writers try to get published in much the same way. They sort of grope their way around, hoping their manuscript will land in the right place.

Writing and marketing can be both fun and challenging, but if you approach them as a professional writer would instead of as a game, your chances of getting published will improve dramatically.

Acting in a professional manner and trying to write like an adult are *not* the same thing. Trying to write like an adult is one of the worst things a young writer can do. One of the best things you have going for you is your youth. Write to express your feelings and your ideas, don't try to mimic what you think an adult writer might do. Believe in yourself, tell the stories you need to tell, and tell them in your own way.

Acting professionally also has nothing to do with age. It means behaving in a courteous, responsible way. It's learning what's expected, and taking the time to provide it. Your interest in reading this book indicates that you're not only eager to get published, but that you're also interested in how to do it right.

This chapter and the next explain the right things to do. If I didn't think you were smart enough and ambitious enough to do them, I wouldn't have spent so much time and trouble sharing them with you. And if there weren't a lot of editors and contest sponsors who believed you could do it, and do it well, the last half of this book would be pretty empty. Here then, are the basics of getting published.

SEND ONLY YOUR VERY BEST WORK

Revise and rewrite as many times as necessary to ensure that what you submit is the best you can do.

Revise and rewrite until each paragraph, sentence and word says exactly what you mean it to say. This type of editing should be a regular part of your practice or training routine. Like a skater repeatedly etching figures onto the ice, a musician practicing to perfect the way he plays a certain tune, or an athlete working to develop both body and game skills, you will improve your writing with practice and fine-tuning.

Consider asking an adult, perhaps a teacher, a parent, or a more experienced writer, to read your manuscript and offer constructive criticism. Listen carefully to their comments, then decide whether you agree or disagree with the advice. Sometimes hearing someone else's opinion will help you to see your material in a new way. Yet always remember that *you* are the creator. You must be the final judge of whether your work is ready to submit. In the end, follow the advice you agree with and politely disregard the rest.

It also helps to hear your material read aloud. You might try reciting into a cassette recorder, then playing back the tape while you follow along with a written version. This often makes it easier to note glitches in construction and awkward words or phrases. If you do the reading, be sure to read what you have *actually written*. Also read it as if you are seeing it for the first time. Don't add a lot of voice inflections as a dramatic actor might. You're looking for places that may need editing, not auditioning for a part in a play! (Play and script manuscripts benefit from a different form of testing. See page 267 for more details.)

It's very easy to read what you *think* you have written, or what you *intended* to write. However, your actual words, not your reading of them, must provide all the drama, action and emotion. Readers should be able to visualize your settings, feel and see right along with your characters just as if they were there with them in the story. *Show*, don't tell, your story. This applies to poetry and non-fiction as well. If you find yourself having to explain what you

---

Author's Tip:

For help planning and editing fiction stories, I recommend that young writers read *Wild Words! How to Train Them to Tell Stories*, by Sandy Asher.

Older students may also enjoy my favorites by author Gary Provost: *Make Every Word Count* and *Make Your Words Work*.

---

meant, then your job as a writer isn't finished.

It's always a good idea to put a piece of writing away, out of sight for a day or two, even a week or more for longer works, before editing it. You'll be amazed at how mistakes you didn't notice before will suddenly jump out at you as if they were waving little red flags. Granted, you may not always have time to let school writing assignments "cool" before turning them in. But take the time before sending a manuscript to an outside market or contest.

MORE ABOUT REWRITING AND REVISING

Rewriting and revising refer to the types of editing that you do to improve the *content* of your manuscripts. Many people use the terms interchangeably. To me, however, rewriting refers to the efforts I make to reword a particular sentence or paragraph to make it say exactly what I mean in the best and fewest words possible. I'm not changing the meaning, only how I'm presenting it. I'll substitute more precise (active) nouns and verbs for weak adjectives and adverbs. I'll fiddle with sentence structure and word placement.

When I revise something, I'm making bigger changes, like taking whole sections of a story or article and putting them in a completely different order. Or I may change my mind about the kind of statement I'm trying to make. Start all over with a slightly different topic. Add a new scene. Twist a plot. Create a whole new story opening or ending. Add or subtract characters. Deliberately lengthen or shorten the manuscript. Sometimes you can revise a previously published manuscript and make it suitable to submit again to a different market or contest.

POLISH AND PROOFREAD

Correct all grammar, punctuation and spelling mistakes in your final copy before mailing it out.

If, while evaluating your work, you discover it doesn't seem quite right yet, rewriting and revision are what you do to fix it. Polishing, on the other hand, prompts you to view the work as a whole, checking to make sure all the parts fit snugly together like a jigsaw puzzle. You want to make sure there are no missing or misplaced parts. As you read it again, forget that you are its author. Try to be as objective and as truthful as possible. (Often not an easy task when editing our own work!) Here are just a few of the questions you might ask yourself:

- Is there a strong beginning that flows smoothly into the middle section, which in turn stimulates the reader and leads him into the climax and ending?
- Do characters sound and act like real people? Could a reader predict how they might realistically behave if they were placed in a different setting?
- Can *you* imagine a setting that would make your characters uncomfortable? Happy? Excited?
- What is the main conflict or problem that the main character faces? What point have you tried to illustrate?
- Have you tied up all loose ends and supported your premise with word illustrations (facts and images) that readers can easily identify with?
- If you have a market or contest already in mind, does the length fall within the word limits set?

Many times the various aspects of the editing process overlap. You might notice and correct problems associated with the above questions during the initial rewriting and revising stage. Or you might get so involved working on small parts of a manuscript during rewriting and revision that you overlook problems that affect the overall presentation. It's like the adage: You can't see the forest for the trees.

The good thing about proofreading is that you don't have to bother doing it until your manuscript is ready for its final presentation. After all, why bother correcting a misspelled word in a first

Author's Tip:

There are many good how-to books on the market that identify and discuss in detail the various parts of a story, poem, article, etc., and how to seamlessly weave them together. Studying these will help you improve both your writing and editing skills. *Writing for Children and Teenagers*, by Lee Wyndham, contains a lot of detailed information suitable for many young writers ages 12 and up, especially those interested in writing fiction. Teen writers working on "adult" topics will also find this book useful.

For honing your nonfiction writing and editing skills I recommend *Words' Worth*, by Terri Brooks, in addition to Gary Provost's books mentioned earlier.

For final polishing and proofing, there is no better addition to any writer's personal reference library than *The Elements of Style*, by William Strunk, Jr. and E.B. White.

draft when it might get cut in the second, third or fourth? It isn't wise to stop to fix typographical errors, look up correct spellings and fret over just the right word or phrase to use while you're trying to be creative. It's too easy to lose your creative momentum. The purpose of first drafts is to get the basic idea down on paper, much like painters first sketch in pencil the basic elements of the picture they plan to paint. You can add the flourishes and details later.

Many manuscripts could be improved if writers put more time and effort into their editing. Yet, be aware that a manuscript can also be ruined by too much editing. Like writing, editing skills improve with practice.

After a thorough polishing, you'll need to go over the material again, looking for technical mistakes such as misspellings or errors in punctuation and grammar that you may have missed. For instance, you want all your nouns and verb tenses to match correctly, and you want to eliminate any unnecessary commas. If the manuscript is already in standard format, now is also the time to look for typographical errors. The typographical error most easily overlooked is a misspelled word you don't notice because you are sure you know how to spell it. Your mind *assumes* it's correct, so your eyes tend to skim over the word rather than see the mistake.

It's a good idea to write or type out a fresh copy of your manuscript after any major editing session. Computers and word processors make this a simple task. Incidentally, although computers and word processors make it possible to edit work directly on screen, many writers still think it's easier to work on a printed copy (commonly referred to as a *hard* copy).

LEARNING TO EDIT

An excellent way to hone your editing skills is to reverse the creation process by re-reading favorite books and stories. After enjoying the overall impression the work makes, try taking it apart. Why did the author choose *this* way to begin his piece instead of *that* way? Identify where the beginning ends and the middle begins. Look for specific words that evoke one or more of the five senses: seeing, hearing, tasting, smelling, touching. How does what the characters say and do help you to imagine them as real people? Try to rewrite a passage using your own words. Is your version as effective as the original work? Can you identify specific things the author placed early in the story that plant certain ideas in the reader's mind and point to things that happen later? What happened during the most crucial point in the story? How did the main character react? What if he had acted differently?

This dismantling process works equally well for nonfiction and poetry. For another perspective, try this process on works you *didn't* enjoy. Try to determine exactly what turned you off. For instance, did you have trouble identifying with the main characters? If so, was it because of the *writing* (story construction, word choice, directions the plot took, etc.), or just because you aren't interested in this type of story? Was the story too predictable, meaningless or absurd?

LOOK SHARP—PREPARE IT LIKE A PRO

Prepare your finished manuscript following the standard formats described in Chapter 3. Proofread again making any needed corrections before submitting your work.

Author's Tip:

Many beginning writers have a hard time understanding both the creative development and the visible changes their manuscripts may go through from draft to polished, properly formatted manuscript to final printed page. In 1992, a marvelous paperback book was published that not only describes in detail how one writer got an idea and transformed it into a book, but also includes reproductions of handwritten notes, drafts in various stages, comments from editors requesting changes, and copies of printed pages before and after final editing.

The book is titled *James A. Michener's Writer's Handbook: Explorations in Writing and Publishing*. Even the youngest writers will find it interesting and learn from it.

Occasionally, editors or contests will want, or allow, manuscripts formatted in a slightly different way. For example, while most editors insist that manuscripts be typed, a few will accept handwritten work. Some contests do not want judges to know any personal information about the entrant, so they will want the author's name and address to appear on the entry form but not on the manuscript itself. The preferred format for individual poems, plays or scripts also varies between certain markets and contests. Under most circumstances, editors and contests will expect to see manuscripts prepared using standard formats.

Plan to submit (send) one manuscript at a time to a market or contest. In other words, do not submit the *same* manuscript for consideration elsewhere until you have received an answer from the one before. Mailing the same manuscript to more than one place at a time is called a "multiple" or "simultaneous" submission. Editors become extremely annoyed when they discover that a manuscript they have spent time and trouble to read is accepted somewhere else before they have had a chance to make their decision. Although some adult writers do make simultaneous submissions occasionally, my advice to young writers is to always stick with the one-to-one rule.

Occasionally writers are encouraged to submit several poems

together to a single editor or contest. This is not a violation of the "one manuscript to one market at a time" rule because you are not asking two people to consider the same material at the same time. Again, read individual guidelines for details.

You may, of course, send different manuscripts out to different markets and contests. In fact, writers are encouraged to have several things "in the mail" at the same time. More about that later.

If you have made only one or two small mistakes per page on a final draft, neatly correct them. To make them as inconspicuous as possible, use a lead pencil or black ink pen. (Editors generally will use colored pens or pencils to indicate where corrections or edits are needed.) Acceptable handmade corrections include:

- Indicating that two letters or words have been accidentally reversed (transposed). [words Two]
- Drawing a thin line through a word or short line that should be deleted. [Word]
- Correcting a misspelled word by drawing a line through it and printing it correctly in neat letters directly above or in the nearest margin. [Corcet *Covrect*]
- Using a small arrow to indicate a missing word or two; add the word by printing it neatly. [Add ∧ word *the*]
- Using the paragraph symbol (¶) to indicate where a new paragraph should have been started
- Placing a forward slash (/) between two words that have run together

If you find more mistakes or if your page has a sloppy appearance, take the time to make a fresh copy. *Then check it again.* This is for your benefit. Because editors cannot meet with you personally and have no idea whether or not you are a good writer, the first impression they get will be from the overall appearance of your manuscript. By sending a neatly prepared and properly formatted manuscript, you will be telling editors and contest judges that you care enough about what you write to give it the best chance of acceptance.

Imagine going out to buy a new pair of shoes. Where would you expect to find the best quality? In a store where the shoes are soiled, mismatched, and thrown in a jumble on a display table for you to sort out? Or in a store where the shoes are neat and clean and paired together for easy selection? This is how a busy editor looks at manuscripts.

Make it easy for editors and judges to read your material. They will respect the time and effort you have taken. When the choice is between two manuscripts of close or equal merit, the one that *looks* better will always win.

STUDY AND COMPARE OPPORTUNITIES—THE WHY

Sending your very best work will not help you get published if you submit it to the wrong place. But how can you tell for sure which is the *right* place?

The answer, unfortunately, is that you can't. Not if the "right" place means the place where your manuscript is guaranteed to be accepted.

But there are ways to determine which are *appropriate* places for you to try; places where a particular manuscript has a good chance of being seriously considered. Keep in mind that an appropriate market or contest for one manuscript may not be an appropriate place to send the next one. And one that is good for your friend may not be the best place for you.

Studying and comparing market opportunities is a multi-step process. It is also a process that needs to be redone from time to time, because the publishing field is not like a stone wall that stays the same year after year. It is more like a meadow. New opportunities sprout like wildflowers while others fade and die away. A few markets and contests last, getting bigger and branching out like strong oak trees as the years go by, but even they go through changes. Editors come and go, staffs may move to new locations, editorial policy changes are made, regular departments and special columns are added or deleted, they may decide to publish more fiction or less poetry or—best of all—raise the rates they pay writers for their manuscripts.

AND THE HOW

First you need to determine which markets and contests are the most appropriate for you. That means understanding which ones accept submissions from someone of your age, writing ability or experience, location and interests. You also need to decide which of these markets are of most interest to you.

Part of this work has been done for you. Of the many thousands of markets and contests open to freelance writers (that means a writer who does not regularly work for the publisher), only those who are interested in receiving submissions from young people (ages 18 and under) have been included in this book. However, not all of these opportunities will be appropriate for each reader. As you read through the listings, you may want to make a list or place a mark next to those that sound appropriate for you to try.

Try not to become overly enthusiastic at this point. Because you are naturally creative, dozens of new ideas for articles, stories and books will suddenly burst like kernels of popcorn in your head as you read through the listings. (Tip: Keep paper and pencil handy to jot down ideas so you won't forget them.) Be selective. For now try to pick from five to fifteen markets and/or contests that seem to want the same types of manuscripts you have already completed or plan to write.

You may want to make two lists, one of opportunities that look good for a specific manuscript, and another of ones that pique your interest or seem especially suited to you.

Next send for the writer's guidelines and/or contest rules from each of the places on your list. If possible, also request a sample copy or borrow one from the library. You don't need to request things from everyone at once, but you should make requests from at least five. That way you'll have a variety to study and compare. Be sure to enclose a self-addressed, stamped business-size (#10) envelope (commonly referred to as an SASE), or whatever the listing says to, with your request.

When the guidelines and samples arrive, read them thoroughly. Study each individually to get a feel for the type of material published. Read *everything*: featured pieces, author blurbs, letters to the editor, editor or publisher's messages, table of contents, even the advertisements. Watch for announcements of special contests or invitations to send your writing. Just as no two writers are the same, neither are any two markets or contests. There are *always* some differences no matter how similar they may look at first.

Ask yourself some questions:

Author's Tip:

If you have friends or classmates[1] who are also interested in getting published, you can share the chore of collecting sample copies and writer's guidelines. Whether you do it alone or with others, be sure to keep a master list of what you have already sent for and received. Note on it the date you received the guidelines and the issue of the sample copy. Send for updated material every year or so.

- Is this what I expected?
- Did I misinterpret the information contained in the listing?
- Do I still think this is an appropriate place to send my work?
- Can I tell how much competition I would have submitting here?
- Would I be proud to have my manuscript published here?
- What new ideas for writing occur to me as I read this?

In addition to all this studying and comparing, you need to take a good, objective look at any manuscript you are planning to submit. Make a list of its identifying features. For instance:

- Is it a short story, poem, script, essay, etc.?
- What is its genre and subject matter? That might be mystery, adventure, humor, science fiction, etc., but could also be sports-related, out-doorsy, or about school or church.
- If there is a main character, how old is he or she? What interests does he or she show in the story? What happens in the story?
- What is the setting for your piece?
- What age reader would it appeal to most? (Someone your own age, younger, older?)
- Do you have illustrations or photographs that would be appropriate to submit with it?
- How long is it?

[1]Collecting, studying and comparing publishing opportunities is a valuable experience that helps young people develop both their creative and critical thinking skills. Teachers should make sure students take an active part in the process, rather than compiling the information for them.

- Has it ever been published before?
- How well written is it? (Do you think it is one of your very best pieces? Or just pretty good?)

Now comes the hard part. Taking into consideration all that you know about your manuscript, of the markets and contests that still seem appropriate places for you to consider, ask yourself two questions:

1. Which one or two places would my manuscript have the *easiest* chance of getting accepted at?

2. Which one or two represent the *higher quality or more prestigious places* (this could be a well-known publication, or one that offers payment, or just one of particular interest to you) that are appropriate for a manuscript like mine, but where my chances of getting accepted may be lower because they receive many submissions, publish only a few pieces like mine in each issue, say that they are very selective, or for some other reason (perhaps it's an adult market) would make it tougher for me?

If you are very lucky, the answer to these two questions will be the same. Most likely, however, you'll have the names of four different opportunities. Do you submit to the easier one, or go for the biggest reward first? That's a choice you will have to make yourself. I know many writers who have almost everything they submit accepted the first or second time out. But they always pick the easiest markets.

Personally, I prefer being rejected by the best and working my way down my list. (*Actually, I prefer getting accepted by the best!*) You'll have to decide for yourself. The important thing is to pick several solid possibilities, so if it isn't accepted by the first place you send it to, you are ready to send it back out right away to the next choice on your list.

If it gets rejected by all four, then start a new list. While you're at it, reevaluate the merits of your manuscript. Could it use a little rewriting or more polishing before you tackle that second list of appropriate opportunities? Did you receive any useful comments on it?

Author's Tip:

....

Writers interested in targeting some of the easier nonfiction markets should read Connie Emerson's book, *The 30-Minute Writer: How to Write and Sell Short Pieces*. It includes dozens of tips and ideas for writing personal essays, humor, opinion pieces, reviews, anecdotes, mini-profiles and more. Be sure to also read about Amy Wu in Chapter 6. She's published more than fifty such pieces in some very prestigious places like *The New York Times* and *USA Today*.

LOCAL, REGIONAL AND SPECIAL OPPORTUNITIES

Some of the best, and often the most appropriate, markets and contests for young writers are in your own neighborhoods, cities and states, or relate to a special interest or circumstance. In every edition of the *Market Guide for Young Writers* I have listed several opportunities that are representative of what can be found in many areas around the country. The TAWC Spring Writing Contest, for instance, is limited to amateur writers in Michigan, but every state has some type of writer's group that publishes a magazine or newsletter, or sponsors either regular or occasional writing contests.

Don't overlook writing a letter to the editor, editorial, guest opinion piece, or a feature or filler story about people and events of interest in your community. Many writers overlook writing nonfiction pieces, yet they are much easier to get published and editors often pay for them. This is especially true of magazines that may publish only one or two poems or short stories, but ten or more columns, tips, articles, how-to's and other types of nonfiction in each issue. Obviously, the more of something they publish, the better the chances of getting that something accepted.

Your local newspaper is also a great place to get a job as a stringer reporter or columnist. Newspapers, especially smaller dailies and weeklies, are always short-staffed. My local paper (and the one where I was first published) is constantly looking for young writers interested in covering school sports and community events.

Whether you reply to an ad or go in on your own, be prepared to answer any questions the editor might ask you. (You may want to do a practice interview with a parent or friend acting the part of the editor.) Try to anticipate his reaction, and any objections that might be raised. What will you answer if you're asked what you want in return? Are you looking for a paid job? (Most likely you would get a set fee. In 1971, when I started, I got $2 for each weekly column published—so don't count on getting rich. On an up note, my column did run above Erma Bombeck's.) Are you willing to work for just the opportunity to get published and learn more about the business? (Tip: If you apply to a non-profit organization, be prepared to donate your services. At a regular business, however, try first for a paying position even if it's a tiny amount. Part-time reporters should receive at least minimum wage for time on the job, but you may not be paid for the time it takes you to actually write your article.)

Figure out in advance how you will present yourself: You need to show enthusiasm, dedication and persistence. You also need to show that you can be trusted to meet deadlines, can accept criticism, are willing to rewrite and polish when necessary, and won't get discouraged or ornery if your section or piece gets moved to a different page or occasionally cut altogether because the editor decided something else was more important (you most likely will not be consulted on this).

Have samples of your work with you, or mail a few of your best pieces with a query letter. Be very selective. They won't be as interested in how much you've written as they will in whether you show real promise as a writer. For local interviews, it's acceptable to take along a scrapbook binder of your pieces (published and/or unpublished). Because the editor may not have time to read through them immediately, bring a few photocopies of your best pieces that you can leave behind.

You might also try local radio and television stations, especially local cable and PBS stations; the community relations directors at area hospitals; or other civic organizations. And don't forget to get involved at school. (Read about a school-based video news broadcast team in both Chapters 6 and 7.)

Special-interest magazines and other periodicals also offer young writers excellent opportunities from time to time. Always be on the lookout for one-of-a-kind contests or invitations to submit material. A few years ago, for instance, The Learning Company, which makes computer software programs for children, and The Tandy Company, which makes Tandy computers, sponsored a "Silly-Story Contest" for students using one of The Learning Company's software programs. It was a fun, one-time contest that drew thousands of entries from eager young writers.

For special-interest magazines you will often be submitting right alongside adults. But if you target publications that are of high interest to you, such as a hobby, computer or pet market (anything that you read regularly), you will be able to compete on equal footing. Many times, because you have taken the trouble to learn the basics of getting published, you'll have a better chance than adult readers who don't know how to prepare a manuscript properly or how to edit their work. *Lifeprints*, which limits submissions to those from writers who are visually impaired, is just one example of a specialty market listed here.

Several resources, such as the magazines *Writer's Digest*, *The Writer* and *Byline*, offer writers updated market and contest information in each month's issue. If you are *very* interested in writing, you might want to subscribe to one of these magazines. *Byline* is the best one of the three for beginning and young writers. But I know writers as young as ten who regularly read *Writer's Digest*.

Writing and marketing are ongoing processes. Try to keep several pieces (to different places, of course) in the mail so if one comes limping home, you can still hope the best for the others.

And don't stop writing while you wait to hear from an editor! Get started on a new project right away.

THE BIG "NO"

Editors will sometimes reject even well-written material. There are a number of reasons, but by far, the biggest is something editors call *inappropriate submissions*. This means that that particular publication or contest *never* uses the type of material that was submitted. The subject of the manuscript may be of little or no interest to that magazine's readers. It may be a short story when only nonfiction is used. It may be hundreds of words over the preferred length. The wording or topic may be too easy or too hard for the readers. The reasons are many but, in general, they make

Author's Tip:

If you've ever had a little brother or sister want to tag after you wherever you're going, then you know how an editor feels when receiving inappropriate submissions. She doesn't have any use for them, and after trying to explain this nicely a few times with no result, she gets frustrated and doesn't ever want to be asked again!

a manuscript inappropriate for that particular publication.

Editors waste a lot of time and energy each month dealing with inappropriate submissions; time they could have spent reading and replying to *your* submission. In fact, so many inexperienced writers (young and old) submit inappropriate material that, like simultaneous submissions, some editors will no longer consider unsolicited manuscripts. (Unsolicited means that the editor did not specifically ask to see the material before receiving it from the author. All of the markets and contests listed in this book will consider unsolicited material from young writers if submitted properly.)

The only way to avoid making an inappropriate submission is to take the time to study the market and contest information carefully. Send for and study the guidelines or tip sheets offered. Buy, send for or borrow a sample issue[2] if you are not familiar with the publication. Then read it objectively to determine if your manuscript would fit in.

Pay close attention to the "Editor's Remarks" and the "Sponsor's Remarks" sections in the listings. Here you will find special advice for submitting material from the editors of that publication or contest. If your manuscript does not closely match their requirements, look for a market that does. You might consider rewriting a manuscript to meet the guidelines of a specific market. This is often possible when a manuscript meets most of the requirements but is either too long or too short, or when the subject and genre are OK but you haven't emphasized the right perspective or angle.

---

[2]Occasionally, free or low-cost sample issues of a publication are not available. This is the exception, however. If possible, make it a point to read one or more issues of a publication before submitting material to it.

EXPECT TO BE EDITED

Once your work has been accepted by an editor (and even some contests), there is a good chance that it will need further editing before being published. This happens to all writers, no matter how carefully they have edited and polished their manuscripts before turning them in.

There are many reasons an editor may edit or make changes to your manuscript. It may have been too long to fit the available space, or the editor may have felt a different word or phrase would make your message easier for readers to understand. This doesn't happen just with books or magazine stories, but with all types of work.

Editors have a responsibility (it's a large part of their job) to edit material when they think it is necessary. Thankfully, most editors will only make minor changes on their own. And most of the time you'll discover that the changes an editor has made in your manuscript have made it better.

Occasionally, you may not like the changes an editor makes. If the piece has already been published, there really isn't anything you can do about it except try to forget what happened and go on to your next project. If you absolutely *hate* the changes made, do not submit to that editor again. There are many other markets to choose from.

Try to view any change from the editor's point of view. If you can't seem to get over it, break a few pencils or kick a few wastebaskets until you calm down. Think long and hard before writing or calling an editor to complain. Consider this message from Dawn Brettschneider Korth, former editor of *Straight*:

> Please tell teens that it's normal to have your work edited. I've had complaints from teen writers when I changed *one word* of a poem — when it was misspelled and used incorrectly! A 16-year-old threatened to sue the company over a poem in which I reversed two lines to make his rhyme scheme consistent. Such scathing letters make editors reluctant to deal with inexperienced teen writers. All we want to do is help them.

WORKING WITH AN EDITOR

When editors feel that all or parts of a manuscript need to be rewritten or revised, they will often make suggestions and ask the writer who submitted the manuscript to make them. If this happens, you will have to decide whether you think making the changes will improve your work. (Please note that even if you change a manuscript according to an editor's suggestions, it is not a guarantee that the revised work will be accepted.)

If you don't understand what you are being asked to do, or if you don't agree with all the suggestions, take time to discuss your feelings with the editor by phone (if invited to) or in a letter. (In Chapter 6, several young writers talk about being asked to edit their work. Read, for example, the essays by Vicki Larkin and Duncan MacKay.)

Be prepared to explain why you think some or all of the suggested changes are unnecessary and to make new suggestions of your own. This give-and-take between writers and editors happens all the time. Don't be afraid of it. It's not very different from the way coaches work with their players. If you and the editor can't come to an agreement about what needs to be done, you can always decide not to have it published there. Most times you will be free to submit the manuscript somewhere else.

All manuscripts get edited, even those by famous authors. It is a necessary, though sometimes uncomfortable, part of publishing.

The more you know about writing, editing and publishing, the easier it will be for you to understand and work with an editor throughout the editing and publishing process.

KNOW YOUR RIGHTS AS AN AUTHOR

When you write something, by law you automatically become the copyright holder (owner) of that manuscript. If an editor agrees to publish your manuscript, he will "buy the rights" to it. Often magazines, newspapers and newsletters buy "first serial rights" or "one-time rights," which give them permission to publish your manuscript one time. Then the rights are returned to you and you may offer the same manuscript to another editor for "second" or "reprint" rights.

A number of publications and some contests buy "all rights," which means that once you agree the publication can publish your manuscript (or artwork, photographs, etc.), the work becomes *their* property (they hold the "copyright") and is no longer yours. You may not send it to another market or contest. Even though you no longer own the copyright, if it is published you will be credited as the author.

Be aware that for legal reasons (and often to make things simpler for staff members) many markets and contests that accept submissions from young people assume all rights to that material whether or not it is published. You will notice that some markets and contests state that policy in their listings. Even if it is not listed here, it will be spelled out on the guidelines or rules sheet, or in a letter or contract sent to you when your work is accepted.

Professional writers and adults who want to be published often advise *not* to sell all rights, if possible. However, the situation is very different for young writers. Because many of the best opportunities for young writers are also the ones that buy all rights, I think young people (and many beginning adult writers) have more to gain from being published by such markets than from retaining copyright to their material. It is a decision that you and a trusted adult should make together. Consider the manuscript in question and the reputation of the market or contest with whom you are dealing. Also keep in mind that many markets that buy all rights will reassign them (give them back) to the writer later upon written request, particularly if the writer is planning to reprint the material in a noncompetitive way.

For example, I once sold all rights to my research and interview notes about farm accidents to a top-quality agricultural magazine. Later, when I wanted to reuse some of the material in a safety article for high school students, I wrote to the editor, explained the situation, and asked for reassignment of my rights. He was happy to comply. He had no further use for the material, and the market I planned to submit to was not in direct competition with his.

On the other hand, especially for teens, it never hurts to try negotiating with an editor. Suggest to him that you prefer to sell only first serial rights. Don't be surprised if he just says, "OK." Buying all rights saves some paperwork, but a publication that

> ### Author's Tip:
> ....
> For young writers (and their parents and teachers) interested in learning more about contracts, I highly recommend *Negotiating a Book Contract: A Guide for Authors, Agents and Lawyers*, by Mark L. Levine. This slim handbook takes you step-by-step through the negotiating process and explores in simple language what the various contract clauses, legal terms and publisher's offers mean.

doesn't intend to reuse your manuscript in some way will often have no objection to buying first or even reprint rights instead.

(Incidentally, I had to ask Matthew Cheney for permission to reprint part of his story, which appears as a sample manuscript in the next chapter, even though the story had appeared in two issues of *Merlyn's Pen: The National Magazine of Student Writing*. However, I needed reprint permission from Landmark Editions for one of Amity Gaige's poems from her book *We Are a Thunderstorm*, even though the book's copyright is registered in her name. I tell you this to illustrate how every situation is different. How did I know who to seek permission from? I asked!)

Negotiating a book contract is more complicated and confusing than dealing with magazines and newspapers. There are many, many things to consider. Most publishing companies offer writers what is known as a "standard book contract." Unfortunately, what is standard at one company is different at another. All writers (young and old) are advised to have any contract checked by a reputable literary agent[3] or lawyer familiar with the publishing industry. All writer's organizations offer contract information and trustworthy advice. (*Note*: Young writers are welcome to join the National Writer's Club, which offers such services to members.)

A number of questions in Chapter 5, "Answers to Questions Young Writers Ask Most," deal with these and related issues.

You should also know that the copyright of a message or library

---

[3]Literary agents seldom represent young writers, and normally there is nothing a literary agent can or would be willing to do for an amateur writer that he can't do for himself.

file of an online information service, such as GEnie, CompuServe or America Online, is usually held by its author. You must obtain the author's permission to use or distribute any portion of a message or file.

Copyrights can be very confusing. More information about copyright law is available by sending $3.75 with a request for "Copyright Office Circular 92," stock number 030-002-00168-3, to:

Superintendent of Documents

U.S. Government Printing Office

Washington, DC 20401-9371

Forms and instructions for registering your copyright with the U.S. copyright office are available free by writing to:

Copyright Office

Library of Congress

Washington, DC 20559

or call: (202) 707-9100

It now costs $20 to register a copyright. Remember, however, you *do not* need to register your copyright. As soon as you put your thoughts down in some type of fixed form (on paper, audio tape, film, computer disk, etc.) your work is automatically protected by law. You are the legal copyright holder until you give it away. Neither ideas nor titles, however, can be copyrighted.

CONTEST TIPS

Contests offer young writers some of the best opportunities to get published. And you'll want to pay just as much attention to writing and editing your entry as you do with any manuscript you are planning to submit. But contests also require an extra amount of care so you don't sabotage your chances before you even get started. Keep the following guidelines in mind.

When entering writing contests, be sure to follow all the stated rules *exactly*. If a contest says you may submit only *one* poem, don't send *two* of your poems. They *both* may be disqualified. And you'll lose any money you sent for an entry fee without any possibility of winning.

If a contest states that entries *must be typed*, be sure to type them. Don't think a judge will overlook the mistakes you make when entering a contest, because chances are the judge will never see your entry.

Most contests have a secretary or someone else to open entries and read them to see if the rules have been followed. Only entries that have followed all the rules will be sent on to the judge or judges.

Don't be a loser before you get started.

Entering writing contests can be an exciting and rewarding experience. To boost your chances of winning, follow these additional tips and suggestions:

1. Send for a complete list of the contest rules, regulations and eligibility requirements.

Unfortunately, space does not allow for all the rules for every contest to be listed in this book. It is best to send a self-addressed stamped envelope (SASE) to receive the rules or guidelines.

2. Follow all the rules exactly.

This includes where your name, address, and other information are to be placed, the number of entries you may submit, and how manuscripts are to be prepared. If the rules do not give specific guidelines for this information, follow the standard formats provided in this book for submitting manuscripts to an editor.

3. Don't forget to include entry fees or required forms with your submission.

Some contests for young people request that a parent, guardian or teacher include a *signed* statement verifying that the entry has been written entirely by the young person. Be sure to include this statement if it is required.

4. Don't limit yourself to contests that are designed just for young writers.

Many talented young writers have placed or won in contests open to adults. However, you have the best chance of winning in contests that are for or have categories open to young people only, especially if they also have age groups; that are specifically or exclusively sponsored for the young people in your local, regional or state-wide community; or that focus on a topic of special interest or importance to you.

5. If possible, try to read the winning entries of an annual contest from the previous year.

Just as reading back issues of magazines will help you understand a publication's editorial preferences, so will studying past winners of a contest. Yet don't let this stop you from entering something that may seem a little different.

For example, Amity Gaige won first place in the 1989 *Written and Illustrated by . . . Awards Contest* for her submission of poems and photographs, *We Are a Thunderstorm*. That same year Adam Moore was named a Gold Award winner for his nonfiction book *Broken Arrow Boy*, which recounted his experience recuperating from a serious accident. Though Adam did most of the writing and illustrating, it also contained some material done by other people. Nearly all past submissions (and winners) of this contest were fiction stories with drawings for illustrations, yet Amity and Adam won with entries that met all the contest requirements but were a little different.

Remember, too, that judges often change from year to year.

6. Don't be discouraged if you don't win.

Most contests award prizes for only first, second and third place. Some also name a number of honorable-mention winners. A judge, like you, has her personal likes and dislikes. Out of the many entries, a judge must choose only a few, and she will make her selection according to what she likes best. Another judge, or editor, might like your work better.

SOME WORDS ABOUT REJECTION

To become a published young writer takes more than enthusiasm and talent. You must also be aware of opportunities. You must be willing to study and follow the guidelines set by editors and contest sponsors. You must understand that while some manuscripts are rejected for poor writing, others are rejected for reasons not readily apparent to the writer. These include: the time needed by a publication to print an issue, the space available, how many manuscripts are received for consideration, the number of manuscripts that have already been accepted for publication, and the personal preferences of the editors, staff and judges.

Rejection is disappointing. It hurts.

But rejection must be put in perspective. The editor or judge has not rejected *you* personally. He has simply picked another manuscript that better suited his needs at that moment — much like you might consider one pair of shoes over another.

You should feel especially honored if an editor or judge sends back any constructive advice, comments or criticism about your manuscript.

Editors are busy people who deal with hundreds of manuscripts each year. They cannot afford either the time or expense to write to you about why your manuscript was rejected. Most times you will receive a generic, preprinted note commonly known as the *form rejection slip*.

The wording on a form rejection is usually so vague it is difficult to tell exactly why a manuscript was rejected. There is, however, a sort of unofficial code many editors use to signal writers that their manuscript has some merit. It is a busy editor's way of offering encouragement. The code goes something like this:

- If an editor *signs* his name himself, then something in your manuscript caught his eye. It may be the flow of your words, your ability to make a point, your characterization within a story, or something else. You are on the right track. Keep going at it!
- If an editor *jots a word or two of encouragement*, such as "good idea" or "nice try," he means your manuscript was better than most but perhaps lacked that certain spark that would have made it outstanding.
- If an editor *writes a few words of advice or criticism*, such as "your characters are a little weak" or "the plot needs tightening up," he means your manuscript was good enough to be given careful consideration. With a little more effort, you may have a winner.

Of course, there are variations on this code. Some editors try hard to encourage promising young writers and will send a short, personal note rather than a rejection slip. Others simply do not have the time to spare. And sometimes a rejection slip that simply says, "Sorry. This does not fit our needs at this time," means just that. They can't use it whether or not they like it.

Rather than dreading a bit of criticism, look forward to it eagerly. It is usually easier to pinpoint minor flaws in a well-written manuscript than in a poorly written one where the trouble is so spread out, it is hard to offer any meaningful help in a short note. An editor who takes the time to offer encouragement, either by praise or constructive criticism, deserves your appeciation. Whether you make use of that advice is up to you.

You may be lucky enough to find yourself a published young writer with your first attempt. Then again, you may need to submit material many times before one of your manuscripts is selected for publication. If you have a strong desire to write, then never be discouraged. With practice your writing will get better and better, and so will your chances of being published.

SET THE RIGHT GOALS

Be careful not to set the wrong goals for yourself. A writer whose only goal is to be published will likely experience many more disappointments than will a writer who hopes to be published one day but whose goal is to enjoy writing and become a better writer.

It is unrealistic to expect everything you write to win a contest or be accepted for publication. Consider how a musician prepares for a performance.

He may continue to take lessons, trying out new pieces, practicing over and over again the pieces he has learned in the past. For his actual performance, he will not play every piece he has practiced. Instead he will pick and choose those he plays and enjoys the most. He also considers which pieces he feels the audience will like hearing.

As a writer, your audience is your reader; your performance is your manuscript. Pick and choose manuscripts you feel represent your best work. And when choosing which markets and contests to submit to, consider what you have to offer that would interest the readers of those publications.

Chapter Three

How to Prepare Your Manuscript

Next to the care and attention you put into creating your work, plus the attention you pay selecting an appropriate place to submit it, nothing is more important than the care you take presenting it to an editor or contest judge. You want your manuscript to look crisp, clean and polished, so the editor will concentrate on what you have written. This is especially important for teen writers targeting adult markets and contests.

However, it is extremely important that you follow the specific guidelines requested by a particular market or contest if they differ from the standards, *especially for contests*. Otherwise, your work may be rejected no matter how good it may be. Worse, some markets and contests won't return an inappropriate submission even if accompanied by an SASE. And *no* market or contest will assume responsibility for unsolicited manuscripts or original artwork or photographs.

With so many variations in policy, it's impossible to give specific advice for preparing all types of manuscripts, artwork and photos. What follows are the general guidelines and formats that most magazines and contests will accept. They are very easy to understand and prepare.

Resist all urges to use scented or colored paper, fancy typewriter type or decorative computer fonts, hand-drawn pictures in the margins, or special bindings, folders or covers for your manuscripts or mailing envelopes. And *please* don't bother concocting any tests for an editor to pass, such as turning a few pages upside-down, backwards or out of order. Many insecure amateur writers (young and old) do this thinking that if a manuscript is rejected and returned to them with the pages still mixed up, it proves that the editor didn't even bother to read their submission.

(This type of writer also prefers to think that editors are prejudiced against them or not smart enough to see what wonderful writers they are; anything to avoid admitting that their manuscript could be improved, or that they chose an inappropriate market, or that it just wasn't possible for the editor to use their work.)

What these writers don't realize is that an annoyed editor will simply return a rejected manuscript in the same condition it arrived. Editors are delighted to discover new talent of any age, but they will shy away from working with writers who obviously do not trust them to do their jobs right.

Remember, there's nothing wrong with being a young, inexperienced writer. But if you are serious about getting published, you don't want to *look* like a young, inexperienced writer. Editors have no time to be entertained by the way manuscripts are prepared. They have barely enough time to read and select submissions. Give your writing the best possible chance of attracting an editor's eye by following the formats outlined here. If you feel you need to overlook or bypass some of the guidelines, be very sure you have a sound reason for doing so.

Of course, for very young writers who will be handprinting their material, the guidelines are less strict. In fact, a few markets and contests, such as *Stone Soup* and the *Written and Illustrated by . . . Awards Contest*, want to see a student's original manuscripts and artwork. Most markets and contests, however, prefer typed manuscripts. The original text and artwork (or photocopies of it) can be included along with the typed version.

GUIDELINES FOR STANDARD FORMAT

Whether you write by hand or type[1], keep these rules in mind.

Write or type on only one side of a sheet of paper. Leave wide

---

[1]Computers and word processors have become so commonplace, at least in the United States and Canada, that typewritten manuscripts refer to those created on any typewriter, word processor or computer. Listings that read no computer printouts or no dot-matrix mean (1) they don't want manuscripts printed on green and white striped computer paper, and (2) they do not want manuscripts printed with dot-matrix printers that do not give a sharp, easily read impression. As long as your dot-matrix printer prints with strong, black type, feel free to use it.

margins of at least one inch on all four sides of each sheet. Use only a standard typewriter pitch, such as pica, or a computer font that resembles typing (such as Courier or Times Roman) and prints 10 cpi (characters per inch). Always print your final draft using a good, clean black ribbon in your typewriter or printer, or use a laser printer. Handwritten manuscripts should be printed or *very* clearly written in cursive using a good lead pencil (for the youngest writers) or blue or black ink pens (for pre- and early teens).

The text of all manuscripts should be double-spaced. This will leave a full line of empty space between each line of type. When using computers, check your software directions. Depending on your software, double-spacing may not appear on your screen even though it will print correctly.

If you write your manuscript out by hand, use lined, white paper. Write only on every other line, especially if you write big or use narrow-ruled paper. (There are some exceptions for poetry, plays and scripts, which will be discussed later.) Smooth-edged tablet or loose-leaf paper is best. Don't tear pages from a spiral-bound notebook, because the ragged edges are a real nuisance to editors.

For typed work, always use regular twenty-pound, white bond paper. Never use erasable typing paper for a final manuscript. It smudges and smears too easily and may give an editor's sleeve an unwanted, tie-dyed effect. For simple mistakes, use a light film of liquid correction fluid or the newer (and neater looking) liquid correction paper. If you need to correct or delete an entire sentence, try press-on correction tape available at office supply stores.

Pay attention to word length limits on fiction and nonfiction, and to line limits on poetry. If you send a manuscript, such as a picture book that has both writing and illustrations, include a second copy of just the manuscript text prepared in the standard format.

Many typewriters and computers can justify (or make even) the right margin. However, editors prefer that manuscripts have a "ragged" margin on the right side. (Note: The pages of this book are justified. For an example of a ragged right margin see figures 1 and 2.)

PAGE 1

You will use a slightly different format for the first page of your manuscript. (See figure 1 on page 47.) At the top of your first page, starting at the left margin, use single-spacing to type your name, address, and telephone number with the area code. (*For contest entries, be sure to check where this information should go.*)

Next type your Social Security number. If you don't have a Social Security number, include your date of birth. Editors must have this information before they can pay writers for material. It is often appropriate to put the exact or approximate word length of your manuscript across from your name, next to the right margin. I also like to include the date I mailed my manuscript. You can easily add this later just before mailing by printing it neatly with a black pen. (Be sure to put the date you are mailing it, not the date you originally wrote it.)

A copyright notice is not really necessary, but it is OK to include it if you choose. Copyright notices are most often placed on poetry submissions, or manuscripts that are being sent to small literary magazines, newspapers, or newsletters that are not copyrighted. This will encourage the editor to include your copyright notice when your poem or other manuscript is published.

With the exception of your first page, plan on twenty-six lines of manuscript type on each page. If you find yourself always typing too close to the bottom of the page, try marking lightly with a pencil where your last line of type should be. Then erase the line later.

Typing the same number of lines on each page will make it easier to estimate the number of words in your finished manuscript. With proper margins and twenty-six lines of type, you will average 250 words to a page.

Drop about one-third of the way down the page and, using capital letters, type the title of your manuscript. Under the title, center the word "by," then on the next line center your name the way you wish it to read in print.

Switch your typewriter (or computer format) to double-space, drop down two lines and begin your story or article. Remember to leave at least a one-inch margin at the bottom.

Editors will use the empty space that you have left on the top

Matthew Cheney
0000 Street
City, ST Zip Code
word count → About xxx words
Date → September, 1990
↗ (000)555-0000
SS# 000-00-0000

— *Your name,*
address, phone,
ss # here

THE NAUGA HUNTERS ← *title*

by

Matthew Cheney ← *author*

Start your story here

↳ Hank, a thirteen-year-old boy with wispy brown hair and spindly legs, spotted his little brother sitting on the floor of the living room, watching a cartoon.

"Hey, Chucky, wanna go nauga hunting?" asked Hank.

"What's a nauga?" asked Chucky, turning away from the television.

"A nauga's a little thing — 'bout the size of a cat — that has big long teeth and a red feather for a tail," explained Hank, with the appropriate hand movements.

"A featha for a tail?"

"Yup, and naugas can change color so we can't see 'em, 'cept for the tail; that don't change color."

Figure 1. Sample story format, page 1

of your first page to write notes to the typesetter or copy editor.

If you wish to include a title page, type it exactly as you would the first page of your manuscript, without including any of the story. It is not necessary to include a title page with a manuscript that is less than six to eight pages long.

PAGE 2, 3, 4 . . .

On each additional sheet, put your last name at the top left-hand corner, followed by a forward slash and a key word from your title, and place the page number at the far right side of the same line. The key title word may also be centered on the line. This is called a "header." (See figure 2 on page 49.) This will help an editor put your story back in order if it gets dropped or shuffled around.

On book manuscripts with multiple chapters, I use both methods. Here's how the header for this page looked in my manuscript:

Henderson/MGYW   Chapter 3   55

At the end of your manuscript, drop down two lines and center the words "The End." This may seem a little silly, but a busy editor or typesetter will appreciate knowing for certain when he's come to the end of your piece. Journalists sometimes center the number thirty (-30-) instead of typing "The End." However, this symbol is not used very often anymore.

Never staple or bind your manuscript together in any way.

COVER LETTERS

If you wish to tell the editor something about yourself or give some added information about your story or article, such as how you came to write it, you may do so on a separate sheet of paper called a *cover letter*. This letter is written like a regular personal or business letter with your name, address, telephone number and date at the top, plus the name and address of the publication to whom you are writing. If possible, locate the name of the editor in a current issue of that publication. Then begin the letter, "Dear last name →   keyword from title   Page number →

Cheney ↙   ↳ NAUGA HUNTERS   " ↳ 8

Hank stood up and jumped on his brother; they fell to the damp ground. His eyes were sparkling and his lips were unfirm. "Would I lie about that, you little . . ." His voice faded as he pulled his arm up to punch Chucky. Chucky was crying now. Hank stood up. "Forget it," he said. "Supper'll be almost ready." Chucky was still on the ground. "You comin?"

Chucky pulled himself up and brushed off his rear end. His face was streaked with tears. "Yup," he said softly.

"Well, hurry up. Then after supper maybe we can go hunt some more naugas. They ain't invisible at night."

"Thought you said they ain't real — like dragons."

"You *believed* me? Boy, maybe you are stupider than you look." He turned around and headed for home, his little brother trying to keep up.

THE END

Figure 2. Sample story format, second through last pages

Mr." or "Ms." followed by the editor's last name. If you don't know the editor's name, simply write "Dear Editor."

Make your cover letter as short as possible, almost never more than one page. Cover letters should always be typed, using single spacing. Use a regular business letter format. Unless a listing suggests otherwise, tell the editor only things that relate directly to the manuscript you are sending. Though editors may be interested in knowing all about you, your family, your friends and your hobbies, they probably do not have time to read about you now. If editors want more information, they will ask you to send another letter. Remember you are trying to interest the editor in your manuscript, not in you.

QUERY LETTERS

Writers send a *query letter* to editors when they want to know in advance whether the editor would be interested in receiving a manuscript about a certain topic. Most editors prefer that young writers send a complete manuscript, though older teens attempting to publish in adult publications may send query letters outlining their proposed article.

Like cover letters, try to keep query letters to one page, and no more than two. *Always* type a query letter, and address it to a specific editor. (You may need to call the publication for the name of the current editor. A receptionist or secretary can give you the information; do not ask to speak to the editor directly.) Include an SASE with your query letter so the editor can respond. If you have been published before, it's a good idea to send one to three photocopies of your *best* pieces, especially if the article (or book) is similar in style or genre.

In one or two paragraphs, briefly describe the article (or book) you have written or plan to write. Give a few pertinent details, especially facts about people interviewed or relevance to current topics. In another paragraph, briefly describe why you are interested in this piece and any *pertinent* credentials you have. Many writers find drafting a good query letter harder than writing the finished manuscript. That's another good reason young writers should concentrate on submitting completed manuscripts. Many of the resources mentioned in this book have sections on writing query letters.

It is unusual for young writers to be represented by literary agents[2]. If you are a serious older teen with a full-length book manuscript, play or script, you may send a query letter to an agent asking if he or she would consider you as a new client. Be sure to enclose an SASE. You may send a short sample of previously published work. *Do not send your manuscript, or a synopsis or outline with your query.* If an agent finds your project interesting, he will write and tell you *exactly* what to send.

---

[2]The best method for a serious young writer to find a reputable agent is through the recommendation of an established author. Many writers' organizations maintain lists of agents.

POETRY

Poems may be single- or double-spaced. Or type your poem as you wish it to appear, double-spacing between verses if necessary. Which you choose will often depend on how it looks on the page. (See figure 3 on page 52.)

Type only one poem per page; include your name, address, and other information on *each* page.

Poems should also be centered on the page. Practice typing the longest line of your poem to determine the correct tab position. Here's a tip for those who have trouble centering poems on the page: Using clean white paper, type your poem as you normally would, indenting one or two tab spaces at the beginning of each line. On a second sheet of paper, type your name and other information where it should appear. When you are finished, cut your poem neatly from the first sheet, leaving as much white space as you can. Now position your poem where it should be and secure it lightly with one or two small strips of clear tape. Send clean photocopies of this "master."

PLAYS AND SCRIPTS

The standard formats for preparing radio and theater scripts often differ from the formats for stories, poems, articles and fillers. It would be best to check with your librarian or audio/video teacher for help locating a sample script. Study it carefully. Notice the differences in typing dialogue, description and sound effects. Use the sample script as a reference when you type your play, radio, film or video script.

Sample scripts may also be found in many language arts books. If you need more help, check with the drama teacher at your school, or ask advice from someone involved with your community theater. Also check the guidelines provided by the markets and contests for additional help.

When submitting a play or script to a magazine, leave the pages unbound and double-space each line of the text. That's because a magazine plans to publish your work on the printed page, very much like a fiction short would be published.

However, most theater groups and contests prefer scripts that are professionally formatted in proper play, script or audio/video

Amity Gaige   Copyright 1990
0000 Street
City, ST Zip Code
SS# 000-00-0000
Birthdate 00-00-00

UNWRITTEN

Out there,
somewhere,
there is a poem
that runs like
a river down the mountain.
It has no name; it has no home
While it would love to sing,
it has no voice.
While it would love to dance,
it has no form.
So it wanders aimlessly,
out there,
somewhere,
in the far beyond.
And despite its promise,
it still remains
unwritten.

Figure 3. Sample poetry format

format and submitted in lightweight folders or grip binders. To allow for binding, set your left margin at 1½ inches.

Older teens interested in submitting plays or scripts to professional markets and contests should consult a reference book such as *The Writer's Digest Guide to Manuscript Formats*, by Dian Dincin Buchman and Seli Groves. This book contains *every single formatting detail* you need to prepare a polished, professional looking manuscript. Guidelines are also included for writing treatments, synop-

Author's Tip:

Since I know next to nothing about play and script writing, I asked Sandy Asher, writer-in-residence at Drury College and an award-winning children's book writer and playwright, to share some tips and resources with you. Read her comments in Appendix A.

Jerry McGuire, video consultant for the National Writer's Club, recommends that you place your copyright notice on the bottom right-hand corner of the title page of your play or script. He also advises you to protect your script by registering it with the Writer's Guild of America. Send a $20 money order and a copy of your script to 555 West 57th St., Suite 1230, New York, NY 10019. They will send you an official certificate, and your property will be protected for ten years.

ses, outlines, concepts and story lines. There is even information for pitching ideas to television and movie agents or producers. The following simplified formats are suitable for submissions to many local and regional markets and contests, and to several of the listings contained in this guide.

In figure 4 on page 55 (page one of Beth Lewis's 1992 award-winning play), notice how the set descriptions and actions of the performers are italicized. If you can't italicize type, use all caps. (See the profile of Beth Lewis in Chapter 6.)

Figure 5 (page 56) shows the first page of *Hefty's*, a short (30-minute) film produced by Dick Rockwell, who wrote and produced the script along with John Prusak. (He is also station manager of WOAK, a cable TV channel at Dondero High School in Royal Oak, Michigan.) Notice how (1) the scenes are numbered for reference, (2) camera directions and set location are indicated in capital letters, (3) actions to be performed are typed, and (4) the way the name of the character who is speaking is centered on the line and typed in all capitals. The dialogue is also indented from both margins. A footer lists the date of the draft, the title and the page number. The wide left margin leaves plenty of room for a binding.

The two-column format shown in figure 6 (page 57) is standard for audio/video scripts.

PACKAGING AND MAILING

If your manuscript is more than four pages long, or if you are including artwork or photographs, use a large manila envelope that will hold your material without your having to fold it.

When addressing your mailing envelope, use the editor's name whenever possible. Such as:

Janet Ihle

<u>Thumbprints</u>

928 Gibbs St.

Caro, MI 48723

You can locate the name of the current editor by checking the masthead, usually located near the front of the publication.

Protect artwork or photographs by placing them between pieces of cardboard. *Never* use a staple or paper clip on a photo. It will cause ridges in the photo and make it difficult to reproduce. *Never* write on the back of a photo with a pencil or hard-tipped pen. Put the information on an address label, which you can stick to the back of the photo. You can also write safely on the back of a photo using a special grease pencil found in art- and office-supply stores.

Affix the proper amount of postage on both your mailing envelope and the SASE or postcard you put *inside* your mailing envelope with your manuscript (see figures 7 and 8, page 58).

SASE: SELF-ADDRESSED STAMPED ENVELOPE

Use a second manila envelope for your self-addressed stamped envelope (SASE). Fold it in half to fit in the mailing envelope. Remember to include enough postage to have your material mailed back to you.

An editor will not return your material if you forget to enclose an SASE with the right amount of postage. Some editors will not even read a manuscript that is not accompanied by an SASE. This may not seem like a good way to do business, but editors cannot afford to pay for the return of manuscripts from every writer who submits material. It would cost them thousands of dollars each

GENIE OF THE LAMP

NARRATOR: The dictionary defines autism as "detachment from reality together with the relative and absolute predominance of the inner life . . . The reality of the autistic world may seem more valid than that of reality itself; the patients hold their fantasy world for the real, reality for an illusion . . ." In other words, "wishes and fears constitute the contents of autistic thinking . . ."

Lights dim and end scene 1.

ACT 1

Backdrops of buildings and lights in a big city. A man, woman and young teenage boy gather around a trash can from where a small fire is giving them warmth in an alley. They are bundled in ill-fitting clothes, torn and dirt-stained. The woman has a scarf over her head and tied under her chin. She also has on a pair of fingerless mittens and open toe shoes. The older man has on a ragged khaki army jacket, but no hat or gloves. He keeps his arms pressed to his side and leans close to the fire. The boy is wearing oversized pants and shoes, and a woman's winter coat that has fur on the collar and cuffs. He is seated on the bare ground near the can, is cradling an old metal teapot in his arms and is rocking back and forth. A female narrator stands center stage dressed in black. A spotlight as she speaks.

GRIFFIN: *(angrily)* Boy! How many times do I have to tell you to get up and warm yourself?

(The boy stares out blankly at the man and continues rocking.)

ANNIE: Now Griffin, don't yell! My head can't take it with you always yellin' all the time. Don't you see the boy's busy? Leave him be.

Reprinted by permission of Very Special Arts; *Genie of the Lamp*, by Beth Lewis, 1991 VSA winning entry. In 1992, the VSA production role of Corey was played by a deaf actress who signed her role.

Figure 4. Simplified sample play format

1. FADE IN

2. EXT. JERRY'S BACKYARD – DAY

   LEGS pumping across an expansive luxuriously green lawn.
   JERRY sprints the final fifty yards of his run and stops.

   He leans forward, breathing heavily, placing both hands
   down on the top of an ancient sundial on a carved pedestal.
   Even his back patio is elegant.

3. INT. JERRY'S LIVING ROOM – DAY

   LOUIS, the family's lifelong servant, anticipating Jerry's
   arrival, pushes aside the luminous draperies covering an
   enormous picture window.

4. EXT. BACKYARD – DAY

   Jerry catches his breath. He appears exhausted but
   purposeful. This is his day. He is preparing for the
   challenge of his life.

5. IN. LIVING ROOM – DAY

   Jerry enters, sweat dripping like champagne from his body.
   He is thirty-something, wearing a yuppie jogging outfit.

   Louis greets him by handing him a towel. This guy is waited
   on hand and foot. Does Louis wipe him too?!

   LOUIS
   Good run this morning, sir?

   JERRY
   Thanks Louis, I'll be ready in a few minutes.

6. INT. JERRY'S HOUSE BATHROOM – DAY

   JERRY – (VO)
   When I think back to that day at Hefty's, I recall
   that I was in the best shape of my life –
   physically, mentally, and gastronomically.

| 2/6/91 | HEFTYS | 1 |

Reprinted by permission of Dick Rockwell, Focal Point Tools '93

Figure 5. Simplified sample film script

VIDEO	AUDIO
A foggy day in London Town.	Fog horns echo through mist-shrouded streets. Carriage wheels clatter on cobblestone.
Sherlock Holmes runs down the steps of his Baker Street home. Watson follows furiously behind.	Footsteps . . . then . . . **WATSON:** HOLMES, WAIT YOU FORGOT YOUR UMBRELLA.
Holmes turns.	**HOLMES:** WHAT IS IT, YOU SAY, YOU BLUBBERING IDIOT.
Watson looks embarrassed.	**WATSON:** MY GOOD MAN, YOU'VE STUMBLED OUT WITHOUT SO MUCH AS A RAINCOAT AND GALOSHES. AT LEAST HAVE THE COMMON SENSE TO TAKE A BUMBERSHOOT AND WEAR YOUR RUBBERS.
Watson tosses Holmes his umbrella. Holmes flinches, misses it and it bounces off the porch railing and lands in a puddle.	**HOLMES:** YOU CONTEMPTIBLE OAF. IF I WANTED SAFE-SEX ADVICE FROM YOU I WOULD WAKE YOU IN THE MIDDLE OF THE NIGHT WHEN YOU ARE MOMENTARILY SOBER.

Reprinted by permission of Dick Rockwell, Focal Point Tools '93

Figure 6. Simplified sample audio/video script

Susie Kaufmann
2151 Hale Rd.
Sandusky, MI 48471

Place
Stamp
Here

Gerry Mandel, Editor
Stone Soup
Children's Art Foundation
P.O. Box 83
Santa Cruz, CA 95063

Figure 7. Sample Mailing Envelope

Stone Soup
P.O. Box 83
Santa Cruz, CA 95063

Place
Stamp
Here

Susie Kaufmann
2151 Hale Rd.
Sandusky, MI 48471

Figure 8. Sample SASE

Author's Tip:

Don't guess. It's important to have your package — manuscript, letters, artwork, photographs and SASE — weighed at the post office or on a reliable postal scale so you will have the proper amount of postage.

Don't seal your package until after you determine the correct postage. This way you can take out your self-addressed envelope and put on the correct amount of return postage. *Do not use postal meter strips on SASEs.*

If you frequently send the same size packages, make a chart to remind you how much postage you'll need.

```
                                              Place
                                              Stamp
                                              Here




              YOUR NAME
              YOUR ADDRESS
              CITY, STATE, ZIP CODE

```

Figure 9. Sample front of a self-addressed postcard

```
(Title of your story) _____

(Date you mailed it) _____

(Who you mailed it to)

_____

_____
                        Received by
_____
                           Date
```

Figure 10. Sample Message Side of Postcard

year! They would rather use the money to pay writers for work that is accepted for publication.

A few of the markets listed state they do not return material at all. You do not need to include an SASE when submitting manuscripts to these markets and contests.

If you are worried that your package may not reach an editor, or if you want to make sure your manuscript did arrive at a market that will not send it back, you may enclose a special self-addressed stamped postcard. (See figures 9 and 10.) Most editors will take the time to mark a postcard and return it to you.

KEEP A COPY FOR YOURSELF

Always make a copy of any manuscript you submit, *especially* to those that won't return your work. It is insurance against a manuscript that gets damaged or lost in the mail. Occasionally, an editor will want to discuss your manuscript with you over the phone. It is much easier when you both have a copy to look at.

Make copies by using carbon paper, retyping a piece, using a photocopier, or by storing a copy on a computer disk.

HANDWRITTEN MATERIAL

If possible, type your manuscript or have someone type it for you. However, some editors who are willing to receive material from young people thirteen and under do not mind receiving handwritten or handprinted material as long as it is neat and legible.

Unless you have excellent cursive handwriting, print your manuscript. Check editors' guidelines for their preference. Use separate sheets of white-lined, loose-leaf paper for handwritten manuscripts. Wide-ruled paper is best if you tend to write big. If you use narrow-ruled paper, be sure to write on *every other line*. It will make it much easier for an editor to read.

Follow the same format rules for preparing each page of your manuscript given for typed material.

Write on *only one side of the paper*. Remember to number each sheet.

Never use paper torn from a notebook. The pages tend to stick together and bits of the edges are always falling off, making a mess. For very young writers, it is OK to use tablet paper with ruled lines. Remember to write on only one side of the sheet.

For all writers, put the pages of your manuscript in order but leave them loose. Never bind or staple them together. (If a teacher is submitting several copies of his students' work, he can use a paper clip on each individual manuscript.)

Make corrections on handwritten material by drawing a line neatly through the mistake, then going on. If you make a lot of mistakes on one page, rewrite the whole page.

Use the same mailing guidelines given for typed material. Follow the market tip sheet for submitting art or photographs.

COMPUTER PRINTOUTS

As personal computers and word processors become more popular, editors are agreeing to read manuscripts prepared on a computer if a letter-quality or laser printer is used for the final draft. The print on many older dot-matrix printers can be very light and hard to read. Sometimes photocopying the printed sheet will produce a copy dark enough to read easily. Keep the lighter print-out as your copy and send the photocopy to the editor. If you use tractor-fed paper, be sure the finished size measures 8½" × 11" instead of larger-size computer paper. And as with traditional typed material, use a good, black ribbon for your final draft.

Follow the same guidelines as those for formatting and mailing typed material. Be sure to number your pages at the top right-hand corner (either by hand or through computer commands). Then, if necessary, remove the pin-hole strips on each side and separate the printout sheets before mailing.

COMPUTER UPLOADS

Formatting for manuscripts that will be uploaded (that is, sent *from* your computer *to* another computer using a modem) depends on two important factors: (1) the type of communications software that operates your modem, and (2) the preferences and requirements of the computer system you want to send material to. Generally, manuscripts are saved and sent in standard ASCII or binary formats with hard carriage returns and line feeds inserted directly into the text.

By using one of these two forms, almost anyone who has access to the same online system can download manuscripts, usually stored in library files, even if they have a different type of computer. For instance, anyone with an IBM-compatible computer system can upload a manuscript that someone with an Apple, Amiga, Commodore, or other compatible brand can download.

(Remember that work uploaded to another computer system is still protected by copyright laws. You can download it to read for your own enjoyment, you can even print it out and keep it to read again. But you *cannot* sell it to others or use it as if it were your own.)

It is very important that you find out how to format a file *in advance*, before trying to upload a manuscript. You will only waste valuable time and money if you don't. On commercial information services such as CompuServe, GEnie and Prodigy, complete directions, guidelines, and additional tips and advice can be found stored in special library files. To find out what library and file has the information you need, leave a message for the system operator (SYSOP) in charge of the special interest group (SIG) that you want to participate in. Also watch for special announcements either displayed on-screen when you log on, or in the printed manual distributed to subscribers.

Procedures may differ for independent bulletin board systems (BBSs). You'll need to contact the SYSOP at each one by modem, through a regular phone call, or by *snail* mail (writing a letter and sending it through the U.S. Postal Service!) to find out individual requirements. Other systems, such as the AT&T Learning Network and BreadNet, also have special requirements and procedures. Contact them individually for complete information.

While formatting manuscript for uploading may differ from traditional markets, you should still follow the general advice given in Chapter 1. Take time to rewrite, revise and polish before sending a manuscript. That means checking and correcting grammar, punctuation and spelling too!

EXCEPTIONS: WHEN AND HOW TO BREAK THE RULES

There may be times when you want to send an editor material prepared in a special way. Just remember to include the *written part* of the manuscript on a separate sheet of paper, following the standard formats as best you can. Then if the editor decides to publish your material, she will be able to give this copy to the typesetter to use.

Here are some examples of when you might consider breaking the standard formats for submitting material:

Situation: You do beautiful calligraphy and your manuscript tells teens how you make extra money by designing and selling personalized stationery.

You might: Prepare your manuscript following the standard formats. Then include as your cover letter a short message written on a sheet of stationery that you have designed.

Situation: Your class has put together a special collection of stories written and illustrated by the students. One of the students, or your teacher, has written an article about the project.

You might: Type the article using the standard formats and include a free copy of your book for the editor to read.

Situation: You have a handicap that makes it difficult to type or write neatly.

You might: Prepare your manuscript as best you can. Include a cover letter telling a bit about yourself. Consider having someone else help you prepare your final copy.

Situation: For a holiday present, you typed some of your poems on special paper, then illustrated or decorated them yourself and hung them in pretty frames.

You might: Retype your poem on a separate sheet of paper using the standard format. Include this with a photograph of your framed poem, or include an extra illustrated poem for the editor.

KEEPING TRACK OF SUBMISSIONS

Once you decide to submit material to an editor or contest, you must also devise a system of keeping track of your manuscripts. This is especially important if you are anxious to get published and will be sending more than one manuscript out at the same time.

One way to keep track is with 3″ × 5″ index cards kept in a file box. Prepare a new index card for each manuscript you send out. (See figure 11, page 64, for a sample format.)

Record the title of your manuscript or contest entry, the date you mailed it (not the date you wrote it), and the name of the market or contest you sent the manuscript to. Under "Notes," you may want to write down the amount of postage the manuscript needed. Include the cost of the SASE or postcard too.

When you receive an answer from the editor or contest, write the date under the "Date Returned" heading. Under "Notes," or

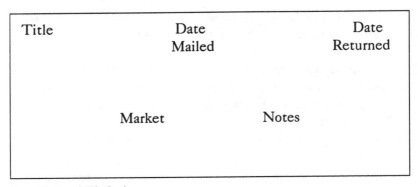

Figure 11. Sample File Card

on the back of the card, mark whether the manuscript was accepted or rejected and any other information such as how much you were (or will be) paid for the piece, and when the editor plans to publish it.

If the manuscript was rejected, select another market from the lists. Mark the new information on the same card if there is room.

If students will be submitting material as part of a class project, one file box may be used to keep an accurate record of all student submissions and editors' remarks.

Similar records may also be stored in a notebook or in a computer file.

MODEL RELEASE FORMS

Occasionally a publication or contest will ask that the author, artist or photographer provide a statement signed by the person granting an interview or photograph, to prove that he or she agreed to the project and understood how the material might be used (such as in a magazine). When the person signs the form, it means that he or she is saying that it's OK to publish the material. Such a form is known as a "model release." Sometimes a market will supply a copy of the model release form they prefer, or you can find examples of them in reference books. However, if only a simple form is needed you can make one up yourself. Here's how:

Using a clean sheet of paper, write your name, address and phone number, and the name, address and phone number of the person being interviewed, photographed, or used as a model. Have that person write a sentence or two that clearly shows he or she understands that the interview or picture might be published or used for publicity purposes. (You could write up this statement ahead of time.) Then have the person sign his or her name and that day's date. Sign your name too. If possible, have another person sign it too, as a witness.

If you are dealing with someone 18 or younger, have a parent or guardian also sign the model release form.

Note that you don't need to provide this form unless the market or contest requests it. But because you may not always know when you'll need to send one, it's a good idea to have a model release form signed by anyone readily identifiable in a photograph you hope to have published.

ADDITIONAL TIPS

Think ahead! If you're really anxious to submit material, don't wait until you have a manuscript in final draft form before sending away for market guidelines, sample copies and detailed contest information. But don't send away for all of them at once either. Choose a few markets and contests that are looking for material similar to what you are most interested in writing. Also consider markets and contests directed toward people your age.

You'll need an easy way to store your market and contest information so that when you have a manuscript ready to submit, you can consult your files and choose where you would like to send it first.

All this information can be kept in a desk drawer, file cabinet, or even a shoe box. An even better method is to make your own personal marketing guide. You'll need a large three-ring binder and a box of vinyl sheet protectors. Top-loading sheet protectors work best. You might also want a package of tab dividers to separate various types of markets and contests, or to file information alphabetically.

When a sample copy and guideline sheet arrive, slip them into a sheet protector for safekeeping. Some sample copies won't fit into the sheet protector. You'll have to store these somewhere else. Put a note on the corresponding guideline sheet to remind

---

Author's Tip

The standard formats and advice featured in this guide will suit the needs of most young writers. For more information about manuscript formats and the marketing process, read *The Writer's Digest Guide to Manuscript Formats*, by Dian Dincin Buchman and Seli Groves. The detailed checklists and submission logs are particularly helpful for anyone planning to do a lot of writing and marketing.

---

yourself where the sample copy is. Insert a reference sheet at the front of your binder to record which market and contest information you have. Also include the date you received the information and the date of the sample copy so you'll know when you need to send for more current information.

Your personal marketing guide is also an excellent place to keep additional notes about writing, the names and addresses of new markets and contests, samples of published material you think is well-written, and even your record of submissions. If you attend conferences or writing workshops, or if published authors speak to your class, store your notes or any handout material in your marketing guide for easy reference.

Chapter Four

Opportunities Online

Imagine writing and getting published without using a single sheet of paper, stuffing one envelope or licking one stamp. Impossible, you say?

Not if you are one of a growing group of writers, publishers and readers using personal computers and telephone lines to communicate with one another. We may still be light years away from becoming a paperless society, but technology has launched a new generation of communication opportunities. Sometimes I wonder what Johann Gutenberg[1] would think of all this.

This chapter introduces you to just a few of the opportunities that have developed in recent years for writers online, such as:

- Markets and contests where you can submit your writing
- Bulletin board systems (BBSs) where writers who share common interests gather to chat, and offer each other help and encouragement
- Electronic libraries bursting with informational and recreational resources; electronic versions of magazines, books and newsletters; samples of works-in-progress
- Ongoing workshops and critique sessions for writers covering all types of writing and genres
- Real-time conferences (RTCs) that allow writers from all over the country — and all over the world — to gather at the same time to chat informally or pose questions to guest speakers

---

[1]Gutenberg is often credited with printing the first book, a Bible, using a machine with moveable type during the mid-fifteenth century. This made it possible to publish multiple copies of books, which previously had to be copied by hand.

Once you become involved, perhaps you'll become a pioneer in this rapidly expanding field.

WHAT IS ONLINE COMPUTING?

Online computing is communicating with others using a personal computer and modem, rather than talking face to face, corresponding by regular mail, or speaking on the telephone. Modems, one attached to each computer and programmed with special communications software, interpret computer messages and files, then transmit the data over regular touch-tone telephone lines using electronic signals. Standard transmission formats have been developed to allow different kinds of computers to read and use the same files, even if they were created on non-compatible machines. For instance, someone using a Macintosh will have no trouble reading a message that I created on my IBM-compatible machine.

ASCII, which stands for American Standard Code for Information Interchange, is the format most commonly used to transmit data electronically. Letters and numbers, simple punctuation (such as spaces, periods, question marks), basic typing commands (such as a tab to indent text, a paragraph or a hard return) and special control codes (to let the other computer know the transfer of data is completed, for instance) are each represented by a special ASCII code.

Facsimile (or fax) machines work in a similar way, but the information sent is printed out by the receiving fax machine. With a modem, however, files can be sent to a host system such as CompuServe Information Service or GEnie (General Electric Network for Information Exchange), where they will be stored until someone retrieves them. Modems also allow two or more people to interact with each other at the same time. For instance, during a real-time conference (RTC) when one person types a message and presses the "enter" or "return" key on her keyboard, the host system (that's the one everyone is connected to) receives the message and then passes it on so that it will appear instantly on the computer screens of all the other people who are participating. For an example, see the transcript of an RTC with best-selling author Michael Crichton in Appendix B.

Author's Tip:

If you are interested in learning more about how computers and modems access online services, an excellent resource is Peter Norton's book, *Outside the IBM PC and PS/2*. Mr. Norton has a talent for explaining the often complex and confusing world of computer technology in an easy-to-understand way. Chapter 3, "Communications Technologies," and Chapter 4, "Modems," provide particularly useful background information.

To learn more about the two largest online services, try *Glossbrenner's Master Guide to GEnie*, by Alfred Glossbrenner, and *How to Get the Most Out of CompuServe*, by Charles Bowen and David Peyton.

WHO'S ONLINE

As mentioned above, an online information system such as CompuServe or GEnie can serve as a host. These systems offer many more services than the few described so far. There are bulletin board areas (called "forums" on CompuServe and "roundtables" on GEnie) for almost any area of interest. They also serve as gateways to huge databases of information that you can search from your own computer. This is particularly helpful when writing nonfiction or researching papers for school. Host systems also offer electronic mail (e-mail) delivery. A letter sent by e-mail will usually appear in the other person's online mailbox within a few minutes, instead of the days it takes regular mail to be delivered.

There are also many private and local bulletin board systems. Chances are you have one in your area. Many computer stores will maintain a BBS so customers can contact them by modem to order new software or equipment, report problems, or meet other people with similar interests. Several writers groups maintain private BBSs that allow members to post messages and hold RTCs.

Even schools are setting up BBSs so their students can communicate with students in other areas. Besides a suitable computer system, modem and communications software, and an available phone line, all that's needed is for the two (or more) schools to decide which one will act as host for the upcoming session.

For our purposes, we're going to concentrate on some of the online writing and publishing opportunities available on CompuServe and GEnie. While CompuServe was the first online information service to offer access to the general consumer (in 1979), the Writers' Ink RoundTable (WINK) on GEnie has established itself as the leading electronic community for writers, according to its founder and leader Jack Smith.

ADVANTAGES AND DISADVANTAGES

There are two major disadvantages with becoming a member of an online service. The first is cost. Fees vary depending on which service you belong to, which areas you access, how long you stay online, what time of day you log on (evenings, weekends and holidays are least expensive), and what you do while online. However, several special software programs can help automate your online sessions. They allow you to write messages offline (when you are not connected), log you on, retrieve any e-mail or messages to you, post your new messages, download any special files you have selected, then log you off automatically. Then you can read your messages and files whenever it's convenient.

CompuServe recommends its communications program called CompuServe Information Manager (CIM) for beginners. Aladdin is used by many IBM and IBM-compatible users on GEnie. Information on these and other programs is available from the individual services.

A second cost consideration is whether or not you must dial long-distance to log on. Telephone charges are billed like any other long-distance call you make (another reason to log on in the evenings or weekends). They are in addition to the connect charges you pay for the service itself.

The second major disadvantage to becoming a member of an online service is that it can be addictive. You've got to watch your time, not just to keep phone and connect charges within reason, but also so you don't neglect your writing, school or family.

Still, most online writers think there are more advantages than disadvantages. The biggest, perhaps, is being able to communicate with other people who understand what it's like being, or wanting to be, a writer. Sheri Sinykin[2], a writer who is an active member of WINK in the children's and young adult books category, put it this way:

> On GEnie, you never know which children's book writers and illustrators might pop in to say hello and share their experiences, problems and excitement about the writing life. Many well-known writers, as well as authors like me who are just beginning their publishing careers, enjoy chatting online almost daily about the ups and downs of our lives and our manuscripts-in-progress. When one of us has a question, someone else is likely to stop by with an answer or two. Some people even upload and critique manuscripts online. My real-life friendships with writers have deepened through speedy e-mail letters and I've made wonderful new friendships with writers — both struggling and published — who I never would have met otherwise.

REAL-TIME CONFERENCES

Perhaps the biggest advantage of participating online is the opportunity to attend a wide variety of workshops and conferences that would normally be out of reach to young people because of cost, location and other restrictions. But online, almost every area of the system is open to young people. Just like in the real world, you will be expected to mind your manners. But no one will know how old you are unless you want to tell them.

That means that you can attend both regular and special RTCs, sitting at a computer and participating by asking questions, posting replies and so on, if they aren't happening too late for your time zone. Or you can do what many members do, download the transcript of the RTC at a later date.

You'll want to check your special interest areas for regularly scheduled RTCs. The Literary Forum, for example, holds a general topic conference on Tuesday nights at 10 P.M. eastern time[3]. On WINK, there's a regular open RTC every Sunday night at 9:30

---

[2]Sheri Cooper Sinykin's children's books include *Shrimpboat and Gym Bags*, *The Buddy Trap*, *Sirens*, and *The Shorty Society* (summer 1994).

[3]This was accurate as of April 1993. Be sure to check for current dates and times.

P.M. Nonfiction writers meet on Wednesday nights at 9:30 P.M., and poets meet Tuesdays at 10 P.M.

Is there an author or publisher in particular you would like to have at an RTC? Then make a suggestion. Forums and roundtables are a lot like local writer's clubs; they depend on active member participation.

ONLINE MARKETS AND CONTESTS

A small sampling of online markets and contests is included alphabetically in the regular listings sections in Chapters 8 and 9. Like all the listings in this guide, they have expressed an interest in hearing from young writers.

Some opportunities, such as *Kopper Bear Press* (see page 195) and *Kids & Computers* magazine (see page 193) are actually traditional publishers who allow writers to contact them using an electronic mail (e-mail) service such as GEnie, CompuServe or America Online. Others, such as Digital Publishing RoundTable (see page 182) offer access to online magazines, newsletters, short stories, poetry, and other types of writing that you can download to your computer to later read on your monitor or print out.

You'll find other, more general areas directly in the listings for GEnie and CompuServe. Again, these forums and roundtables (commonly referred to as SIGs or special interest groups) have each said they welcome submissions and participation by young writers. It was not possible for me to contact every one of the various SIGs individually. If you have a special hobby or interest (anything from aquariums to zoology, casual or technical) be sure to check in the information service directory that comes with your membership for additional forums, roundtables and SIGs to participate in. Similar groups might also be found on other information services such as America Online or Prodigy.

To locate appropriate markets for your work, it's best to check the descriptions of the various sections (or categories) and libraries within individual SIGs. For instance, in the Writers' Ink Round-Table on GEnie, there is a special category (#5) just for young writers. Topics include "Round Robin" stories and "Humorous Short Story Exchange." Young poets may be more comfortable, or

Author's Note: Proceed With Caution

Just as you should any market or contest, study and compare online opportunities before submitting material. There are vanity publishers and subsidy presses you'll want to avoid.

Also be aware that there are a large number of self-publishing opportunities available online. Some, like uploading your stories or poems to forum libraries, provide benefits similar to contributing to school anthologies or Young Author Day projects. Others, however, more closely resemble the self-publishing ventures described in Chapter 1 under "Ego Alert!" Enjoy yourself, but don't get so caught up in sharing your work with the world (either on paper or electronically) that you forget the long-term goals you have set for yourself as a writer.

find more expert help, participating in Category 30, the "Poet's Retreat."

On CompuServe, the primary forum for creative writers is the Literary Forum. But other forums offer a variety of opportunities as well. For instance SYSOPS (that stands for system operators, the people who manage each area) in the Outdoor Forum, Motor Sports Forum, Computer Graphics Forums (there are several), and the Comic Book Forum all say that young people are more than welcome to join in. Even the Legal Forum has a library file written by a young student. Dann Marvin, a 9-year-old, wrote about his experiences visiting some court proceedings.

Contest opportunities can pop up unexpectedly. In February 1993, for instance, the Student Forum offered members a chance to win a $25 CompuServe usage credit in a new creative writing contest. The idea was sparked by the upcoming book *What Do We Mean When We Say Love?* Members were asked to submit 300-word compositions, which could be serious or humorous, but had to be as creative and original as possible, explaining what love means to them.

Joshua Hauser even started an online publishing opportunity himself by suggesting that interested members write a community story. He started things off by writing:

Author's Note:

At least one company even offers a paperless bookstore. While this particular option has yet to catch on with the general publishing community, some, like SoftServe Paperless Bookstore manager N. Neil Schulman, feel it's an idea who's time has come. SoftServe is available on the Writers' Ink Round-Table on GEnie.

It was a dark and dreary day in the big city, but since I was in a totally different city, it didn't affect me. I was making breakfast when the phone rang.

Other writers then added to the story.

News about online writing, art and photography contests are often featured in special messages (called banners), which scroll by whenever you log on to a service or SIG. To access the rules and regulations for each contest, you need to go into the SIG that is sponsoring the contest and download the special library file containing the information. If you don't know where to look, you can post a message to a SYSOP and one will reply within a day or two.

ONLINE GUIDELINES

The guidelines for preparing traditional manuscripts and art apply equally well to the more traditional online markets and contests. That means spending time writing, rewriting, revising and polishing your stories; checking for grammar, spelling and punctuation mistakes; and making sure you are submitting an appropriate manuscript to an appropriate place. Many markets that accept electronic submissions have posted their guidelines in various libraries. The two best places to check are in the libraries of writing-related areas such as the WINK RoundTable on GEnie and the Literary Forum on CompuServe.

In addition, remember that most library files must be sent (uploaded) in standard ASCII format. You won't have to worry about margins and headers and page numbers. But you should understand that ASCII does not recognize special features (called attributes) such as boldface type or underlining. If you want to emphasize a word or short phrase TYPE IT IN CAPS or *place it between asterisks*. To indicate that something should be underlined or in italics, such as the title of a book, place it between two underline characters: _Market Guide for Young Writers _.

Don't forget to include your name and e-mail address on all files that you upload. It is also recommended that you add the standard copyright notice at the beginning or end of every file you upload. (This applies to library files or special text sent as a manuscript, not to ordinary chit-chat type messages.) To indicate your copyright notice, type the word "Copyright," the year the manuscript was created (put in fixed form, such as when you typed it) and your name. Here's an example:

Copyright 1993 Kathy Henderson

Check your wordprocessing software manual to find how to save your text in ASCII format. Sometimes this is called generic DOS. By the way, graphic files are usually quite large compared to straight text. They should be uploaded separately, using an acceptable graphic format.

Don't be shy about asking questions. SYSOPS, like Jack Smith (WINK on GEnie) and Jan Stimson (Student Forum on CompuServe) agree that the only dumb questions are the ones that aren't asked!

ETIQUETTE ONLINE

Because time *is* money online, the messages members post are usually brief and informal. Unlike the care you should take polishing a final draft or writing a cover or query letter to an editor, don't worry about minor misspellings or typos and lapses in punctuation and grammar.

On the other hand, messages also tend to be clearer and more concise, a fact that even Pulitzer Prize-winning writer and film critic Roger Ebert[4] has noticed. During a visit to the Journalism Forum on CompuServe he said, "For some reason, most of the people on CompuServe in the forums I visit are very good writers. Maybe electronic mail helps you become concise because of the cost and memorable because of the competition."

If you have a reason to post a long message (perhaps you are sharing what you learned at a workshop you attended) preface it by giving readers fair warning. Here's an example:

To ALL

Kathy Henderson recently did a writing and publishing workshop at my school. I thought you might enjoy hearing some of the advice she gave us.

* *

WARNING — LONG MESSAGE

* *

Then continue with what you want to share.

Fellow online members will appreciate the courtesy you've shown. They can download the message if they are interested or send a break command to bypass it.

COPYRIGHT PROTECTION AND UPLOADING

Bear in mind that copyright law applies to the messages and other files you download from online sources just as it does to printed, taped, and other fixed methods of creative work. Chapter 5 contains additional information regarding copyright.

---

[4]Readers may know Ebert, an internationally known film critic, as half of the Siskel and Ebert team. He is also a former teacher and magazine editor. A complete transcript of his seminar visit is available in Library 3 "Free-lancers," of the Journalism Forum on CompuServe. The file name is EBERT.TXT.

Author's Note: Special Offer From WINK

Jack D. Smith, head SYSOP of the Writer's Ink RoundTable (WINK), headquarters of The Electronic Writers Association on GEnie, has made a special offer to readers. After joining WINK, send him an e-mail message using the WRITERS.INK address. Introduce yourself and mention that you saw this offer in the *Market Guide for Young Writers Fourth Edition*. You'll receive a two-week free flag to the WINK RoundTable. That means you can read and post bulletin board messages, upload and download files to the libraries, and take part in real-time conferences *free* of GEnie connect charges while in the Writer's Ink area. (Offer does not cover telephone billing charges.)

If you are already a GEnie subscriber, simply post an e-mail message to WRITERS.INK in the usual way.

If you would like to take advantage of this offer, have a parent or teacher use the following sign-up procedure:

1. Set your communications software for half-duplex (local echo) at 300, 1200 or 2400 baud.
2. Dial toll free: (800) 638-8369 (or in Canada: (800) 387-8330.) When you see CONNECT on your screen, quickly type HHH. (You must use all capitals.)
3. At the U# = prompt, enter XTX99003,WRITERS and press Return or Enter on your keyboard.
4. Have a major credit card ready (U.S. residents can also use a checking account number). You will be prompted for the necessary information.

Note: You'll want to capture what appears on the screen to a disk file so you can review it offline later. Be sure you know how to open a log file (also called "screen capture") before your modem dials the telephone number. Your account will be activated within a couple of days. Then you can request your free flag from Jack Smith using GEnie mail. You'll also receive a GEnie membership kit through the mail.

For voice information about GEnie (in other words, to talk to a real person), call (800) 638-9636.

Chapter Five

Answers to Questions Young Writers Ask Most

QUESTIONS ABOUT GETTING PUBLISHED

Why should I include an SASE?

SASE is the abbreviation for self-addressed stamped envelope. All editors and most contests insist that writers include an SASE with their manuscript. The editor will use it to send you an answer, or to return your manuscript if it is rejected. To prepare an SASE, write your name and address on the front of an envelope as if you were mailing it to yourself. Put the same amount of postage on your SASE that you put on your mailing envelope. *Example*: If it costs you $.52 to mail your manuscript, you must also put $.52 on your SASE. Put your SASE inside the mailing envelope with your manuscript when you mail it.

Special note: Always use regular postage stamps on your SASEs. Do not use metered postage tape or the post office may not return the envelope to you. This is because the metered postage tape will show the date you origi-nally mailed the manuscript or letter, rather than the date when the SASE was mailed back to you.

I sent a self-addressed stamped envelope with my manu-script but never received a reply. What should I do?

It often takes an editor four to eight weeks to respond. If you have waited this long, send a polite letter to the editor asking if he received your manuscript and if a decision has been made. Be sure to include an SASE or self-addressed stamped postcard for a reply. Remember that some markets receive so much mail that they have a policy not to respond at all unless a manuscript is accepted for publication, or if it wins an award in the case of a contest. Check the market listing or guidelines. If a market says, "Does not respond" or "Does not return submissions," you do not have to enclose an SASE. If you want to make sure an editor or contest has received your manuscript, enclose a postage-paid *postcard* addressed to you. (See figure 9, page 59.)

If you still receive no answer from a market that normally responds and returns manuscripts, I suggest you write one more time saying that you are withdrawing your manuscript from consideration and would like it returned to you immediately. Some professionals feel that if an editor hasn't responded within a reasonable time (normally about two or three months) writers should feel free to simply submit their manuscript elsewhere without bothering to notify the first editor.

Most editors try to be as prompt as possible.

Can I send a manuscript to a publication that is not listed in *Market Guide for Young Writers*?

For various reasons, not all publications that consider material written by young people are listed in this guide. Some editors have asked not to be listed because they prefer that only their readers submit material. If you have read a notice in a publication asking for submissions, you are considered a reader and may send them your submission whether or not they are listed in this guide. Be careful to follow their guidelines.

Editors who currently receive more submissions than they can handle or use also sometimes ask not to be listed in a particular edition.

There may be other publications I was not aware of, or that were too new at the time this edition was printed, that may also consider your manuscript. (*If you discover a market not listed, please send me their name and address so that I may contact them to see if they would like to be included in future editions.*) Send your suggestions to: Kathy Henderson, MGYW, c/o Writer's Digest Books, 1507 Dana Ave., Cincinnati, OH 45207.

Feel free to check other resources such as *Writer's Market* or *Literary Market Place* for additional market and contest opportunities. Several writer's organizations, such as the National Writer's Club, and many trade magazines for writers, such as *Byline*, *The Writer*, and *Writer's Digest* are also useful sources of current market and contest information. Note, however, that it will be harder to tell in these resources which opportunities are practical for young writers to target.

Why don't you include the editor's name and phone number with all the listings?

Phone numbers are only listed when the editor includes the information on the survey sheet that is returned to me *and* indicates he wants it included with the listing. (For examples, see the listings for *Stone Soup* and *Merlyn's Pen*.) Most editors do not want their phone number included because they fear having to answer too many phone calls from people who should be sending their questions by mail. If you have a legitimate reason to call, you can usually locate the phone number on the guidelines sheet or masthead in your sample copy.

The same criteria applies to including the name of an editor or contest coordinator. If you send for guidelines or a sample copy *before* submitting material as advised, you will find out the names of editors and contest coordinators.

Can I send the same manuscript to more than one magazine at the same time?

Sending the same manuscript to more than one market at the same time is called a multiple or "simultaneous" submission. It is not recommended for either adult or young writers. However, you may send different manuscripts to separate publications at the same time. Be sure to keep a record of which manuscript you sent to which market.

Most contests want only new material that has not been published or submitted to another contest or market before. A few contests (for example, see *NWC Novel Contest*) state in their guidelines that you may also submit entries to a publisher. The only way to know for sure is to read the directions.

Why does a listing say "send holiday or seasonal material six months in advance"?

It takes several months to collect, edit and print each issue of a publication. Therefore, editors must consider material several months in advance of the issue's scheduled appearance. Often editors are reading Christmas stories in July and surfing stories in December. This is called the "lead time." (Pronounced like "reed.") Different publications have different lead times. Generally, a magazine's lead time is much longer than the lead time for a newspaper.

What is an International Reply Coupon?

International reply coupons (IRCs) are redeemed at post offices for postage, similar to how subway or bus tokens substitute for coins. The *value* has been paid for in advance. Writers need to send IRCs instead of putting postage stamps on their self-addressed envelopes (or postcards) when submitting manuscripts to foreign markets. For instance, U.S. postage cannot be used by people in other countries, including Canada, to mail a letter or package back to you. You also couldn't mail a letter *from* the United States *to* Canada with a Canadian stamp. Sending IRCs instead of stamps allows an editor in one country to purchase the appropriate stamps to respond to a writer in another country.

If you wish to submit to a foreign market, ask a postal clerk for the appropriate amount of International Reply Coupons to enclose with your self-addressed envelope.

Can my friend and I send in a story we wrote together?

Usually this isn't a problem, especially when submitting manuscripts to markets. Some contests, however, insist that an entry be the original work of one writer. Again, it's important to check the guidelines.

Why doesn't my favorite magazine publish more poems by young people?

A publication is limited in how much material it can print in pbeach issue. This is usually determined by the amount of advertising used or, in the case of publications that carry no advertising, a predetermined number of pages. You might try writing to the editor and explaining that you would like to see more poems (or short stories, or whatever) by young people. Also, look for more opportunities to publish your work in your local area. You may even want to consider starting a newsletter of your own or arranging for a sponsor like Margaret Larkin did. See her profile on page 142 and the one on Carole Trapani, page 139, for ideas.

My story won first place in a writing contest. Can I send it to a magazine to be published too?

Some contests retain the copyright to entries and some do not. The rules should state when and if you may submit your manuscript elsewhere. For instance, NWC contests say that you *may* submit contest entries to a market. However, The Ayn Rand Institute College Scholarship competition guidelines state "all entries become the property of The Ayn Rand Institute." An entry submitted here, whether or not it wins, *cannot* be submitted anywhere else. That's because the manuscript would no longer be *your* property. By entering it, you agreed to relinquish (that means to give up) your rights to it. Be sure to consider this when deciding where to submit your work.

Do I have to subscribe to a magazine before I can send them a manuscript?

It depends. Some magazines want material only from their current subscribers. One of these is *Authorship*. Subscribers can usually find submission guidelines in current issues. Some magazines prefer submissions from readers, though not specifically subscribers. If you don't have these magazines delivered to your home but read them in your school, library, church, etc., you are still considered a reader and may submit material. However for most magazines, newsletters and newspapers you do not need to subscribe before you submit material.

I don't own a typewriter. What can I do?

Some editors will accept handwritten manuscripts if they are legible, which means neat and easy to read. Almost all markets for teens and adults, however, require manuscripts to be typed. You might try borrowing or renting a typewriter (perhaps at school), or find someone who will type your manuscript for you. Consider saving your money to buy a used typewriter, or a no-frills word processor or computer system if you can't afford a new one. The point is, if you are serious about getting published, you will find a way to get your work typed. Don't bother complaining that such policies are unreasonable to writers who don't own typewriters or don't want to find other ways to get their manuscripts typed, as some frustrated beginning adult writers do. Expecting manuscripts to be typed is no more unreasonable than expecting someone who wants to play hockey to get a pair of ice skates.

Remember that nowadays "typed" means it can be produced with either a typewriter or computer, as long as the final printout is legible. When using a typewriter or dot-matrix printer, make sure to use a good ribbon that produces solid black type. Light print is not only very hard to read, it does not fax or photocopy well.

My story is 1,927 words long but the magazine I want to send it to only accepts stories 800 words long. Should I send it anyway?

You have three choices: (1) Cut, revise and polish your story until you get it down to the 800-word limit, or close to it. A little over, say 50 words, is usually acceptable. This type of editing usually produces an even better manuscript. (Stories may always be under the word limit.) (2) Look for a different publication that accepts longer stories. (3) Send it as is and take your chances. Obviously, the first two suggestions are the best to follow.

Remember, do *not* go over the maximum word limit when entering a contest. Your entry will be disqualified.

When the magazine published my story, they changed some of the words and left some parts out. I liked it better my way. Why did they do that?

There are several reasons an editor may change your story. It may have been too long to fit the available space, or the editor may have felt a different word or phrase would make your message clearer for readers to understand. This doesn't happen just with magazine stories, but with all types of work. Editors have a responsibility (it's a large part of their job) to edit material when they think it is necessary. Thoughtful editing can make a good manuscript even better. Thankfully, most editors will only make minor editing changes on their own. If they think more changes are needed, they will make suggestions and ask the writer to make them.

Unfortunately, if a piece an editor changes has already been published, there really isn't anything you can do about it except go on to your next project. However, when an editor requests that you make some changes in your manuscript before she will consider publishing it, you will have to decide whether making them will help your work or not. If you don't understand what you are being asked to do, or if you don't agree with all the suggestions, take time to discuss your feelings with the editor by phone or in a letter. Be prepared to explain why you think some or all of the suggested changes are unnecessary and to make new suggestions of your own. This give and take between writers and editors happens all the time. Don't be afraid of it. If you and the editor can't agree on what to do, either she will decide not to publish it or you can decide to submit the manuscript somewhere else.

All manuscripts get edited, even those by famous authors. It is a necessary part of the publishing process.

Note: If you self-publish your work, it should still be edited. Rewriting and revising and polishing are key steps to producing quality work. You may be able to do all the necessary editing on your own. However it is much wiser to enlist the help of someone with editing experience.

A story I sent to a magazine was rejected. But the next issue had a story almost like mine. I think they stole my idea. What can I do?

First, because of a publication's lead time (see page 81) it is very unlikely that someone stole your story. Second, many writers have the same idea for a story, although they do not write the story in the same way. Your story was probably rejected because the editor had already accepted the one you read before your manuscript arrived. Try sending your story to a different market. And get busy writing new ones. Ideas, by the way, are not protected by copyright. Many of us have similar ideas, but we write them in different ways.

I'm afraid someone will steal my story and publish it if I send it to an editor. Is there some way I can keep people from stealing it?

It is very unlikely that anyone will steal your story, especially if it is unpublished. When a story is stolen (someone pretends that he wrote it and gets it published or enters it into a contest), it is called "plagiarism." Plagiarists are usually found out, and can be taken to court.

There is a poem that I really like but it has no author's name on it. Can I submit it?

No, especially if you hope someone will think that you wrote it. That would be plagiarism. *Someone* wrote that poem, and it wasn't you.

Are there any other exceptions?

Yes, there is a situation when you *may* submit something you saw published in one publication to another. A good example is *Reader's Digest*, which publishes many short, usually funny, items published in other magazines and newspapers. The difference is that the person submitting the material, called a "clipping," does not pretend that she created it herself. If you submit this type of item, always give credit to the person who wrote it and the publication where it was originally published. If no author was credited, identify the author as unknown or "anonymous."

My dad says that charging for sample copies is just a way for magazines to make money by selling extra copies. Shouldn't they be willing to send them to writers free so we can see what type of material they publish?

A few do. They're more likely to be ones hoping that once you see a copy, you'll want to subscribe. But most publications simply can't afford to send a free copy to every writer who wants one. Saving money to send for sample copies is not always easy. How-

Author's Tip:

Plagiarism is a serious offense. It means to use or submit someone else's work as your own original work. Plagiarism often hurts innocent writers in ways that are not always apparent.

For example:

Several years ago I was one of fifty judges who evaluated entries in a large student writing competition sponsored by the *Detroit Free Press*. Many of the entries were so well written that some judges (many were public school teachers) were genuinely surprised, yet pleased, at the level of talent displayed by the young entrants. Then, halfway through the first day of judging, I read an entry that I knew was plagiarized material. The student had copied two chapters from a juvenile novel by Dorothy Haas. Not even the names of the characters had been changed.

Immediately the judging atmosphere changed. Judges who moments before had been surprised and delighted to discover well-written manuscripts among the hundreds of entries were suddenly wary and suspicious. Whether consciously or unconsciously, we all feared the same thing: Was this another plagiarized entry? Can such a young student really write this well?

If the student who submitted this plagiarized entry thought no one would be hurt by the deception, he or she was wrong. True, no harm was done to Mrs. Haas, the original author. But consider the harm done to all the young writers whose work was judged after the plagiarized entry was discovered. The most talented young writers were hurt most, because their entries drew the most suspicion and thus may have been given lower marks than they would have been given the day before.

ever, if you are serious about writing *and* publishing, it's money well spent. In some ways, it's almost like paying for lessons to learn how to play the piano better.

It's not necessary to send away for every sample copy that's available. Concentrate on the publications you really think you can sell your work to. Also, remember you can read issues of many magazines for free at the library. You may also be able to get samples of old magazines from waiting rooms at some businesses. My kids are now too old to want a subscription to *Highlights for Children*, so I take home old copies from my chiropractor's office — with permission, of course.

Should I enter a contest if I don't really think I have a chance of winning?

That depends. If you just write and write and never bother to consider how revising, rewriting and polishing your work might make it better, and then you pick just any contest to enter, you might think you had no real chance of winning. And you'd be right. There wouldn't be any point to entering in the first place.

On the other hand, if you've taken the time to write and then edit until it's the best work you can do, and you've gone to the trouble to find a contest that is appropriate for the type of manuscript you've written, you still might think you don't have a chance — if you lack self-confidence. It's true that you might not win, but you'd be wrong to think that you didn't have a chance. If you don't enter, you'll miss the benefit of the experience and a chance at placing. And for some contests, such as the *California Young Playwrights Contest*, you'd miss out on receiving a free, detailed professional evaluation that could help you become a better writer.

Do I have to submit to magazines only for kids, or can I send material to the ones my parents read, too?

A number of magazines for adults regularly publish material from young people. Some are listed here. You'll need to judge for yourself whether a publication not listed would consider publishing your submission. I can't think of *any* circumstances where it would be wrong to express your opinion on a certain topic as a letter to the editor.

Why should I bother sending my material to a publication that doesn't pay for it?

As a young writer, you should be more interested in gaining writing and submission experience than in making a lot of money. Very few writers of any age get rich by selling their manuscripts. You will gain valuable experience with every "sale" you make to a publication, whether or not you are paid in cash for your efforts. It is hard for poets, in particular, to find paying markets for their work. Of course, you can choose not to send material to a publication that does not pay young writers. It is entirely up to you. (Beware, however, of markets and contests that want *you* to pay to have your work published!)

If this advice still doesn't make sense to you, pretend for a moment that you want to become a Major League Baseball player earning a million dollars a year when you grow up. How much do you expect to be paid while playing Little League?

Why do some magazines pay a lot for manuscripts, some just a little, and some not at all?

How much a publication pays for a manuscript varies greatly according to the publication's operating budget and editorial policy. In general, the markets in this guide that normally pay for material, pay the same rates to young people as they do to adults. Note that publications that include advertisements often, though not always, pay at least a little for accepted manuscripts. The money that companies pay for advertising space increases a publication's operating budget, making it more likely to pay for accepted manuscripts.

On some guidelines I've read "pays on acceptance," and on others "pays on publication." What's the difference?

A publication that "pays on acceptance" will send you your check soon after your manuscript is accepted. Markets that "pay on publication" wait until they have actually printed your manuscript before sending you a check. Waiting for a "pays on publication" market to pay you is sometimes very frustrating. It may take a year or longer before your manuscript is published. When you need to decide between two markets with similar guidelines it makes sense to submit first to the one that "pays on acceptance."

Do I have to cash the check I got from a magazine? I want to frame it.

By all means, cash it. Consider framing your printed piece or a photocopy of the check instead, to signify your first "for pay" sale.

What does it mean to get a "$500 advance against royalties"?

Normally, when a writer sells a manuscript to a book publisher, he receives a contract. Among other things, the contract tells how much money he will earn for every book that the publisher sells. This is usually based on a percentage of the book's selling price. For example, if the writer's contract says that he will earn 10 percent for each of his books the publisher sells at retail for $10, the writer will receive $1 for each book sold. (When you go into a store and purchase something, the price you pay is the *retail* cost.) This percentage of sales is known as "royalties."

Sometimes royalties are based on the publisher's *net* price, instead of retail cost. In other words, the price the publisher actually sells the book for, rather than the price listed on the cover. For instance, bookstores buy books from publishers at less than the cover price listed. (Bookstores pay the *net* price rather than the *retail* price.) This allows the bookstore to make money by selling the books to customers at the retail price. In the example above, if the publisher sells the $10 book at net for $5, a writer earning a 10 percent royalty based on net would earn only $.50 for each book sold.

Royalties are normally paid out to writers twice a year.

[Question: How much money would a writer make on a book earning 10 percent royalties based on the retail price for a book that sells for $6.95 if one thousand books are sold?

Answer: $6.95 \times 1,000 \times 10\% = \$695.00$

What if the 10 percent royalties was based on a percentage of *net*, and the publisher sells each $6.95 book for $3?]

Because it often takes a year or more between the time a writer sells a manuscript and when copies of the book begin selling, publishers often offer writers an *advance against royalties*. An advance is a certain sum of money that the publisher gives to the writer when the contract terms are agreed upon, but before the book is actually published. This is not free or extra money that the writer gets. When the book is finally published and copies are sold, the publisher will deduct the amount of the advance from the total royalties due to the author.

Therefore, a $500 advance against royalties means that a writer will not receive any money earned from royalties *until* his royalties exceed $500. That's the ugh side of advances. However, writers always try to get as big an advance from their publishers as they can against royalties (preferably based on retail) because the good part is, you get to keep all of the advance money even if your book doesn't sell well enough to earn you any royalties.

Winners of the *Publish-A-Book Contest* receive a $500 advance against royalties. Prism Awards winners, however, receive a $500 cash award *plus* royalties. *National Written & Illustrated By . . . Awards Contest* winners receive royalty contracts.

An article I submitted was rejected because they had printed a similar piece a few months before. How can I know what subjects have been covered without reading every back issue of every magazine I'd like to submit to?

This happens most with information or how-to articles. For magazines to which you, your friends or neighborhood library subscribes, take time to scan at least the table of contents of several back issues. For other publications, have your school or public librarian show you how to use two reference collections called *Readers' Guide to Periodical Literature* and the *Children's Magazine Guide*. Both list articles published in many publications by subject, title and author. These and similar resources are often available on library computer systems or through an online information source such as CompuServe or GEnie. Finding information is much easier and quicker by computer. However, be sure to check with an adult before using an online information source because you have to pay access fees.

However, don't worry too much if your subject has been covered recently if you've written an essay or opinion piece. Editors often repeat certain subjects if the writer presents a different or interesting viewpoint.

What is a "theme list"?

Some magazines and contests plan issues around a certain topic or theme, such as medicine, sports, dating, Colonial America, holidays, etc. Most listings will specify if a publication or contest follows a theme list. The deadline dates for submitting material will be included to help you meet their lead time. (For examples see the market listing for *Cobblestone* or the contest listing for the *Publish-A-Book Contest*.)

I'm confused about submissions. Do I send my original manuscript and keep the copy or do I send the copy and keep my original?

Generally, you would send your original manuscript and keep a copy. Note that "original" here means both something new you created on your own *and* the final draft you made of it. Markets and contests that accept handwritten work by young people, like *Stone Soup*, are more likely to want the actual work you created and not a photocopy or a copy retyped in standard format. Markets and contests that only accept work in standard typewritten formats don't really care if they receive the original or a copy, as long as what they receive if clear and easy to read.

The most important point to remember is *never* to send the only manuscript you have. *Always* keep a carbon copy, photocopy, disk copy, extra handmade or typed copy, computer printout or the original, just in case something happens.

Note that some contests specify to send originals, others say send a copy.

What should I do with material that is rejected?

First of all, try hard not to take it personally. Manuscripts may be rejected for many reasons, and some have nothing to do with how well, or poorly, they are written. Re-read your work and see if you can improve it. If you like it the way it is, look for another market. Make certain that you have followed all of the guidelines and any theme or deadline requirements. Remember that even famous writers have material rejected. Some manuscripts are not bought until the fifth or even thirtieth submission. The key is to keep trying. And to keep writing new material.

What does "copyright" mean?

For writers, "copy" means their written work. (Don't confuse this with making a copy of something.) "Right" refers to the person who has the authority to sell or offer a certain piece of written, drawn, photographed or computer-created work for possible publication. When you write something, you automatically become the copyright owner by law. If an editor agrees to publish your manuscript, he will "buy the rights" to it. Sometimes, magazines buy "one-time rights" or "First North American rights," which gives them permission to print your manuscript one time. Then the rights are returned to you and you may offer the same manuscript to another editor for "second" or "reprint" rights. A number of publications and some contests buy "all rights," which means that once you agree the publication can print your manuscript (or you submit to that particular contest), the work becomes *their* property. They hold the copyright, and it is no longer yours. You may not send it to another market or contest. Even though you no longer own the copyright, your name will be listed as the author if the manuscript is published.

You should also know that you hold the copyright to messages or library files you create on an online information service such as CompuServe. You cannot use messages or files created by other people without getting their permission.

Copyrights can be very confusing. See page 38 for more information on them.

Should I include a letter with my manuscript when I mail it to a publication?

If you would like to tell the editor special information that is not included in your manuscript, you may send a short, one-page letter. This is called a "cover letter." Often this is not necessary. When an editor receives a manuscript prepared in standard typewritten format, she assumes that you are hoping it will be accepted for publication. Note that some markets and contests want you to include a cover letter, particularly if you are under 18 years of age. For more information, see page 48.

Is a cover sheet the same thing as a cover letter?

Not exactly. While a cover *letter* may also serve as a cover *sheet*, many contests use the term *cover letter* to mean the form that should accompany an entry. (For two examples, refer to the contest listings for the *Nationally Written and Illustrated By . . . Awards* on page 249 and the *North American International Auto Show Short Story Contest* on page 251.)

What is a query letter?

Writers send a query letter to editors when they want to know in advance whether the editor would be interested in a manuscript about a certain topic. Most editors prefer that young writers send a complete manuscript, though older teens attempting to publish in adult publications may send query letters outlining their proposed article. For more information see page 50.

Someday, if you've sold several manuscripts to the same editor, you may be surprised to receive a query letter from that editor, asking you to write on a certain subject. The editor will feel confident doing this because he is already familiar with your work and knows that you can be depended upon to complete a writing project. Of course, it will be up to you to accept the assignment or not. Most of the editors, contest sponsors and young writers profiled in this book received queries from me asking them to contribute.

What does "solicit" mean?

"To solicit" means to ask for something. A publication that *solicits* poetry is indicating that it wants to receive poetry submissions to consider for publication.

A *solicited* submission means an editor has either specifically asked a writer to submit a particular manuscript, or agreed in advance to consider a manuscript when it is submitted. For example: If you query (ask) an editor if she would be interested in seeing your manuscript about "What Kids Can Do to Protect the Environment," your manuscript becomes a *solicited submission*.

The opposite, or *unsolicited submission*, refers to a manuscript that is just mailed to an editor without his prior knowledge and approval. In other words, the editor hasn't asked to see it. Unsolicited submissions waiting to be read and answered are often referred to as the "slush pile."

What does "in-house" publication mean?

When a company or organization publishes something intended primarily for its employees or members, such as a newsletter, it is often referred to as an "in-house" publication. In other words, it is not meant for the general public. A student school newsletter is a good example of an "in-house" publication.

Some people also use the term "in-house" to mean that all the work done creating a publication is done without assistance from outside sources. You may hear, for example, "We did it all in-house."

What's a press pass, and how do I get one?

A press pass is an identification card or badge. Writers, especially journalists and TV or radio reporters, use press passes to attend special events, especially when they want to gather behind-the-scenes information or interview someone special. Publication staff members and writers on assignment (told by an editor to pursue a specific topic for an article) can request a press pass from their editor. For example, members of your school yearbook staff get a type of press pass to attend sports and other activities free, in order to get information and photographs.

Read about Amy Wu on page 126. She used a press pass to attend the 1992 National Democratic Convention. The profile of Jill Bond, co-editor of *The Bonding Place*, also has information about obtaining a press pass.

An article I read in a writer's magazine said to be polite to editors. One tip was to compliment the editor who will read the manuscript you submitted. What exactly should I be complimenting her on?

First of all, the article you mentioned referred to complimenting an editor *after* she has contacted you and, unfortunately, rejected the manuscript or idea you submitted. Many rejection notes and letters will contain the editor's name. The author was suggesting that writers send the editor a short note saying, basically, "Thank you for taking the time to read my manuscript and considering it for publication."

Sometimes writers who get rejection notices write nasty letters back to the editor, no matter how kind the editor tried to be. So I'm sure many editors would prefer receiving a nice thank-you note once in a while instead. However, I don't think this is necessary unless an editor has sent you a very personal letter that offers some words of encouragement or advice for improving your manuscript.

What is the "Genre's Trade Journal"?

The word "genre" means a specific type or kind of writing. Science fiction is one genre. So are picture books, cookbooks, romances, biographies, even comic books. Every type of writing can be considered a different genre.

Many professions have magazines (also called journals) devoted specifically to them. For instance, doctors have magazines about medicine. Mechanics have magazines about fixing cars. Writers and editors have special magazines for their professions, too. You're a writer and you read *Writer's Digest*. The "Markets" section of *Writer's Digest* often lists the names of editors. (Editors and publishers also have special magazines, such as *Publishers Weekly*.) So, one example of a writer's "genre trade journal" would be *Writer's Digest*.

I'm afraid I won't know what to do if my book manuscript gets accepted and the publisher sends me a contract. Will the publisher decide not to publish it when they find out I'm just a kid?

Publishers are interested in publishing good books. They really don't care what age the author is, as long as the author acts in a responsible, professional manner (re-read the beginning of Chapter 2.) Contracts can be confusing, but don't be afraid of them. If there is something you don't understand (and there probably will be) talk it over with your editor. Also get some outside help from a trusted adult. The main things to look for in a contract are: What rights does the publisher want to buy? How much will you be paid, and when? What is the deadline for you to turn in a final, polished manuscript? What other responsibilities does the publisher expect from you (for instance, if your book will have photographs or illustrations, who pays for them, you or the publisher)? What happens if the editor does not like your final manuscript? How will the copyright be registered? Must you give this editor first choice for accepting your next book? See the additional advice I offer on page 35.

QUESTIONS ABOUT ELECTRONIC COMMUNICATIONS

I write on a computer at school with special software that helps me make up stories. Can I send my story to a market or contest?

Many computer software programs help students learn how stories are put together by showing part of a story onscreen and asking them to fill in missing parts. They encourage creativity and help students learn new words. But they really do not help students create original stories. These stories are not suitable for submitting to regular markets and contests because the work is not entirely your own.

Occasionally, someone will sponsor a special writing contest based on one of these programs. In 1988, for instance, The Learning Company and Tandy Corporation (the company that makes the computers sold by Radio Shack) sponsored a "Silly-Story" writing contest. Everyone used the same story "shell" that came with one of The Learning Company's software programs, filling in the story blanks with creative nouns, verbs, adjectives and adverbs.

My teacher has tried to upload some of our stories to the Literary Forum on CompuServe, but we can never find them listed in the library section. Where are they?

Literary Forum SYSOP Janet McConnaughey says that people uploading files often forget to include line feeds or carriage returns at the end of *each* line of text. That means you need to press "enter" or "return" as *each* line of type gets to the edge of the screen. Most word processors automatically wrap words that go beyond the screen to the next line. However, you'll need to do this manually for manuscripts you want to upload. Just remember to type as if you were using an old typewriter, the kind with a handle you have to push at the end of each line.

(Check individual online systems for the maximum number of characters that can be included in one line of type. This is sometimes referred to as "number of columns." A typical width is eighty columns.)

For additional help, check both your word processing software manual and the manual that explains how to use your communications software. Also, it's a good idea to post a message to SYSOP on any bulletin board before uploading your first files, for advice about which library to use and for other information. State in a few words what your file contains, such as the topic or genre, to help the SYSOP give you the best answers.

Do I need my own user ID number and password to log on to a computer system like CompuServe or GEnie?

Generally, students within a classroom or school may share one user ID number and password, as can all the members of a family. For instance, one student logs on using her teacher's account to request submissions from CompuServe's Student Forum members for an electronic newspaper project. However, the subscription will only be registered under one name. If you spend a lot of time online, you or your parents may want you to have your own account for tracking purposes (like when your parents want to blame you for the high phone bill that just arrived). As you would for any other hobby, consider paying all or part of the expense involved.

Regardless of whose account you are using, *make sure you have received permission before logging on.*

How can I use my own name online if I'm using my dad's or my teacher's account?

On GEnie, users may use nicknames to sign messages. (Tanya Beaty uses "Oracle" as her nickname on the Writers' Ink Round-Table.) After you log on to a bulletin board or real-time conference, use the /NAM command to enter a new name. This nickname will appear (along with your normal GE Mail address) in each message you leave in that board. If, for instance, you are the only one using that account to access Writers' Ink, the nickname you have chosen will remain the same. If your dad accesses other areas, he can use a different nickname there. Once you choose a nickname, you won't have to go through the process again unless you want to.

CompuServe prefers that users always use their regular names, first and last, rather than nicknames. (Actually, they insist a first and last name be used, but they are nice about it.) But instead of your dad's name being listed, you can change it to show your name instead for a particular forum. How you do this depends on which software you are using — CompuServe recommends that new users use CIM (CompuServe Information Manager). With CIM, select the "special" menu and then choose "options." Backspace over the current name and type in yours. If you don't want to bother changing the name (or if someone, like your dad or your teacher, doesn't want you to) consider this method instead: Sign messages and identify files with your own name, then add the name of the person who has the subscription. This is the name that will appear next to the User ID number anyway. For example: John (Joe Smith's son).

The directions will vary, but most online information service or bulletin board systems allow you to change the name used during that session. This is especially useful when participating in online conferences. Many communication software packages also let you automatically change the name used online.

How can I tell what stories are written by kids?

Sometimes you can't, unless the manuscript was uploaded as part of a contest that had special categories for different ages. That's one of the advantages of communicating online! No one can discriminate against you because of your age, sex or background, because no one will know (unless you tell them). Young writers who want their ages known can add the information to the uploaded file, in the file description, or in the keywords area.

If you're looking for files written by kids, look for addresses within the files or descriptions that indicate a school or class. Example: Written by students at Perry Middle School.

You can also post messages on the bulletin board stating your age and interests and inviting other members to contact you. Finding online pen pals is a popular BBS feature these days.

I'm having trouble uploading and downloading files. Where do I get help?

First, make sure you've read your manuals. If a parent or teacher can't help you, leave a message to the SYSOP in the special interest group (SIG) you're trying to access. You can ask for help at your local computer store. Also, many software manufacturers and online information systems have toll-free numbers you can call for help.

Is there any way to save on connect charges when I want to log onto a computer information service?

Several software packages can help you "automate" your sessions by allowing you to log on, go straight to the SIG you want, automatically up or download a file, then log off—all with the push of one or two keys. These are often referred to as "navigation" programs.

Several packages are available for CompuServe users, including AUTOSIG and TAPCIS for MS-DOS users (IBM and compatible systems); CompuServe's Information Manager and Navigator for the Macintosh; ST/FORUM for the Atari ST; and WHAP! for Amiga users. GEnie users with IBM or IBM-compatible systems can use Aladdin. (A version for Macintosh systems is under development.) Most of this software can be downloaded directly from the computer service and tried out for free. Note that you pay connect charges while downloading the file. (Normally, you can upload to any service without connect charges.)

WRITING TO ME

Here are some guidelines for those who would like to write to me:

1. Please include an SASE with your letter when you write. You will get a quicker response. If you don't include an SASE, remember to write your return address on your letter!

    I receive many letters each year from students and teachers that I cannot respond to because there is no return address on their letters or envelopes. Even though I want to respond to the letters, I can't, because I don't know where the writers live.

2. Tell me a little about yourself, such as your age, school, and the kind of writing you like to do.

3. Feel free to ask me *specific* questions. Here, for example, are what three students at Warrensburg Elementary in Warrensburg, Illinois, recently wrote to ask me:

Where do you get your ideas?
What made you become an author?
What is your favorite animal?
Did you write any books about your childhood?
What is your favorite book you wrote?
(By the way, my favorite animals are my calico cat Page and my horse Spanky. My favorite book that I wrote is this one.)

4. Please ask me questions that you are interested in knowing. Don't, for example, ask the same thing everyone else in your class is asking. If everyone wants to know the same thing, send one letter like the Warrensburg students did.

5. Please do not ask me to give you answers to things you can easily find in my book. That's why I wrote the *Market Guide for Young Writers* in the first place . . . so you would have the answers. It is very bothersome to receive six letters (especially all from the same class) that say:

Dear Ms. Henderson: *(or: To Whom It May Concern)*
I am in the 5th grade, and am planning to send some things for publication. I need to know the requirements—handwriting, paper size, etc. Thank you.
    Sincerely,

    So and so young writer.

Unfortunately, I receive several packets of such letters every semester.

6. If you include a sample of your work, please limit it to five pages. I especially enjoy receiving photocopies of things

young writers have had published. *However, I do not publish writers' work myself.*

7. Please be patient while you wait for me to respond. I try to answer within two weeks, but sometimes it's longer. In addition to writing, I also help do morning and evening chores on our dairy farm and sometimes travel to speak at schools and conferences.

8. Occasionally things get lost in the mail, so if you don't hear from me after a while, feel free to write me again. Don't forget to include your address on *both* your letter and envelope, in case they get separated. Please include an SASE if possible.

Send letters to me % Writer's Digest Books, 1507 Dana Ave., Cincinnati, OH 45207. You may also contact me via GEnie or CompuServe. My e-mail addresses are:

On GEnie—K.HENDERSON
On CompuServe—71660,3100

May I write to other writers?

I can't speak directly for other writers, but generally, yes, you may write to other writers. It's always a pleasure hearing from readers who have enjoyed our work. If you don't know where a writer lives send your letter to the company that published his or her book, or to the magazine where you read about the writer. Your letter will be forwarded if possible. Note that it may take several weeks for a writer to receive a letter forwarded from the publisher. I once received mail *one year* after it was sent to a publisher with whom I used to work. So, please be patient.

PART TWO

Chapter Six

Young Writers in Print

You've come to my favorite part of this guide, where I get to introduce a new group of young writers who have found from a little to a lot of publishing success.

Even before I finish working on one edition of *Market Guide for Young Writers*, I've already begun to collect information and references for the next. I never grow tired of meeting young writers or of reading and hearing about their experiences. Many people have asked how I learn about young writers in so many different parts of the country and with such different backgrounds. (Each new edition features a different group of young writers; a total of thirty-two so far. One young writer, Mike Snyder, was profiled twice because he was the one who gave me the idea for the guide in the first place. I wanted readers to see how well he'd done after following the marketing advice in the first edition (1986). Another nine successful young creatives are featured in the first edition of *Market Guide for Young Artists and Photographers*.)

Finding young writers is the easy part. Many write to me each year, and not only from the United States. Letters have come from young writers and teachers in Canada, England, Australia, France, Belgium, the Netherlands, Germany, Puerto Rico and the U.S. Virgin Islands, Malaysia, Japan, Spain and India. They occasionally send samples of their work, share good and bad experiences they've had marketing and entering contests, want to know more about me personally, or ask for more information about writing and marketing. Some I "chat" with on the Writers' Ink RoundTable on GEnie or in the Student Forum on CompuServe. Many of their questions find their way into new editions.

I also learn about talented young writers by asking for recommendations from the editors and contest sponsors I'm interested in featuring. It's not always possible, but I prefer to feature both an adult and a young writer with ties to the same market or contest. This gives you, the reader, a unique two-sided look behind the scenes.

The hard part comes when I must decide on the few I can invite to contribute to each new edition. I try to have different parts of the country represented, as well as writers from different backgrounds, writing and publishing experiences, and ages. Because I encourage young writers to take advantage of opportunities in their own areas, I also look for young writers who can highlight a small, local or specialty market or contest.

But most important, each young writer essay *must* have three things: (1) something of value to share with readers, (2) some words of inspiration or encouragement, advice about becoming a better writer or marketing tips, and (3) a different style and way of presenting themselves. I always ask them all to share at least one good and one not-so-good experience. And, of course, I have to get their submissions in time to meet my book deadline. But if you asked them, they would tell you that I give very few guidelines about how to write their essays. What I give them is a skeleton. They must construct a strong body.

The most fun, however, is when I receive everyone's photo since I rarely know what anyone looks like in advance! And of course, it's also fun right now, when I get to introduce them to you. I know you'll enjoy meeting them as much as I have. It's a unique treat this time to also share a bit of young writer history from someone as successful as Stephen King.

STEPHEN KING
Former young writer
Bangor, Maine

Stephen King (one of today's most famous and prolific writers) started writing in his youth. The following is a reprint of a story that was self-published in the "magazine" written and published (photocopied and stapled!) by Mr. King and a boyhood friend. They produced several, but to his knowledge, only one copy of each still exists. When they sold them for $.10 to $.25 to the kids at school, Mr. King realized for the first time that one could write something and get paid for it. School officials eventually made them stop.

In a 1986 letter to Carol Fenner, managing editor of Flip, *a student literary magazine no longer published, he had this to say about his story:*

This has been very painful for me but I have managed to dig up the rotting body of one of my stories written as a teen of about thirteen. I think your readers will see what a really dreadful story it is, but I think they will also see maybe the first delicate sprouts of what has become the world's bestselling Venus flytrap. If you don't want to use this story, I'd be delighted. But for what it's worth, you have my permission.

Unfortunately, the issue of Flip *that was to have featured Mr. King's story was never published due to lack of funding. I'm grateful to Ms. Fenner for her cooperation in helping me access this story and to Mr. King for allowing me to reprint it here.*

THE HOTEL AT THE END OF THE ROAD

"Faster!" Tommy Riviera said. "Faster!"

"I'm hitting 85 now," Kelso Black said.

"The cops are right behind us," Riviera said. "Put it up to 90." He leaned out the window. Behind the fleeing car was a police car, with siren wailing and red light flashing.

"I'm hitting the side road ahead," Black grunted. He turned the wheel and the car turned into the winding road spraying gravel.

The uniformed policeman scratched his head. "Where did they go?"

His partner frowned. "I don't know. They just—disappeared."

"Look," Black said. "Lights ahead."

"It's a hotel," Riviera said wonderingly. "Out on this wagon track a hotel! If that don't beat all! The police'll never look for us there."

Black, unheeding of the car's tires, stamped on the brake. Riviera reached into the back seat and got a black bag. They walked in.

The hotel looked just like a scene out of the early 1900s. Riviera rang the bell impatiently. An old man shuffled out. "We want a room," Black said.

The man stared at them silently.

"A room," Black repeated.

The man turned around to go back into his office.

"Look, old man," Tommy Riviera said. "I don't take that from anybody." He pulled out his thirty-eight. "Now you give us a room."

The man looked ready to keep on going, but at last he said: "Room five. End of the hall."

He gave them no register to sign, so they went up. The room was barren except for an iron double bed, a cracked mirror, and soiled wallpaper.

"Aah, what a crummy joint," Black said in disgust. "I'll bet there's enough cockroaches here to fill a five-gallon can."

The next morning when Riviera woke up, he couldn't get out of bed. He couldn't move a muscle. He was paralyzed. Just then the old man came into view. He had a needle which he put into Black's arms.

"So you're awake," he said. "My, my, you two are the first

additions to my museum in twenty-five years. But you'll be well preserved. And you won't die.

"You'll go with the rest of my collection of living mummies. Nice specimens."

Tommy Riviera couldn't even express his horror.

TIM AND RYAN JESSOP

Directors, Providence Elementary
  Broadcast News Team
Providence, Utah

Unlike the rest of the young writer profiles in this and past editions, this one by the Jessop brothers wasn't written and submitted by them. Instead, they chose to be interviewed, reporter-style, by phone.

Tim, now 11, has since moved up to the Spring Creek Middle School, which doesn't have a school video news program. He didn't realize how much he enjoyed the program at Providence Elementary and the leadership role he played until he left it behind. Ryan, who served as assistant director under his brother, still participates as a member of the broadcast news team. Both brothers feel that students can learn more about the news, both on and off the air, by being involved with a local project such as this one.

You can learn more about this school broadcast news program by reading the profile of Vaughn Larson on page 152. Mr. Larson is the media specialist at Providence Elementary and serves as the program's executive producer.

MG: What do you like best about being part of your school's broadcast news team?

Ryan: It's fun.

Tim: The thing I liked was the control. I like to be in charge of things. We both felt like we could handle all the little problems that could come along.

Ryan: We also learned how to get along with people better.

MG: How long are your broadcasts?

Ryan: Each one is five to ten minutes long, depending on how many stories we have.

Tim: Plus, it takes about thirty to forty-five minutes to set everything up for taping. We use a computer to do some of the backgrounds and air graphics.

MG: What sort of news do you usually include each day?

Tim: We cover state events if they are of local interest, and school activities like awards. We sometimes reported on news that was happening in our city, especially if there was some sort of controversy or voting going on.

MG: Who decides what stories get on the air?

Ryan: The editors do. But we all get a chance to express our opinions. And all of us do some work as reporters.

MG: As directors, did you ever run into any particular problems along the way?

Ryan and Tim together: Yes!

MG: Can you give an example?

Tim: One of the biggest problems for us was trying to decide who to pick for certain jobs. Most of the boys wanted to be sports writers and a lot of the girls wanted to be anchors. We just had to pick who we thought would do the best job.

Ryan: Some other problems were mistakes in the writing. The anchors could not understand what the newswriters had written. This really showed everyone how important it is to write clearly.

MG: Any other examples?

Ryan: Well, to catch errors in our stories, we would read them to other people and they would try to see if anything important had been left out.

Tim: That was really helpful.

MG: Why do you think it's important to learn to write news stories?

Tim: It helps your writing skills. It helps you to work on the major points of a story and not get too caught up in parts of the story that are not as important. It helps make your stories more interesting to the reader.

Ryan: It helps me to look for details and make sure that I haven't left anything out of my story.

Tim: The reason our news programs are so good is because everyone works so hard. Everyone helps us figure out some of the problems that come up. Even when we argue, we still all pull together.

MG: Have you always been interested in writing and editing?

Ryan: I like writing stories.

Tim: I found it quite interesting. I'm more interested in writing now than I was before. I've learned to enjoy watching the news.

MG: Do either of you plan to be journalists when you grow up?

Tim: Being a journalist wouldn't be a bad job, but I want to be a dentist.

Ryan: If professional basketball doesn't work out, I'll look into it.

MG: Final question. Do you have any advice you'd like to give?

Tim: I think more schools should do their own broadcast news. It's a lot more interesting than watching Channel One. That's boring. No one pays much attention to it.

VICKI MAY LARKIN
Young Writer
Saginaw, Michigan

Vicki Larkin's experiences are typical of many eager young writers today. Most typical, she is part of a family of avid readers and has enjoyed both peer and adult encouragement toward her writing. Also quite typical, Vicki has had several publishing successes in local and regional markets. To her credit, she responded to the editorial advice of the editor she made her first submission to and revised her story's ending. And she accepted the editor's further revisions with grace.

Not to detract from Vicki's writing skills in any way, it's also true that her early success, even in a well-known national publication like Creative Kids, *stems as much from her eagerness as from her talent. As she matures as a writer, attempting more challenging projects and submitting to more competitive markets and contests, it's likely she'll meet with more rejections than she has so far. That's to be expected. As long as Vicki remains open to constructive criticism, keeps rejections in perspective, works with an attitude toward improving her writing, keeps reading and writing, and keeps submitting suitable manuscripts to appropriate markets, she'll continue to add publishing credits to her résumé. Even if Vicki loses interest in creative writing and publishing, she will always remember these early experiences fondly.*

She and her mom publish a newsletter that provides additional editorial training, encouragement and opportunities to publish in the broadest sense — the act of sharing one's work with others. It's a wonderful, low-cost playground for any budding young writer. You might want to compare Vicki's remarks with those of her mom, Margaret Larkin, who is profiled in Chapter 7. (See page 142.)

My name is Vicki May Larkin. I'm 11 years old and in the sixth grade at Swan Valley Middle School, Saginaw, Michigan. My favorite subjects in school are math and reading.

I have a pretty big family. There's my mom and two sisters. Amber is 10 and Melissa is 15. They like to write, too, and have had items published. There's also my dad and my brother Adam, who is 17.

I have always loved reading and writing. I told my mom my first story, "Bear Soup," when I was only three years old. Mom used to tell me to slow down when I was telling her my stories so she could write them down for me. She still helps me by editing my stories and encouraging me to keep writing. She sends out manuscripts to various markets for all of us, her included.

So far I have had six things published in different newspapers, magazines and newsletters. I had my first manuscript published when I was 10. It was a short story titled "The Wishing Rock" in *Thumbprints*, which is a monthly newsletter published by the Thumb Area Writer's Club. After I sent my story in I received a note from the editor asking me to work on my ending because it was "a little flat." After I revised it, it was published. The editor had made only a couple little additional changes to my story.

The second item published was a poem in *Creative Kids* magazine. I have received lots of rejection slips but I keep writing and trying to get them published.

Along with reading and writing, I love to make crafts and babysit. I enjoy sports with my friends, too. Someday, I would like to be a well-known author and an art teacher.

I like to meet authors. Sometimes they come to our local library or school. I receive encouragement and pointers on how to improve my writing from them. Nate Aaseng, author of *Full Court Press*, read one of my published stories and told me, "I wish I could have written like that when I was little." You can imagine how proud that made me feel!

My mom and I publish our own newsletter. We call it *Ink Blot*. She is the editor and I'm the assistant editor. We collect submissions from our local elementary, middle and high school students. We have used submissions from others as well. We also put small artwork in it.

I am glad to get free copies of the publications my work is published in. I liked the T-shirt I received from *Cappers* for a piece that ran in "Space Place," their special department for young writers. But I would like to start earning money for the things I write so I'll have money for college and a car when I'm older.

KATE HACKETT
1992 5th-Grade winner of the Jon Douglas
   Essay Contest
Pacific Palisades, California

When 11-year-old Kate Hackett, a student at Corpus Christi Elementary School, went to live in Poland for seven months with her parents and 9-year-old sister Stephanie, she didn't know that a year later she would win an essay contest for sharing her impressions of the people she met.

She attended the American school in Warsaw, but lived in a Polish community and her classmates came from forty different countries. Her mother Claire says that Kate was terrific at learning to communicate in Polish, and she was often sent out to do the shopping, which gave her a chance to meet many people in the neighborhood. They were in Poland because her father Michael, who teaches in the theater department at UCLA, had received a special invitation by two Warsaw theater groups to direct two plays. One of them, An American in Warsaw, *was a musical about the songwriting careers of George and Ira Gershwin. Kate's parents co-wrote it especially for the occasion.*

But it was more than Kate's unique experience that caught the judges' eyes, says contest coordinator Carole Trapani; it was that she used her own experiences and observations to compare how people react to freedom. She took a topic students are frequently asked to write about, and in less than 350 words added a special, personal touch to it. Other winners did the same thing. "These essays always seem to be more original and creative," says Mrs. Trapani.

In the following brief essay, Kate talks about how her interest in reading sparked her interest in writing and her involvement in the contest.

One reason I enjoy writing is that I love to read. I like trying to create stories as interesting as the ones I have read. One author who really inspires me is C.S. Lewis and his *Chronicles of Narnia*. It amazes me how he could create a whole new world and make it seem so real yet so magical. I have also read J.R.R. Tolkien's *The Hobbit* and *The Lord of the Rings* series.

All of my family writes. My mother keeps a journal and my

father writes plays. My sister enjoys writing for school and at home. I especially like writing poetry and short stories. I try to capture scenes, feelings and ideas in my writing. With my poetry I like to challenge myself to see if I can rhyme it correctly, get the rhythm right, and have it still make sense.

I have entered the Jon Douglas contest for three years — in third, fourth and fifth grades. In third and fourth grade I only won honorable mentions, but in fifth grade I won first prize.

My winning essay was on freedom. I had recently returned from Poland where I lived with my family for seven months. Until three years ago, Poland was a communist country, but I was able to see the Poles learning how to use their new freedom. In my essay I tried to focus on what I had seen.

A lot of people we got to know there were afraid of speaking out in public and sometimes even in their own homes. They forgot that they weren't a communist country anymore and worried that a spy might hear them. But then they'd remember and talk about how things have changed. It was interesting to see how they reacted to advertising, which hadn't been allowed before. In fact, a lot of the people from the United States when we were there came to teach them how to do it. The people were also just getting used to having a supermarket in their own neighborhood.

I really enjoyed writing my essay and every year there has been an interesting topic. If you win, you march in the parade on the Fourth of July. It makes you feel excited about writing, and you feel that you can achieve very hard goals.

DUNCAN MACKAY
Young Writer
Waterloo, Ontario

Duncan MacKay, author of "Biggest Fish in the Pond," was a Canadian Prism Award winner for Humor in the 7-10 age group. He lives in Waterloo, Ontario, where he enjoys reading, skiing, badminton, hockey and playing the clarinet. But most of the time you can find Duncan fishing. He loves to fish! He's such an avid fisherman that he started raising his own worms.

Duncan speaks both French and English, but he prefers English. He says the best advice he ever got about writing was to write about topics you're familiar with and that's when he discovered he was bursting with story ideas.

There I was standing in front of a large audience in the Ontario Science Centre in Toronto, Canada, handing out trophies to the 1990-91 Prism Award winners from across the country. The previous year, I had been an award-winner in the humour category for my story, "Biggest Fish in the Pond."

Winning this award has led to many exciting adventures. I have had the opportunity to do readings for children at various workshops; visit schools to talk to kids about writing; and I even had the chance to visit my local Board of Education to talk to sixty teachers about creating a good writing environment in the classroom. Perhaps the biggest adventure of all was when my Prism Award story was filmed at a local trout pond by the Canadian Broadcasting Corporation (CBC), as part of a national documentary on The Prism Awards.

It was in grade six when something good happened to my idea of writing. That year my English teacher was one in a million! I had never been so productive while having so much fun in class. Writing was not a chore because Mrs. Kathy Lewis made it both interesting and enjoyable. We didn't just *write* stories and hand them in; we sat in circles with our classmates and critiqued each other's work. Heated arguments erupted, but that made us more creative. In fact, that became the most fun part of the writing process. I don't think any of us realized just how much this helped our work, because we were too busy having a great time!

In February of that year Mrs. Lewis gave us an assignment: to write a story on the topic of our choice. While I was wondering what to write about, I remembered something important she had once told us. She told us some advice given to her by author Welwyn Katz, which was to write about topics we were familiar with. That might have been the best advice I have ever been given.

As soon as I got home from school that day, I wrote my story on the subject I know best—fishing. I wrote it quickly because I had so many ideas. I didn't realize that so many ideas were in my head until I sat down to write.

I have always found watching fishermen just as interesting as fishing itself. Fishing is not only a sport for catching fish—it attracts a large variety of people who have a common interest. When they get together at a pond or beside a river, the fun starts. There is so much to write about.

When I finished the story, I showed it to Mrs. Lewis. She encouraged me to enter it in The Prism Awards annual program. So I did.

Several months later Lucy LaGrassa, the founder of The Prism Awards program, phoned with perhaps the greatest news I've ever received. She told me I had won one of the awards. Winning was the most incredible feeling I have ever had. The closest thing I can compare it to is the feeling of hooking into a large trout!

Then, the hard part came. Lucy asked me to lengthen my three-page story into a novelette[1]. When Lucy sent a copy of my original manuscript back I couldn't believe all the edits she had made. Some of them seemed odd at first, but when I started to write, taking these edits and suggestions into account, they started to make sense. I was given two weeks to add twenty pages to my story by developing characters and the plot. This task was more difficult than any school assignment I had ever been given. But soon the book took shape, and after several more drafts, it was off to the publisher. What a feat!

I'm now writing more poetry than stories. I think this is because I don't have high expectations of myself, the way I do with my

---

[1]The term *novelette* means a very short novel.

storywriting. When I try to find ideas for stories, I find that I'm looking for a masterpiece, but poetry comes so much more freely. I am now gaining more confidence. In fact, I have just recently entered a local poetry competition. If I don't win, I won't be disappointed the way I would have been if one of my stories was unsuccessful.

One day, I know I'll write more stories and have them published. But for now, I'll concentrate on poetry.

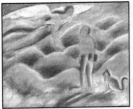

NATALKA ROSHAK
Young Writer, Prism Awards winner
Ontario Province, Canada

Natalka Roshak is bilingual, speaking both French and English fluently. After winning the 1992 Canadian Prism Award in science fiction for children ages 11 to 14, for her story "Gulububble," she went on to win the Alberta Poetry Award. Her favorite activities include talking to her friends, working with her friends, entering (and winning) National Science Fairs, jogging, playing the piano, and working out math puzzles with friends. She likes to read Shakespeare, Margaret Atwood, Robert Heinlein and Issac Asimov's editorials. Now that her secret goal of getting published has been met, she looks forward to doing it again!

I started writing when I was very young; before that I just made up stories. I read a lot of books, so it was natural that some of the stories I made up landed on paper. Almost without meaning to, I created in my mind an image of myself as a person who was good at writing. It was fun, and whether these stories were literary gems or not (pick B), writing them was a pleasure. Rough and unpolished, they were effortless, like breathing.

Gradually, I started to get recognition from the outside world. Teachers were so moved by my stories that they asked me if I was crazy. I was told to submit, to keep writing, to join this writing club, to do these exercises, to try writing this dialogue.

Well, that was fun, too. I started to take writing more seriously. I would spend hours on a story, playing with the music in the words. For a long time I kept the same style of slightly insane narrative because it seemed so successful with people reading it. Then my teacher got fed up with it. And this, too, was good because I learned to write with different voices.

Basically, I was feeling pretty confident about writing when I wrote "Gulububble," which my teacher entered in The Prism Awards competition. Because you're reading this, you know it won. Of course, I had no idea, until I received the fateful phone call from Lucy LaGrassa.

I thought it would be so simple, at first! I went and got the award, got my fill of public recognition, and expected a nice, beautifully illustrated book to pop magically out of the works. Instead, the award really meant more work. This, too, came to pass, and it was good because by arguing with my talented editors I learned exactly what makes a story work or not work. For the first time I learned how to control the images, as well as the words, that I had heretofore simply blurted onto the page. Then I went back and learned how to do this without ruining the story. Simultaneously, Lucy was sending me writing opportunities like this one — more practice, more recognition.

In this way, The Prism Award is one of the best things that can happen to a writer. It offers exposure and practice working with the publishing process, as well as seasoning a writer. Working with Lucy taught me skills to supplement raw instinct and brought me an awareness of the devices used in a story. Thanks, Lucy!

MATTHEW CHENEY
Young Writer
Plymouth, New Hampshire

As an eleventh-grader (he's a student at The New Hampton School in New Hampton, New Hampshire), Matthew has already accomplished a great deal as a young writer. He's been editor of his school's literary magazine and he twice received the school's T.H. White Award for creative writing. In addition to being published several times in Merlyn's Pen, *Matthew has been published in* The Thundering Grasshopper Review, *which he says is "a charming, if strange, little magazine from South Dakota." In addition to his successes, Matthew has collected dozens of rejection slips too.*

Matthew's first published story, "The Nauga Hunters," which appeared in the October/November 1990 issue of Merlyn's Pen, *was recently excerpted in an English composition textbook from Glencoe, a division of McGraw-Hill.*

Teen writers especially will find practical, encouraging and insightful advice from Matthew in his essay below. I also used parts of "The Nauga Hunters" to illustrate what properly formatted manuscript submission pages look like. (See pages 47 and 49.)

Robert Parker said, "Writers write." This is the best advice any young writer may get. I've taught a couple of times in local schools, and usually the only diference between me and the students is that I don't stop writing and they only do it in the classroom. The wordsmith learns to use words by putting them down on paper one at a time.

Writing something coherent, however, isn't so easy. I've been writing since before I could read. I would draw picture books and tell the story to anybody who happened by. In the third grade I had a teacher who was obsessed with writing and who made us write every day. I found that once I started I couldn't stop—I took my notebook home and filled it up and bought another and filled that one up. I got a computer and filled more than twenty disks before getting a computer with a hard drive. Writers write.

Publication doesn't make you a writer, it just makes you a writer who happens to have caught the eye of an editor. Anybody can do that, once they learn the basics and then get lucky enough to find a responsive editor. It took me years. If you want to be published you must *never* give up. I have a plastic bag filled with more than one hundred rejection slips from almost every state. After two years I stumbled upon *Merlyn's Pen*, sent them my best story ("The Nauga Hunters") and got an acceptance. The first page of the published story, framed, sits in the window in front of my computer as a monument to persistence. A year later I had dozens of new rejection slips and a single acceptance—from *Merlyn's Pen*—for "Starry Night."

Since then I have submitted less and less to magazines because the urge to publish has diminished. I still write the same amount, and I've gotten two more acceptances from *Merlyn's Pen* and one from a magazine in South Dakota, but I'm taking a sabbatical and honing my skills. Once you've had a degree of success, don't let it go to your head. You can always do better, and good writers will.

There are some mistakes to avoid. I started submitting fiction to magazines when I was in sixth grade. ("The Nauga Hunters" was accepted when I was in the eighth grade, and published a year later) and I made almost every mistake a beginning writer can make. I was going to tell you some of these mistakes and how to avoid them, but I realized that all I would be doing was quoting *The Elements of Style* by William Strunk, Jr. and E.B. White. This is one of the few books a beginning writer needs. (Master those skills and you're ready for *The Art of Fiction* by John Gardner, *The Poet's Handbook* by Judson Jerome, or any other specialty guide.) Remember, though, that classes and books can only teach you so much. Writers write.

Don't worry about being rejected by a magazine or receiving criticism from an editor or teacher. If you don't agree with them, ignore the advice. Criticism is seldom meant to hurt you, it's meant to *help*. I spent three weeks in Pennsylvania at a writing workshop three or four years ago, and I was stupefied to find the other kids responding to criticism by becoming defensive. I was overjoyed to have somebody willing to help me write better. Have humility. If the critic is right, then fix your manuscript. If the critic is wrong, don't change anything. You, in the end, are the person in control of your work.

I've found that one of the greatest assets to my writing has been my interest in drama and acting. I've been acting since I was in third grade. Some of my own plays and scenes have even been performed in school. But as an actor, if you are going to grow and expand your repertoire, you've got to learn about *character*. People.

I've watched people for as long as I can remember. I sit in restaurants and airports and classes and don't talk to anyone because I'm observing how the other people move, their gestures and speech patterns, what they talk about. Good actors learn to mimic people. As an actor I've also learned to pay attention to dialogue. My best fiction is dialogue-heavy, "The Nauga Hunters." A warning, though: Don't make the mistake I made with "Nauga Hunters" and write a majority of the dialogue in dialect, the way people really sound. "Ah em gonna go now 'n' git me some grits tak cook fer breakfust" is unnecessarily hard to read. Don't force your readers to become translators. You can still use contractions and such slang as "gonna," as long as you use it *in moderation*. A character has a southern accent? Write: "He spoke with a deep southern drawl." It works, and it doesn't disrupt the flow of the words.

Acting in and directing plays has also shown me the world of writing plays. Condensing action to only a few sets, scenes and characters is a challenge that forces you to focus your work, but there's a lot of freedom in plays. You don't have to be realistic at all. Read plays by Samuel Beckett or Harold Pinter or Christopher Durang—realism is seldom their primary objective. There is also, if you're able to get the play produced, a tremendous thrill to seeing your work come to life. I haven't written much fiction or poetry recently because I've been writing plays. There is a thrill greater than simple publication, and it is the thrill of hearing your words spoken by actors, your story presented to a theater full of people. (There are, alas, few frustrations greater than hearing your words mangled and misinterpreted, your story shredded by inept direction and performance. It's a risk.)

In the end, though, there is little advice one artist can give to another. Do what you love. If you don't love what you're doing, find out what you *do* love and do that instead. Joseph Campbell called it "following your bliss." Do your best, and if you can't do your best, try harder. Writer's block is no excuse — I'm seldom free of it, but it doesn't stop me from putting something on paper.

Writers write. And if you want to be a writer, you too will write.

BETH LEWIS
1992 Very Special Arts Young Playwright
   Winner
Merrit Island, Florida

*It was 18-year-old Beth Lewis's admiration of a
classic play that sowed the playwright's seed within
her. But it was the challenge of the Very Special
Arts Young Playwright competition that fed her
talent and motivated her to follow through. Beth's success winning a major
competition such as this in a genre that was new to her was not an accident.
As you read about her experiences, note the effort she made to learn about
how plays are constructed. Also note how much research she needed to do
in order to write credibly about autism, a medical condition she knew nothing
about.*

Performances of Beth's play, Genie of the Lamp, *were included in
The John F. Kennedy Center's "Imagination Celebrations" staged in Dallas
and Fort Worth, Texas; Colorado Springs, Colorado; and in Washington,
D.C.*

Ever since I can remember I have kept a journal, and I think
my love for writing first took root in its pastel pages. Each journal
I completed was an accomplishment for me; as if with each crisp
clean book a new phase of my life began. It wasn't until I took a
creative writing class in my ninth-grade year that I realized the
remarkable things a person can create through words. I had always
enjoyed reading, and I believe that reading and writing go hand in
hand. Now, for the first time, my work was actually being read by
teachers and other students. I am so thankful that I was blessed
with wonderful English teachers who encouraged and inspired me
to continue to write.

My love for literature was a foundation for my writing. As a
junior in high school I read *The Crucible* by Arthur Miller. I was so
excited and moved by the play that I became determined to write
a play of my very own. Later my English teacher gave our class
information about the National Young Playwright Awards sponsored by Very Special Arts. The plays were required to address
some aspect of disability in society, so I wrote my play entitled

Genie of the Lamp about the wishes and dreams of a homeless autistic boy. Because I knew absolutely nothing about autism, I spent many days after school in the library doing research. Finally, with much apprehension and at the very last minute, I sent my play to Very Special Arts. Then I waited desperately for months to hear from them.

I was overwhelmed when I learned that my play had been selected as one of the two plays to be produced at The John F. Kennedy Center for the Performing Arts! The Lord truly had answered a prayer.

Since then I have gained confidence in my writing. Whether my work is award-winning or not, I treasure each word because it is an outward expression of who I am.

I want to encourage anyone who has an interest in writing to explore every aspect of it and to consider it a great door of opportunity and adventure. Before labeling yourself a poet or a playwright, try your hand at short stories or satires. You may be surprised at the variety of work you can produce as long as you remember not to limit yourself.

There are millions of readers in the world, and the fabulous thing is . . . perhaps they are just waiting for exactly the unique words you have to say. Keep writing!

AMY WU
Young Writer
Thornwood, New York

Few young writers can match the publishing efforts of 17-year-old Amy Wu — more than five hundred submissions in four years, garnering her more than fifty acceptances, some in very prestigious places.

Although she has had several poems and essays published, it is her interest in sharing her views on current events and issues in guest columns and editorials, as well as numerous letters to the editor, that have been the key component to her success.

Unfortunately, her track record also shows 450 rejections. Many of them came early. "Like any novice who plunged into the confusing world of publishing, I did many things that now seem foolish to me," Amy now says. "During one period, I printed out dozens of copies of my works, sending them randomly to various publications. I cried when photocopied rejections poured into my mailbox. I questioned my talent as a writer, but every so often an encouraging note from an editor would keep me going."

Just before this edition went into production, Amy wrote to say she'd been invited to the Asian American Journalists Association "Face Value" benefit at The New York Times. *Quite an accomplishment for a teen writer. But she seemed even more thrilled about attending* The New York Times *Spring Literary Luncheon at the Plaza, where she will meet such authors as Sue Miller and Wendy Wasserstein. She received a free ticket after sending in a collection of her writings.*

I always feel a sense of exhilaration and peace when I face a blank sheet of paper. My pen becomes my sword and my mind becomes a channel to another world known as the imagination.

My love for books and powerful imaging stem from the fact that as a child I was always very sensitive and quiet. As I grew older, I acknowledged my quietness with some shame and humiliation. I wanted so much to stand tall like my classmates, with my head held high.

The written word became the way I spoke for myself as I grew into early adolescence. I spent days at a time sitting on the threadbare easy chair in the library familiarizing myself with literary names such as Chaucer and Wolfe, Mailer and Updike.

I am now 17 years old, but I was 13 when I first entered the publishing aspect of writing. I began writing poetry in eighth grade. What boosted my confidence in submitting was when I sent in a poem entitled "The Path," which was accepted for publication in the National Library of Poetry's anthology, *Of Diamonds and Rust*. It was through my poetry that I began to discover the type of writing that I enjoy most and seem best at producing.

The local newspaper, part of the chain of Gannett Suburban Newspapers, first published one of my opinion pieces about stereotyping people of various races. I began to write more and more opinion pieces on topics ranging from politics to the environment. How exhilarated I felt when I first saw my name in print. It is a feeling that I will never forget.

I believe that a person who is serious about writing and sees it in their future must be willing to put in a lot of hard work, accept rejection and not get discouraged. In my four years of freelance writing I have sent about five hundred submissions to various magazines, newspapers and even publishing companies, but I have been rejected countless times. Many of these rejections are printed on postcards and are very impersonal. But certain editors have also written me letters of encouragement. For example, one of the assistant editors at *Seventeen* magazine wrote telling me how she admired the way that I continue to try for publication. She also said that she enjoyed reading my essays and, after reading my letter to the editor in *The New York Times Magazine* concerning MTV, she asked me to write a short column about MTV for *Seventeen*. She also said that she would be happy to read anything I sent her.

Being published, however, is the reward for hard work and a lot of time spent trying to become a better writer. I can truly say from my experiences that if you write just for an editor, or just for publication, what you write will not be as good and as beautiful as what you write from your heart. If you write from your heart not only will you be pleased with what you write, but what you write will likely have more affect on others. I discovered a few years ago that when I would write about my Chinese mother and her relationship with me—a Chinese-American daughter—these stories came out well with a nice flow to them. These are the types of stories that have caught the attention of various markets such as *Creative Kids*, *Mini-World Magazine* (a Japanese publication), *Iowa Woman*, *Youth Magazine*, and *Sassy*. These stories come from my own experiences, and straight from my heart.

When my friends and classmates ask me how many times I have been published, I tell them fifty and counting. They are shocked and tell me that it is amazing. Then they ask why getting published seems so easy for me. It's difficult to explain, but the truth is, writing is not easy and getting published doesn't just happen. Every day I write at least something, whether it is in my journal or on my computer. When I submit it takes even more time to write cover letters and make sure that the manuscript is neat and polished. The process is long, but the rewards can be great.

I have discovered that some big adult market publications welcome young writers' contributions, if what you say is profound, from your own experience, and can be related to the issues in society. Last July I wrote a column for *USA Today* about my experiences of being stereotyped as an Asian American. And the Gannett Papers published a guest column I wrote about Chelsea Clinton and how hard it must be being 12 years old and growing up before the public eye.

My advice to young writers is not to give up. The writing business is difficult. There are thousands upon thousands of people sending in their writing. The key is to master good writing first and then the rest will follow.

As a young writer I still have so much to learn. Some books that have helped me are William Zinsser's *On Writing Well*, and Strunk and White's *The Elements of Style*.

I can't live a day without writing. I use the written word to express my thoughts and feelings, to set my imagination free, and to bring others into a world that they have not yet entered. My goal in the future is to be a columnist for a newspaper such as *The New York Times*, and to perhaps expand my writing into short stories. I'm an avid reader; my favorite writers are Amy Tan and Garrison Keillor. I believe that with hard work and a little luck anything is possible . . . especially in writing.

TANYA BEATY
Young writer and GEnie onliner
Lynchburg, Virginia

Tanya Beaty, an active member of the Writers' Ink RoundTable on GEnie, who goes by the nickname "Oracle" online, is shy about the major publishing success she had in 1992. Marion Zimmer Bradley, whom Tanya calls "one of the grande dames of science fiction," decided to include one of her short stories in the ninth Sword and Sorceress *fantasy anthology.*

You'll get a sense of her lighthanded style in the essay that follows, but first here is how Tanya describes the events leading up to that success. It's an excellent example of what can happen if you keep your eyes open to possibilities and make the effort to open doors for yourself.

"Bradley's anthology was one of the best things that has ever happened to me. I had read, in the introduction to one of her previous Sword and Sorceress *books, a passage about Ms. Bradley receiving manuscripts. She asked, if I recall correctly, prospective contributors to write for guidelines before they sent anything in.*

"I was interested so I wrote the publisher, asking for information. They forwarded my letter to her, and she in return sent the guidelines to me. I pondered a bit, and then wrote a story tailored specifically to those guidelines.

"It's interesting, because before I sent it in, I had lots of people telling me to get ready to accept the rejection notice. People who were creative writing majors gave me various odds on the possibility of the first manuscript I handed in getting accepted — and none of them were very good.

"Months passed. I didn't hear a word. No notice, no returned manuscript. I finally realized that the manuscript must have gotten lost in the mail, must never have made it to Ms. Bradley.... Then one day in the middle of May, I arrived home from school to find a large manila envelope waiting for me. I was curious. What was this? I had put the story so far from my mind that it was a shock to realize I was holding, in my hand, a contract between myself, Tanya Beaty, and Marion Zimmer Bradley, one of the grande dames of science fiction."

The only previous publishing credits Tanya had were poems in school literary magazines and a poem in the program for the Dade County First

Annual Ecology Forum, a panel discussion between students and scientists on the ecology of South Florida.

She is currently one of the youngest freshmen attending the Randolph-Macon Woman's College in Lynchburg, Virginia.

When people ask me where I learned to write, I look at them blankly and say that I learned in school, along with everyone else.

A few will persist. "No, where did you *learn* to write?"

Ah, I see. They want me to give them some mystical formula, some quick, easy way to a best-seller. Add some eye of newt, boil, and *poof!* Instant best-seller.

That's not the way I learned to write. Talking with my friends (authors in their own right) on GEnie, an online network I have an account with, I found that neither did they.

So how does one learn to write?

Bring two cups of water to a boil, add dragon's blood . . .

Whoops. Not that way.

Read anything. Books, magazines, encyclopedias. It really doesn't matter what you read, as long as it has words. One of my favorites is the *Oxford English Dictionary*. It's one of the best ways I know of to pick up new words to broaden your vocabulary. People will look at you oddly the first time you say "panjandrum," but it's worth it in the end. Before you can write in a language, you've got to know that language. Intimately. You need to have a large vocabulary; you need to know the correct word that will describe exactly what you want. Not only that, you've got to know the different meanings of the same word. See how they're used in varying genres.

I've found that it also comes in handy during games of Trivial Pursuit. You'll be one of the most popular people around when it comes time to pick teams.

Reading a variety of things, from the classics to fantasy, poetry to prose, will also familiarize you with the differences in writing styles. Some styles will be very expository, and tell everything. Some will be minimalist and tell little, relying on the reader's imagination. The reader is always taking some part in the process of words, whether following closely or just letting the author dictate the direction his thoughts go. Re-read your favorite books and see what you like. Do you enjoy having things described to you in great detail, or do you prefer to cultivate your own images?

Write. Every day. I can't emphasize this part enough. Most people claim they can't write. Wrong. Everyone can write — it's a matter of getting your thoughts on paper. That's the part that stops most people; you place a pen in their hand and they freeze. They shake their heads and say, "Uh-uh. No way." If you really want to write, don't let this stop you. Learn to record your thoughts. Keep a journal. Experiment with it. Use different voices, different points of view. Try something you've never tried before. You can't go wrong. Write down little phrases that you've heard elsewhere — on television, perhaps, or something someone said — that have stuck in your mind. I keep a little book of my favorite quotes by my bed. *Any* type of writing will help. Believe it or not, replying to posted messages on the GEnie bulletin boards helps me write in a concise and clear manner. I don't want people to misinterpret any of my messages, so I watch what I say in my reply.

Then go back and read what you've written. Do you like it? Does it convey the point you're trying to get across? I often find that if I ignore my work for several days, then go back to it, I can judge it with a less biased eye. Or I bring new ideas, or a fresh viewpoint. This is the point where I begin to tighten my sentences, cutting out anything that's superfluous. This is also the time when I'm ready to have the work critiqued.

Something all writers must do is develop a high tolerance for criticism. Taking criticism is hard for many people to do — and writers lay themselves open to it.

No, we don't love torture. But criticism is not supposed to be negative and degrading, it is supposed to be helpful. Keep that in mind when giving or taking criticism. Learn whom to ask for criticism. Your friends can give you an opinion on how interesting it was, but remember one thing: They are your friends. They like you. Most of the time, they don't want to hurt your feelings.

Granted, sometimes a friend will give objective criticism, but she's *my* friend and you can't have her.

On a serious note, I will often show my friends my work and ask them where they got confused, but for helpful criticism, I ask the users on WINK, the Writers' RoundTable on GEnie. Writers themselves, they will give me objective criticism when I ask for it. I value their opinions because I know any comments made will be helpful and objective.

Learn to take criticism as well. When someone critiques your work, they are not making a personal judgement. If they are, you asked the wrong person. Realize that you and your work are two separate entities. You asked for comments on your work, not your personal life. Anything that is less-than-glowing praise should not be taken personally.

Finally, don't get impatient. If you're looking for fame and fortune, you've got a long wait. It takes a while to refine your style, and until then, you'll make mistakes. You might even (gasp!) write some really bad stuff. But keep working on it, and soon you'll be able to look back and say, "Gosh, this is really bad! Did I write this?"

Actually, I meant to say, "Gosh, I could really rework this into something good!" Really I did.

Chapter Seven

Editors Are Real People, Too

In this chapter you'll have an opportunity to meet six editors, a real estate agent who moonlights once a year as a contest coordinator for local young writers, and the artistic director of a unique and thriving inner-city family theater with the blood of a young creative still coursing through his veins. They not only come from very different backgrounds, they also came to their present situations following very different routes. You'll also learn about the founding of the Very Special Arts Young Playwright Program at The John F. Kennedy Center for the Performing Arts.

In their own words, the editors and contest sponsors share a bit of personal history, some advice and encouragement to help you become better writers and more successful marketers of your manuscripts, and a few specific tips on submitting to their particular market or contest. This insight will help you master how to study and compare opportunities. As they represent only a handful of the wide variety of top-notch writing and publishing opportunities available to young writers, you may want to read the editor profile sections in editions two and three.

I think you'll find it particularly interesting to peek behind the scenes at some of the same markets and contests described by the young writers in Chapter 6. Compare Matthew Cheney's remarks with those of *Merlyn's Pen* editor Jim Stahl; Duncan MacKay's and Natalka Roshak's to those of Lucy LaGrassa, Canada's Prism Award founder; young writer and *Ink Blot* assistant editor Vicki Larkin's to those of *Ink Blot*'s publisher and editor Margaret Larkin (who just happens to be Vicki's mom); hear how executive producer and Utah media specialist Vaughn Larson caused the only missed airing of the school broadcast news show directed by Tim and Ryan Jessop; glimpse two perspectives of the Jon Douglas Company's annual Fourth of July Essay Contest with Kate Hackett and contest coordinator Carole Trapani; and notice how closely the goals and experience of Beth Lewis meet those upon which the Very Special Arts Young Playwright Program was founded.

Learn about the ambitious dreams of Jeff Church, artistic director of The Coterie Theatre in Kansas City, Missouri, who took a direct route to his present position by founding a still-flourishing theater in his Colorado hometown at age 15. Jill Bond will introduce you to *The Bonding Times*, the newsletter she publishes and edits with her husband. But first, meet Arun Toké, an electrical and electronics engineer turned energy auditor and environmentalist. He is the founder and editor of *Skipping Stones*, an international magazine filled with the writings and art of children from around the world.

ARUN NARAYAN TOKÉ
Editor, *Skipping Stones*
Eugene, Oregon

Arun Toké is an electrical and electronics engineer turned editor, energy auditor and environmentalist. He co-authored a textbook on Energy, Economics and the Environment *while teaching at Vermont Technical College. He has also written* Song of Winter Wonderland, *illustrated by children in Randolph, Vermont. Arun speaks Marathi, Hindi and Spanish, as well as English. He enjoys photography and the outdoors. He edited* Cookstove News, *a quarterly journal on appropriate technology and energy conservation, before founding* Skipping Stones *magazine in 1988.*

Skipping Stones has a widely scattered readership that reaches every state of the Union as well as twenty-five other countries. Pen pal requests come from Africa to the Ukraine. Mr. Toké estimates that hundreds of pen friendships have begun through Skipping Stones *pages.*

In addition to selling traditional subscriptions (see listing page 205), he provides low-income discounts and some free subscriptions to schools, libraries and nonprofit organizations working with low-income youth anywhere in the world. Mr. Toké says, "We try to send Skipping Stones *to Africa, Asia or Latin America for free, whenever we can afford it. Many of our subscribers share in this worthwhile expense by sending a little donation." More than 65 percent of the world's children cannot subscribe to a magazine that costs $15 a year.*

When I came to the United States in August 1971 to attend graduate school, it felt as if someone had just thrown me in the cold waters of cultural shock. I had spent all of my youth in India. Everything was different — culture, climate, economy, food, geography, language, lifestyle and, of course, the religion. My new life here was not at all like anything I had experienced in India. I was away from my family and friends in India. Naturally, I saw life in the United States with wide eyes and a big ?WHY? Luckily, I had learned some English in the schools I attended in India.

Since then, I have lived and traveled extensively in the Midwest, Northeast, Southeast and the Pacific Northwest, as well as in Canada, Mexico, Central America and Europe. During my 500 + km walk in Central America and 3,000 + km bicycle trip in Northern Europe, I came across numerous cross-cultural experiences that I still cherish. During these years, I have also witnessed many situations where cultural insensitivity was displayed or racism practiced, knowingly or unknowingly. And, too often, I have also observed cultural biases and insensitivities against nature and the environment!

As I journeyed through my childhood into youth and beyond, I have come to realize more than ever before that we do not make the best use of our youth—our plentiful and energetic resource. Our modern society brings up kids more as consumers, a burden or liability on the family. But in some cultures the children and youth play an important economic role by helping the family in various daily and seasonal tasks.

I have had no formal training in editing, journalism, publishing or business. Yet I started *Skipping Stones*. Why? I felt that there was a need for a multicultural publication for youth. A forum for communication among children from different lands and backgrounds. To validate our youngsters' experiences. And to help facilitate an awareness of our cultural and ethnic heritage. To promote an understanding and appreciation of our ecological and natural richness. Our survival and our well-being depend on how well we welcome cultural diversity and ecological richness.

Have you ever felt that you do not really count? Do you sometimes feel that you have no voice? At *Skipping Stones*, we invite children and young adults to share their cultural or traditional celebrations, concerns, daily life experiences, feelings about special places and things, experiences and critical thoughts on contemporary social issues through their artistic expressions. Articles, cartoons, drawings, jokes, letters to the editor, paintings, paper cuts, photos (preferably black and white), free or structured poems, questions for Dear Hanna (or other readers), riddles, songs and stories are all appropriate forms of submissions. Try to write short pieces and be space-conscious. About 500 to 700 words maximum. Do ask yourself: "How effective have I been at conveying what I started out to tell?" Review your writing and get comments from your teacher, parents or someone you trust before sending it on. This will improve the chances of your submission getting accepted. Send your manuscript handwritten, if you have good handwriting. It stands out that way. Illustrations are always a plus.

You can ask for a sample issue ($5) or our guidelines for submissions by sending an SASE. It makes good sense to see how different *Skipping Stones* is before you send us something for publication. Regular departments that welcome your contributions are: Dear Hanna, Book Reviews, Noteworthy NEWS, Rhymes and Riddles, Networking, Pen Pals, Cultural Collage, and *Skipping Stones* Stew.

You can contribute to our upcoming features on family, Afro-American heritage, songs from around the world, your favourite recipe, substance abuse among young people, adoption, animals and other beings, understanding world religions. . . . We always look for fresh ideas from our readers. If you have traveled to another country or region, you may wish to share your discoveries. Think of photos, drawings or paintings as *illustrations* of what you want to share.

We do not publish fiction for the sake of fiction. It needs to bring in ecological, cultural or social understanding. Stereotyping other cultures is something you want to avoid. Be original, creative and expressive!

You can use your native language to express yourself. We try to publish side-by-side translations in English whenever possible. We welcome writings in *all* languages. We know that *Skipping Stones* must be multilingual, not only to communicate but to preserve the flavor of other cultures. One can learn a lot about a culture through the language.

We especially encourage youth from underrepresented populations. Tell us about your family or cultural background. Where did your parents or grandparents live? Have you any special experiences to share about your childhood? You can also send a black-and-white photo in a natural setting. Do send an SASE if you want your work returned. And it's always a good idea to write your name and address on each page, and on the photographs you send. Just in case things get lost in the paper shuffles.

We also publish writings and art by adults that might enrich your lives by sharing their insights into the human experience. We have published stories, articles and photos from rural Mexico to

Moscow, from China to Chicago, and from India to Uganda.

As we enter our fifth year of publishing, we continue to broaden our horizons as we attempt to expand the horizons of our young readers.

Because we are not a for-profit publishing house, we need not worry about advertisers or about maximizing short-term profits. We are able to attract volunteers for translating, editing, proofreading, mailing and other routine tasks.

At times, parents or teachers write us, "How I wish a magazine like *Skipping Stones* existed when I was young." Our satisfaction comes from being of service to the young people of the globe. We try to provide as much space to as many of you as we possibly can. Share your lives with others and enrich yourself in the process.

CAROLE TRAPANI
Coordinator, Jon Douglas Essay Contest
Pacific Palisades, California

Carole Trapani is neither an editor nor a writer, which makes her unique among the adults featured in this edition. Nevertheless, her interest in young people and encouraging their creative efforts led her to promote the idea of a writing contest to her co-workers at the Jon Douglas Company, where she works as a real estate agent.

Despite the responsibilities it adds to her already busy schedule (her young son Dominic takes acting lessons and has appeared in Pepsi and Burger King commercials), Mrs. Trapani is committed to this project. It is an excellent example of a relatively simple, yet quality writing project sponsored at the local level. Because the project is limited in size (open only to students from specific schools) and scope (essays must relate to a specific theme each year and must be no longer than 350 words), yet offers awards to a relatively high number of entries, students compete on more equal terms and face less overall competition. This, plus distinctive public recognition of the winners, makes it a rewarding and inspirational experience for the whole community.

Pay close attention to Mrs. Trapani's advice for writing a winning essay. Notice how personalizing your entry and following the rules are as important to winning a small, local contest as they are when entering a larger, national one.

Pacific Palisades, a small community near Los Angeles, is nestled between the Santa Monica Mountains and the Pacific Ocean. The Fourth of July is celebrated here with a parade of marching bands, home-made floats, local celebrities, motorcycle acrobatics, and the usual assortment of clowns. In 1989, I had just joined the Jon Douglas Company, a large southern California real estate firm. At that time our company did not sponsor a marching unit or float as did other local businesses. I suggested to co-members of our firm's Community Affairs Committee that our company sponsor an essay contest for local elementary school children grades three through six. Winners would make up our marching unit.

Each year the parade has a theme, and the topic of the essay would relate to that theme. The first contest topic was "What Freedom Means to Me." That was in 1990. In 1991, the theme was "My American Hero" and in 1992, "The American Dream . . . What Is It and How Can I Share It." Flyers announcing the contest are delivered to the six local private and public elementary schools. Essays are limited to 350 words and are judged on the following criteria: following instructions, creativity, originality, correct usage and grammar. Each essay is scored without identifying data (other than grade) by at least three judges, and then the scores are totaled.

The first- and second-place winners, plus ten runners-up from each grade, are invited to march in the parade. Our marching unit is one of the most colorful in the parade. Fifty happy and smiling children decked out in red, white and blue Jon Douglas t-shirts and carrying red, white and blue balloons, all marching under the banner "Jon Douglas Essay Contest Winners," make a very colorful, patriotic and enchanting group! The kids love the event and so do the proud parents watching from curbside. For two years in a row, the parade commentator has stopped our unit to interview one of the winners.

First-place winners receive a $50 gift certificate (second-place winners, a $25 gift certificate) from a local children's bookstore, an engraved medal on a neck ribbon, a Jon Douglas t-shirt, and a certificate of recognition. First (and sometimes second) place essays are printed in the local newspaper in a full-page spread.

Words of advice for writing winning essays?

1. Write from personal experience. Each year the winning essays have been those drawn from personal experience. These essays always seem to be the more original and creative. For example, in 1991 the third-grade winner, Hilary Kerrigan of Palisades Elementary, chose her baby-sitter, Beatriz Hernandez, as her "American Hero" because she worked many jobs to earn money to send to her husband and family engaged in the struggle in El Salvador. In 1990, Palisades Elementary fifth-grade winner Rumi Mayeda, writing on "What Freedom Means to Me," wrote that "Freedom to me is like riding a bicycle for the first time. It's hard to stay on it without falling off. But, once we learn to ride it, we never forget

it. In the same way, once we learn what freedom of ideas, speech or action is like, we can never forget it."

2. Follow instructions exactly! Ten points are given for following instructions; zero points if entrants do not. Unfortunately, each year well-written essays that might have been winners are not *only* because ten points are lost because the essays are over the 350-word limit, or because they are written in cursive and not typed or printed as instructed.

Although the Jon Douglas Annual Fourth of July contest is small and limited to children attending our local schools, it has generated large rewards in unexpected ways. For many of our winners, ours is the first contest they have entered and won. It is a joy to hear their excitement when they are told, "Congratulations, you're a winner!" and to see their smiles when proudly marching in the parade. Some of the parents have told me that their child never thought they had a chance to win any contest and were bursting with pride and new-found self-esteem when they learned that their essay was an honorable mention winner. This past year our contest received national attention when well-known author and columnist Richard Reeves wrote an article on our winning essays. His column, which reprinted parts of several winning essays, was carried in hundreds of newspapers across the country.

MARGARET LARKIN

Editor, *Ink Blot*

Margaret Larkin has been writing since she was a child. Like many young writers, she even enjoyed school writing assignments, especially if she got to choose the topic (something many students often don't admit to their non-writing friends). Her interest in writing continued through high school, where she worked on the school paper. But after graduation she went to work, dropping the idea of a writing career.

Years later, however, her children's interest in reading and writing rekindled and reshaped her old desires. While helping them research publishing opportunities, she began self-publishing a small newsletter that featured creative work by her children and other young writers. Soon daughter Vicki (whom you read about in Chapter 6) was helping as assistant editor.

This type of small, local effort provides a big opportunity to young writers. Through hands-on experience they learned both the joys and difficulties of being an editor and publisher. Relying mostly on old-fashioned technology — typewriter, paper, scissors, tape, glue and photocopier — the newsletter is relatively inexpensive to produce. For those with a computer and printer, the task is a bit easier.

Young writers eager to get published may want to look for a similar opportunity in their own community. Check with your school or public librarian, since they usually know the active writers in the area. If no one is currently publishing a local newsletter for writers, consider starting one yourself or with classmates and friends. Or consult with the editor of your local newspaper to see if a special column could be featured in the paper on a regular or periodic basis.

As a child I loved to read and write stories. Sometimes I wrote by moonlight if I had an idea in the middle of the night. I still seem to get my best ideas after midnight. During high school I had brief thoughts about becoming a writer. But when I graduated and went to work, thoughts about a writing life were left behind. After marriage, and before our children came, I again turned to writing, occasionally mailing out a few short stories to publishers.

But when only rejection slips came back, I got discouraged and, once again, put my writing aside.

My daughters grew into avid readers and writers. It was their interest in writing that rekindled my own writing ambitions. As they, at ages 8, 9 and 13, wrote poetry and stories, we began looking for markets for their writings. We searched for information, and found *The Writer* magazine and *Market Guide for Young Writers* at our local library. We followed the formats outlined to prepare our manuscripts, and chose markets carefully following their guidelines.

The first response was from *Thumbprints*, the monthly newsletter published by a writer's club in a neighboring county. The editor wrote a short encouraging note to my daughter Vicki. I noticed how much this personal touch from an editor inspired her to do her best. With each letter of acceptance the level of excitement grew. We received many rejection slips, but the few pieces that were accepted kept the words flowing.

Seeing my children so excited about writing thrilled me. I kept a notebook of the how-to-get-published information I collected. Soon I began to wonder if other children would be interested in a creative writing class after school.

I spoke to Dennis Miner, principal of Shields Elementary School, where two of my children attended. He was very supportive and as pleased as I was when twenty-four students signed up for my ten-week "Writers' Workshop" class. I spent many hours preparing projects, themes and information for my young writers. They had so much enthusiasm and shared so many beautiful ideas and a variety of writing styles. The nervousness I'd felt in the beginning melted away.

As part of the workshop, the young writers shared their works with other classrooms at school. This not only gave them exposure but also an opportunity to practice their public speaking. We also compiled their efforts into spiral-bound books, including artwork, for the school libraries.

With so many stories and poems, I looked for more ways to share them with others. I met with the editor of our local weekly newspaper, *The Township Times*, and asked how to obtain a column for my workshop writers. He said we needed a sponsor to cover the cost of publishing the column. Many businesses are willing to do this as advertisement to create goodwill with customers. I asked a family friend, co-owner of a funeral home, if he would be interested. He sponsored our column for eight weeks!

I made sure every student was featured in print. I encouraged them to edit and rewrite. I tried to tell them to write with feeling, write what is in your heart, put yourself into the story to make it more personal.

I also made sure they knew the importance of proofreading their work, checking for grammar, spelling and typing errors. Even asking someone else to help proof it. When the workshop finished and the newspaper column ended, I was left holding the rest of my students' writings. I needed a new outlet. They were masterpieces of talent and creativity.

In January 1992, my daughters and I met with Janet Ihle, editor of *Thumbprints*. We discussed how she published her simple, six-page newsletter. Her suggestions and encouragement prompted me to start *Ink Blot*. With my former students' permission, I typed up my first issue and presented it, with my ideas, to several area school principals who, agreeing it a worthwhile project, offered help photocopying issues.

I put large manila envelopes in the offices of each of the four schools in our district to collect writings from the students for *Ink Blot*. Copies were distributed to the schools, and also to the local public libraries and area hospital waiting rooms. As each issue was printed, I tried to improve it. It was very difficult rejecting some of the items sent in. Sometimes it was because they were negative against society and I wanted to promote a more positive attitude. Some items were copied from other publications and not original work. Others needed to be edited extensively for spelling errors or incomplete thoughts.

I had such high expectations for my newsletter; it was a great disappointment when the flow of submissions began to decrease. With school over in June, I suspended publication for the summer.

Ink Blot continues, published sporadically as soon as I receive enough material for another issue. We encourage original submissions, even from outside our local area. If you are asked to write an assignment for school and it receives good comments, put it in the mail to *Ink Blot*. We welcome them.

My advice to writers of all ages is to keep at it. After twenty years of attempts and failures, I have had two items of my own published at last. This just goes to prove that if you stay with it you can succeed. *Don't give up!*

JILL BOND
Co-editor, *Bonding Times*
Lake Hamilton, Florida

Jill Bond and her husband Alan founded Bonding Times *in 1990 as a quarterly publication for Christian families. But it was their interest in home schooling that prompted them to include a special section, "Our Literate Legacy," and to sponsor the annual "Kids Write Contest." Says Mrs. Bond, "When we realized that children educated at home don't always have the same access to national contests that encourage student writers and artists, we decided to sponsor our own." Now not only do home schooled children have a special place to publish, the many contest winners share more than $5,000 in cash and U.S. Savings Bonds annually.*

Mrs. Bond also provides additional "in-house" publishing opportunities and encouragement to her own children, all home schooled, and advocates that other parents do the same, whether or not their child is home schooled. For instance, when son Reed at age 8 asked where butter came from, "Principal" Dad assigned him to find out and write a report. Instead of the standard, boring *research report, Reed surprised them by presenting his findings on butter and its production from a dairy cow's point of view. With help from Mom and Dad, he published it in book form. The title:* Betsy's Butter.

While the Bonds make considerable use of their personal computer, kids can "publish" just as well (and often more artfully) with regular paper, pencils and crayons.

Here Mrs. Bond shares some of her own experiences growing up as a young writer. In addition, she gives advice for getting—and keeping—the creative juices flowing. Her best advice: Writing doesn't have to be boring. Not even school assignments, no matter what kind of teacher you have.

My mother remembers that I couldn't wait to learn to write and was quite nagging and persistent about it. As a child, I organized the other kids in printing a newspaper. Always wanting to learn more, I later accepted the election as editor of our school's paper and then of our yearbook. I found I not only loved writing, but I also had a knack for editing, layout and publishing.

I must admit, though, I was bored with the standard fare of public school writing assignments. And rightly so. Who in the real world reads book reports? In the real world we read book reviews. We don't normally read history reports; we read the newspaper, editorials and stories. With the exception of the work of a few excellent teachers, many of us were taught to hate writing.

The "Two Gun Times," one of my favorite "newspaper" projects, chronicled the events for one week in an imaginary Western town in 1892. I wrote the lead news story, the advertisements and a sports page, and even included an essay about a new-fangled, sure-to-be-a-failure game Easterners were playing: basketball. It was a wonderful adventure into writing that not only earned me an A+ in junior high journalism, but proved to me that there was more to writing than those dreary homework assignments. Just because the teacher was boring didn't mean that the angle, or the way that I developed the assignment, had to be.

At *The Bonding Times*, we want to encourage you and your interest in writing. Following are a few pointers that helped me and can help you further develop the skills you already possess.

Are you an avid reader? That is a hallmark of a good writer. (I read all of *Gone With the Wind* when I was only 9 years old. It is sort of a family tradition, as my mother also read it when she was 9.) Read and analyze the writings of others. Try to find ways to improve their work. Pretend you are a reporter and interview the author. Then answer the questions as if you were the author. For example, "Why did you choose to reveal the main character's fatal flaw so early in the book?" Keep a log book of your favorite works and why you like them.

Write.

Not only write on paper in proper English, but write in your mind as you're drifting off to sleep, waiting in the dentist's chair, or riding in the carpool. Pretend you are the announcer and you're narrating a film about whatever you're doing . . . write the script.

Punctuate conversations. Warning: Do this silently or you might offend someone. While you're listening, add the statement after the quotes. It will help you become more observant and help your dialogue to be more believable. Here's an example: You hear your mom say, "Come in here." Mentally think (as you're rushing to her), "she screamed," "she pleaded," or "she demanded." It's a fun little game to play that will help you realize how real people talk and use words.

When you write in your mind, it's part of pre-writing—one of our most valuable tools as writers. Next, let your thoughts fly. Here's an example: Jot down on paper, as fast as your fingers can fly, your idea, the angle, and any clever word uses, so you don't lose the great idea. Don't worry if it's not a complete sentence. Don't worry if it's a run-on sentence. Just get the idea on paper or reword the same sentence different ways. You can come back to it later.

So many wonderful ideas for stories are lost in the maze of stopping to look up the proper spelling, the quirk of some grammar rule, or the hangman's noose of penmanship. To avoid this, I highly suggest you recruit someone like Mom or Dad to take dictation. They can probably write faster than you and then you won't use a watered-down word because you can't spell the perfect word that is brimming with connotation and style. You won't use "bunch of boats" because you can't spell "flotilla." Download the story in real words from your mental tape. You can always go back and smooth out the rough phrases and polish the style.

Nobody around to help? Then try using a tape recorder. Just don't lose those wonderful ideas that come to you.

Once you develop those ideas, consider sending your work to us. We'd love to read it and perhaps publish it for others to enjoy. Send for our writer's guidelines first.

Also, if you have a great idea for an interview, article or essay and could cover it better from an "insider's" angle, write us a query letter. If we like your idea, we'll send you an "on assignment" cover letter. Use it to help get a "press pass," which is one definite advantage writers have. Writers with press passes get into the most interesting places, such as to see a space shuttle land, or meet a celebrity or important politician, or behind the scenes at the theater.

[*Author's note*: Young writer Amy Wu, profiled on page 126, used a press pass to attend the 1992 National Democratic Convention.]

MAXINE PINSON
Editor, *Savannah Parent*
Savannah, Georgia

Of all the people profiled in this edition, Maxine Pinson is the only one with whom I had prior contact. We first exchanged letters in March 1987, after she'd written to me eager to share news about her daughter Celia's experiences getting her work published. Celia, then 12, was indeed a talented writer, as is her younger sister Melissa. Every few months I'd receive another note or two, and delightful handmade holiday cards from Celia. But I sensed in those letters that Mrs. Pinson, herself, was yearning to become a published writer. Someday she'll grow her own roots, I thought.

So it was no surprise to me when a letter arrived one day that announced Mrs. Pinson's unusual entry into the publishing field. I'm pleased to share her story with you in the pages of the Market Guide for Young Writers, *the same guide that once offered a profile of Celia.*

Each of us is granted special gifts, seeds of talent and unique ability planted within us. When these seeds of our potential begin sprouting, they grow rapidly; strong root systems develop when the seedlings are recognized, acknowledged, fostered. Unfortunately, like the neglected flower I once discovered, God-given gifts sometimes remain dormant and untapped until circumstances cause blooming at the most unexpected moment — and late bloomers can be just as beautiful.

I recall, as an awkward and introverted sixth-grader, sitting through classes and tuning out my teacher while writing zany rhymes about my classmates. My rhymes made my classmates laugh, and I discovered that I could say things through my rhymes that I was embarrassed to convey verbally. Later, as a senior, I became absorbed with my school newspaper; however most of my contributions were behind the scenes and unrecognized. Little did I know how valuable my hands-on journalistic experience would prove during mid-life!

Journalism was in my blood by the time I entered college, but not the encouragement and self-confidence that I needed to pursue it. I'll never forget the thrill of an English professor reading a haiku I'd written. I still remember it word for word. How I wished such encouragement had come sooner and with more consistency. But it had not, and my continuing lack of confidence stomped out the words wrestling to get out of my head. After my freshman year in college I closed my box of writing desires and shoved them into a closet. Twelve years later, my 4-year-old daughter began pulling them out.

As my young daughter began sharing her own creative tales with me, I typed and compiled them for her. Eight years later, I helped her submit, and many of her writings were published. She was even featured on the cover of *Reflections*, a national poetry magazine for students. I resolved that I would give her the encouragement to develop her writing talent that I had not received.

Before long, my daughter was scribbling down story after story, with me cheering her on all the way. I gathered information about publications that accepted children's works and sought out writing contests for her. When a magazine arrived with one of her stories or when she won a contest, my jubilant squeal was louder than hers. I was so proud of my daughter; but, eventually, I realized that I was also attempting to recapture dreams of my own — dreams I thought were lost forever.

When my daughter was asked to be a staff writer for a teen newspaper in Atlanta, I had an opportunity to meet another editor. Then, when the publisher of the teen paper decided to expand and start a parenting publication in our hometown, I was asked to edit the paper. At first I was hesitant. My degree is in elementary education, and I did not feel qualified for such an undertaking. However, an unusual set of circumstances made me reconsider, and incredible opportunities began to surface. Within three months I was editor, publisher and owner of *Savannah Parent*, the publication I was initially afraid to become involved with — and my daughter was editing *my* work.

As publisher and editor of *Savannah Parent*, I enjoy providing a forum for local children's creative drawings and writings. My younger daughter, also a published writer and illustrator, helps select submissions appearing on the "Creative Expressions" page each month. She sometimes assists me with the layout. *Savannah*

Parent usually sponsors a couple of contests each year for children, and lists national contests open to children.

I will always be grateful that, through my daughters' introduction to the publishing world, I also had the privilege of discovering first-hand that "editors are real people, too." I was able to observe the creative ways through which they enabled my daughters to feel special and affirmed, in addition to providing genuine encouragement for them. Inspired by "real people editors," I now try doing extra little things to make the children whose work appears in *Savannah Parent* feel special.

Parenting papers are popping up all over the country. However, most of the ones I've seen do not have a children's page. Yet, I believe that most editors would consider adding a "Creations" page if enough interest was indicated. I am always amazed at how few parents help their children send in their work, even though I print most of the submissions I do receive. I usually must solicit work from local schools to fill the "Creative Expressions" page.

It is important for children to share their work, and parents can do a lot to help them.

VAUGHN LARSON
Executive Producer, Providence
   Elementary Broadcast News
Providence, Utah

*Vaughn Larson is the media teacher at Providence
Elementary School in Providence, Utah. On the
first day of work he was informed that he would
be in charge of the school enrichment program,*
which involved a weekly activity for all fourth and fifth grade students. Not
only was this a shock, but he had no ideas of what to do with these students.

*The secondary schools in the district had just installed Channel One, and
the idea occurred to him that elementary students could produce their own
video news programs. But could young elementary students write, edit and
operate audio/video and computer equipment? The answer is yes. Just ask
the staff at The Valley Channel, a local television station that even allowed
students to fill part of its air time.*

*With the push for integrated curriculums, cooperative learning, and the
teaching of life skills, this program addresses many skills that students will
be required to have in the coming years.*

The purpose of this project is to help students become better
writers. However, in the process, we hope that students will gain
an appreciation for a free press, become more informed about current events, develop critical thinking skills, and gain technology
utilization skills.

Students form a production company that produces a weekly,
seven to ten-minute news broadcast. The teacher, acting as the
executive producer (another way of saying that he is in charge
but does very little work on the production and is there to offer
suggestions and answer questions), begins the process of job selection. A general vote is taken to select a director who will oversee
all aspects of the production. Depending on the size of the class,
the director may select an assistant director. Students then lobby
to the director to fill job slots such as editors (world, national,
state, local, school, sports, special features). Again, depending on
the size of the class, editors may have staff writers who are responsible for writing and selecting stories from their respective areas.

Set designers, camera operators, video engineers, audio engineers and anchors (selected by audition) fill out the employee docket.

Students are taught lessons on newswriting, addressing such issues as the "Five Ws" (who, what, when, where and why), plagiarism and fact versus fiction. Channel One and CNN's Newsroom are very helpful for students to view.

Training the technical staff is a bit tricky at first, but the students love the equipment and are not at all scared of it, which is at times good and at other times bad. Generally, mistakes are made early and are eliminated after a few trial and error runs.

The fun part of the project is the day of filming. The editors are frantic doing rewrites to meet time frames. The director is still waiting to see if the set designers can get the backdrop to stay up. The anchors are not really sure if they are pronouncing Bosnia-Herzegovina right. The technical staffers are having second thoughts about when they are to switch from live video to graphics — is it before the story on the new playground equipment, or after?

I don't know how it happens, but I do know that in all the years we have done this (we began during the 1987-88 school year), there has only been one week that a newscast has been cancelled. And it was my fault. I didn't get the equipment hookups connected properly.

The research on such writing programs is very clear. Students improve in areas such as organizing and synthesizing information. They are better able to distinguish between fact and opinion. Student writing becomes more clear and forceful. These broadcasting students are on their way — move over, Dan Rather and Diane Sawyer!

JIM STAHL
Editor, *Merlyn's Pen: The National Magazine of Student Writing*
East Greenwich, Rhode Island

Since its founding in 1985, Merlyn's Pen: The National Magazine of Student Writing *has become one of the most highly respected publications featuring the work of young writers. It is dedicated to maintaining high literary standards, publishing only the best work of young writers and, thus, encouraging readers to set high literary standards as well.*

In the following essay, founder and editor Jim Stahl recalls how much his own experiences as a student influenced the philosophy and goals Merlyn's Pen *was founded on. In addition, he shares his opinions on why getting published can seem so difficult, why conformity in fiction is the kiss of death, and what to do about rejection letters.*

I attended many suburban public schools, typical places where the unspoken mood was: I'm nothing, you're nothing. Teachers felt chained to their textbooks, curriculums, and the whims of poorly trained principals; students lived in fear of a bad grade. The classrooms felt like cages! No one — teachers or students — felt safe enough to experiment, to try out what they knew. No one even trusted what they knew. It felt unsafe.

These memories shaped the launch of *Merlyn's Pen*. It would be a place where the telling of one's own story and where one's singular talent, intellectual interests, unique slant, and dedication to crafting these into a story would all be welcome.

Bureaucracies (schools among them) can't possibly encourage such singular, uncapped thinking. Such thinking and writing is too *unpredictable*. Bureaucracies require that we march to the same dull beat. But good fiction, to be good, *must* be unpredictable! It must create its own beat, so a magazine like *Merlyn's Pen* was needed to allow new beats to be heard.

Our educational goal at *Merlyn's Pen* is to improve the image of student writing. Writing by students has taken a bad rap, and teachers and librarians have largely ignored its usefulness to student readers.

Many magazines of student writing have helped sustain the impression that students can't write. How? By publishing nearly everything in sight. Some journals seem to have no standards at all, no high expectations for their authors (or their readers). They function almost as bulletin boards in a public square, displaying every citizen's effort, every sentiment that someone took the effort to post. Bulletin boards serve very important functions, as do magazines that reward effort at all cost, but good fiction is not among the goals served by these magazines. Adult readers don't allow carefree editing in the magazines *they* read; why encourage free, poorly edited, unpolished expression in the magazines we promote to young adults? I think over-sentimentality about children's "expression" has something to do with the problem.

With so many other magazines promoting free, unshaped expression, *Merlyn's Pen* need not be about that. It's more about encouraging and printing the important fiction of this new generation. It's about showing young people, their parents and teachers, too, that teens themselves have a part (perhaps a responsibility) in shaping this new genre called "Young Adult Literature."

Young people often ask me why becoming published is so difficult. To be honest, I must tell them that writing that is good enough for national publication quite often (1) says something differently, (2) invites scrutiny of the author, (3) represents a singular point of view, and (4) calls attention to itself. These are often the *last* things most teens wish for themselves! To be hip, to dress like one's friends, to speak as other teens speak, to have opinions and entertain oneself according to the peer group is *mandatory behavior* in school. Teens doing otherwise risk being outcasts. Conform or die!

In your fiction, though, conformity is the kiss of death! Publishable fiction demands that you lay bare your heart, speak in your *own* voice (which may at times be strong, at times weak, at times weird, at times stupid), call things as *you* see them and risk embarrassment. How many teens — how many adults — are willing to risk such exposure? Not many, and I believe that's why so few of us write publishable material.

Here's an example: One of my students gave all her female characters "long, silky, blonde hair." The hair was always "feathered," the style at the time. Well, clearly this is the hair the author wanted for herself (advertisements at the time stressed this), and this is the hair she felt her characters would need in order to be liked by readers! This particular writer wasn't alone: All the girls in her class wrote about girls with long, silky, feathered hair. Such hair may get your characters a date, but it won't get them into print.

Ever wonder why so many successful male action and adventure stories are written by girls? Readers like to *connect* with adventure characters; they want to see how they *think* and *feel* in relation to the events that befall them. Boys are afraid to show feelings. (Rightly so, showing them in our culture is considered weak; much better to be cool, unmoved, James Bondian, unfazed, wooden.) Readers, though, (unlike moviegoers) can't relate to wooden characters. So many great adventure stories about boys have been written by girls. Girls seem more willing to let their male characters loosen up, respond, dance, shed a tear or two. Readers need to see characters' feelings before readers will empathize. Who wants to empathize with a block of wood?

Young writers also want to know what to do about rejection letters. If the editor is kind enough to write comments on your work, read between the lines. Realize that the editor has condensed her entire impression of your story into twenty or thirty words, so each word is probably loaded with implication. To make the most of the editorial comment, show it around. Ask another writer, a teacher or a parent to help you unpack the comment: But demand honesty from them. False praise from others and blaming the editor won't bring you any nearer to getting published.

There are, of course, other things young writers ask me. I trust, however, that what I've shared will help you, as a young writer, improve your approach to your craft. We are particular about what is published in *Merlyn's Pen*. It has become, as I had hoped, a place where one's own story, one's singular talent, one's intellectual interests, one's unique slant are not only welcome, but encouraged. Many young people are capable of writing good fiction. You can read their work in the pages of *Merlyn's Pen*.

LUCY LAGRASSA
President, The Kids Netword
Concord, Ontario

Lucy LaGrassa, who started writing as a child, lives in metropolitan Toronto and has been a professional writer and editor for more than fifteen years. Her career as a publisher and trainer of child authors began five years ago when she founded The Prism Awards program and The Kids Netword training and book publishing programs. Canadian children ages 7 to 14 have an opportunity to enter the world of authorship every fall by submitting their most ingenious and creative piece of writing. Official entry forms are widely distributed to schools, libraries and associations across the country. The form outlines the rules and lists the story categories, which vary annually.

Winners of The Prism Award join The Kids Netword Training Program, where they learn about being professional writers. They are also given a $500 cash award from Scotiabank and a trophy — a crystal prism. Winning works are considered for publication as part of The Kids Netword series of books. But what really excites the winners, and Mrs. LaGrassa, is the long-term support offered by The Kids Netword.

In the following, Mrs. LaGrassa shares how her own experiences as a young writer influenced the founding of The Prism Awards and The Kids Netword. You'll read about how guilty she felt when her first poem was published. She was sure it would have been rejected if the editor had known she was only 10 years old!

Sometimes it seems so long ago that I was a child scribbling hour after hour, huddled over my desk, often into the wee hours of the morning. I was fascinated with words. I was fascinated with feelings. I was fascinated with behavior. I was fascinated with people. I was fascinated with the things I saw and heard. It seemed like there were so many things that fascinated me that there wasn't enough time or paper to write them all down.

By the time I reached high school I was devoted to my diary, not because I wanted to keep track of everything I did but because I wanted to review, to evaluate, to understand the world around me. "Just what is life about anyway?" I kept asking myself. Soon, no daily account was complete until I had written what I called "Today's Saying." It was a poem that explained something I discovered that day that I thought was profound. Not one day could go by without my intense desire to learn something new and something wise. Of course, this was all just personal reflection. But I enjoyed the challenge and it taught me to observe, to listen and to understand behavior with an acute ear, an acute eye, an acute heart and an acute soul. Little did I know these same things would serve me well in the years ahead when I decided to work with young writers.

I didn't start out deciding to be a writer or an editor or a publisher. After all, it seemed like one of those romantic professions that only a romantic without much common sense would pursue. And it wasn't something that just happened. I became a trained journalist and editor not because I wanted to be a writer, but because I was still looking for something new to learn every day. I became a political speech-writer not because I wanted to be a writer, but because I was intrigued with politics. I'd say that for me, becoming a writer was something that evolved from nurturing seeds of writing talent with a zest and love for the truth about life!

At the age of 10, on a whim, I sent a poem to a university literary magazine to see what would happen, and it was published. I couldn't believe it! This was good news and bad news. The good news was that someone liked my poetry! The bad news was that I believed that if they had known I was only 10 they wouldn't have published it. Rightly or wrongly, I felt guilty about that for years. Many years later I came to appreciate the beauty of my poetry and went on to win a number of international awards. It helped tremendously, of course, that family and friends coveted my poetry like prized jewels.

These seem like idle thoughts, but these are the things that helped create the foundation of my understanding and my ability to develop programs for children. I knew that there were children bursting with God-given talent but who had no direction. There was no publishing house set up to work seriously with children; no place where they could be trained professionally; no place where they could be professionally published; no place where they could be professionally marketed as legitimate authors. It was important to me to create a program that would let children be accepted, respected, honoured and established among the country's finest authors for their own genuine talents.

The Prism Awards program was designed to open this avenue for children. There is one winner in each story category in ages 7 to 10 and in ages 11 to 14. So if there are five story categories there are ten winners. An editorial team at The Kids Netword works with these ten winners. They learn to develop story lines, characterization, detailing, subplots, parallel plots and much more. Most importantly, they learn the fundamentals of good communication and how to do it in an entertaining way.

But the program would only be half a sandwich without The Kids Netword publishing program. Air Canada, one of Canada's largest airlines, commissioned a collection of Prism Award-winning books and intends to be a long-time supporter of the publishing program. The Prism Award winners who have their books published also receive royalties.

Now with thousands of books by Prism Award winners in the hands of children, either on board the airline, in the classroom or in the library, professional child authors have become an established and valued part of the literary community in Canada. Adults and children alike can now enjoy the world from the eyes, ears, hearts and souls of professional child authors whose works burst with honesty, integrity and great entertainment.

After all, it is not the age of the author that matters; it is great ideas that are ageless and timeless.

JEFF CHURCH
Artistic Director of The Coterie Theatre
Kansas City, Missouri

At age 15, Jeff Church founded the La Junta Children's Theatre in his Colorado hometown. He still returns there annually to direct a show. Later, as playwright-in-residence at The Kennedy Center's Theater for Young People, he started a "roundtable for young playwrights," where interested young people gathered to learn play writing.

Now, as artistic director of The Coterie Theatre in Kansas City, Missouri, Jeff Church at 32 is working to redefine children's theater. "We are an inner-city theater, and for the African-American community we now have begun to fill needs both cultural and social. This is fully reflected in the casting of every play," he says. Categorizing The Coterie can be a challenge. They commonly produce such lighthearted fare as Winnie-the-Pooh *back-to-back with Fugard's* My Children! My Africa! *But the theater's staff and board are proud of the stretch and elasticity they get from their audience. "They* know *we don't offer typical children's theater," says Mr. Church proudly.*

In the following, Mr. Church shares some of the guiding objectives and goals of The Coterie. In addition, you'll read how he has incorporated the roundtable idea into "Reaching the Write Minds" workshops, and learn what he finds artistically stimulating. Young playwrights looking for direction and inspiration will find it here.

At The Coterie we continue our aggressive search for strong and unusual plays needing a second or third "refinement" production after their premiere. For playwrights, this is a real issue — especially in youth theater at this time — because a quick and cheap commission has taken the place of a producer paying a royalty or reading a developing script.

We're proud that, for example, this year's two AATE distinguished play awards went to James Still's *Amber Waves* and Pam Sterling's *Secret Garden*, both of which received their second and third production with us in 1991. Now, in 1993, we're producing the new adaptation of a kids' cult classic, *Bunnicula*, first seen in

Chicago, and Joanna Blythe's strong but little-seen adaptation of *Anne of Green Gables*. We're also staging a one-woman show, *Blazing the Outback*, starring controversial local Kansas City author/mother Marlo Morgan, who is said to have been taken by Australian aborigines on a four-month "walkabout" with no preparation — and then learned the secrets of the planet. It's startling and terribly compelling at once, containing a desperately important message about the earth, no matter if Morgan's highly debated story is truth or fiction.

We are newly emphasizing a number of one-of-a-kind community and educational programs that allow us a high degree of person-to-person interaction, something The Coterie has never tried before in its thirteen-year history. "Reaching the Write Minds" is a five-hour in-service for schools, designed to light a fire under students who are selected for our specialized dramatic writing sessions by their school district.

Now in its first year, "Reaching the Write Minds" is already the largest city-wide writing project in the area. It has bolstered our access to inner-city students. The personal contact we made has led to the extraordinary onstage performance by Victor James II, who played Malcolm X's bodyguard Rashad in *The Meeting* this past fall.

To give a voice to emerging young playwrights, fifteen motivated students from the "Reaching the Write Minds" workshops will be invited to be on our "Young Playwrights' RoundTable." Late this spring (1993), our plans are to convert our loft rehearsal room in Mel's Artspace into theater performance space exclusively for dramatic material written by teen writers and performed by paid professional actors. Exciting ideas, such as kids, parents and teachers having to roll dice to determine their price of admission, are being planned. (If the show sells out, there will be an instant cast party after with pizza donated!)

We have been the catalyst for other ongoing community relationships such as: a program for Catholic suburban churches to meet with sister inner-city churches at a performance and use the theater afterwards as a place to talk and interact; and a program called KC-PACT where pregnant substance abusers in recovery regularly meet and interact with a Coterie Theatre director and teen women from the Young Playwrights' RoundTable.

In addition, we fully anticipate having a new and researched education program in place this summer, which is to offer classes using recent, successful drama education techniques, such as live art for teens. For younger students, by using themes such as the environment, we'll program topic-based participatory classes where the teacher/artist creates a role and remains in it the entire session.

For us, success is the creation of programs that grow out of a need in the community, that knit us into a school and public fabric, and that can be administered by artists who can see how their work contributes to the artistic core. On a practical level, it is important to us that new programs don't burden our small business office staff with heavy paper trails and incoming phone calls! Success is the creation of a season that gets tremendous response from identified constituents we wish to serve.

Working with young playwrights, like the roundtable I started at The Kennedy Center, is a trend I hope continues and expands. It doesn't cost any money; you just gather them together in the best possible way—through submissions, probably—and start meeting to get them into play writing. We want a variety of ages so that we can eventually produce a whole entertainment by young people for young people. And I don't mean to say those tired things with "adolescent angst."

It's always fun to look at things in a way that seems fresh. What doesn't stimulate me, artistically, is a set with a big couch right in the middle to signify a living room; if that's the set the script calls for, I toss it away and don't read it. But if the couch was, say, burnt so there was only the frame of the couch . . . anything that seems fresh, wacky or strange. Writers should avoid putting familiar characters in settings they are familiar with!

Plus, I like scripts that offer the best words you can give me and that are sparse enough to let me do the sets and costumes. And you have to keep truthful to the script and make acting choices that are energized, not passive. For example, if a character is bored or lethargic and the script says that, you don't *play* boredom, do you? You play it with energy, with the kid stabbing at mom saying, "I'm bored!"

In short, a play must harness our emotions. For The Coterie, we like the play that features a young protagonist, and insist it contain three-dimensional performances. If we can consistently find ways to offer up the familiar in a new light, or the unorthodox in an accessible way, we feel we succeed.

PROFILE OF VERY SPECIAL ARTS YOUNG PLAYWRIGHTS PROGRAM

"Only when every child in our society can be assured the opportunity to share in an appreciation of the arts can all of us claim a share in the wonder of the talent, the creativity and the joy of every child."

JEAN KENNEDY SMITH
FOUNDER AND PROGRAM CHAIR,
VERY SPECIAL ARTS

ABOUT THE VERY SPECIAL ARTS YOUNG PLAYWRIGHTS PROGRAM

Very Special Arts is an international organization that provides programs in creative writing, dance, drama, literature, music and the visual arts for individuals with physical and mental disabilities. Founded in 1974 by Jean Kennedy Smith, Very Special Arts is an educational affiliate of The John F. Kennedy Center for the Performing Arts. It seeks to promote worldwide awareness of the educational and cultural benefits of the arts for all people. Very Special Arts programs can be found in all fifty states, the District of Columbia, and many countries around the world.

Of the many programs that Very Special Arts offers, the Young Playwrights Program is targeted to students interested in writing. The Very Special Arts Young Playwrights Program invites students between the ages of 12 and 18 to express their ideas and feelings about disabilities in plays. This program has been designed to encourage students to think and write about disabilities in contemporary society.

As long as you are between the ages of 12 and 18, you are eligible to submit a script to the Very Special Arts Young Playwrights Program. Entries may be the work of an individual or a group of students, but the script must address the issue of disability. The script may be written from the student's personal experience or from another person's experience.

You should ask yourself these important questions while writing your script: Does my play address and incorporate the topic of disability in a meaningful way? Will the audience be able to gain new insights about dealing with disabilities? Will my characters' circumstances draw a strong emotional response? Is the plot of my play interesting from beginning to end?

Each entry is read by drama professionals associated with Very Special Arts. They narrow the choice to five or ten finalists, which are then reviewed by a panel of award-winning directors and playwrights. One or two scripts are selected for production at The John F. Kennedy Center for the Performing Arts.

Every student who submits a script receives a certificate of participation. The young playwrights whose scripts are chosen, and their teachers, will travel to Washington to participate in rehearsals and will be honored at the premiere production of their play at The John F. Kennedy Center for the Performing Arts.

If you are a student who aspires to be a writer, or simply one who enjoys written expression, this is a wonderful opportunity. You are invited to learn more about the Very Special Arts Young Playwrights Program and to receive an entry form and informational poster by writing to: Young Playwrights Coordinator, Very Special Arts Education Office, The John F. Kennedy Center for the Performing Arts, Washington, DC 20566.

(*Author's note*: This profile was prepared by the staff at Very Special Arts.)

PART THREE

Chapter Eight

The Market List

On the following pages you will find the market listings for young writers. Yet many of the best and most accessible markets are not listed here. They are the publications you are already familiar with, such as your hometown newspaper, the regional magazine insert that comes with the daily paper, your own school or church publication, and the special publications sponsored by clubs and organizations you belong to. And for those of you who are members of online information services, don't forget to check what's available in your special-interest areas. They are all potential markets for your work. You may submit material to them using the same formats and advice you have learned here.

Be sure to include a short cover letter when you first submit to a local or regional market, especially ones not listed here. Tell the editor where you are from and include a *brief* bit of personal history. Include such things as the name of your school and the grade you're in. You may want to add a line or two about your writing and publishing desires. However, as previously noted, don't waste time telling the editor what a great (or miserable) writer you are, or that you have enclosed (or want to send) a great story, poem or article. And you usually shouldn't bother mentioning how great (or yucky) your family, friends or teachers find your writing.

Local editors, like editors elsewhere, are usually opinionated when it comes to submissions. If you *are* a good writer and *have* submitted a really good manuscript, the editor will know it without your telling him or her. If the editor doesn't agree with your assessment of your writing ability, no amount of boasting will convince him otherwise. Editors in general are skeptical about working

MARKET LISTING CHART

SEC.	YOU WILL FIND	PAY SPECIAL ATTENTION TO
1	Name of Publication. Mailing address for manuscripts, guidelines and sample copies. Brief description including how often it is published, the age range, and interests of its readers.	Who reads this publication and the general theme followed in each issue.
2	Types of written material, art and photography, that are considered for publication. Specific material that is not accepted.	Any special columns or departments written exclusively by young writers. Any specific types of material that are never used.
3	More detailed information to help you write and prepare your manuscripts. Payments offered; rights purchased. Word limits; line limits for poetry. Availability of guidelines and samples.	Any special instructions for submitting manuscripts. Whether you need to include a signed statement from your parents, teacher or guardian.
4	Advice and helpful tips especially for young writers, quoted directly from the editor.	What the editors say they do and do not want from young writers.
5	Subscription rates. Subscription mailing address when it differs from the editorial office.	Included as an extra service for young people, parents and teachers.

SAMPLE MARKET LISTING

1 _____ **THE ACORN,** 1530 7th St. , Rock Island, IL 61201. For young people in grades K-12, published six times a year.

2 _____ **Publishes:** Fiction, nonfiction, articles on any subject of interest to young people. Uses 4″ × 5″ black ink drawings on any subject. Uses material from adult authors, as well as young authors, but work must be slanted to students in grades K-12.

3 _____ **Submission Info:** Handwritten material OK if readable. Prefers standard format. Maxiumum length for fiction and nonfiction 500 words; 200-word limit for articles; poetry up to 32 lines. *Always* put author's name, address, age or grade on manuscript. Submissions will *not* be returned without SASE. Reports in one week. Pays in copies. Guidelines available for SASE. Sample copy $2.

4 _____ **Editor's Remarks:** "Just be yourself. Write your feelings; dare to be different. You never know when what you have to say might be of help and encouragement to other young authors."

5 _____ **Subscription Rates:** One year $10 (six issues: February, April, June, August, October, December).

with people who think too highly of themselves or their work. Let your work speak for itself.

The biggest benefit of submitting work to this type of market is that if a local editor likes your work and finds that you are willing to listen to his comments and ideas, and you can accept editing without much fuss, you may just find yourself being hired to do special writing assignments.

UNDERSTANDING A MARKET LISTING

Markets, which include secular and religious magazines, newspapers, newsletters, theater groups, book publishers and other opportunities, are listed alphabetically, including those accessed through online computer services.

Each listing contains three sections of information to help you understand (1) the type of publication it is, (2) what material it will consider from young people, and (3) the preferred formats for submitting your work. There are also two optional sections. "Editor's Remarks" are directly from editors or their guidelines sheets. They provide additional information to help you understand and evaluate whether or not the market would be an appropriate place for you to send your work. "Subscription Rates" has been included as an extra service, because so many of the publications listed are available by subscription only.

New additions to this edition's market listings are preceded by a checkmark (✔). Markets that are of special interest to young people are preceded by a star (*). Markets that require an entry fee are marked with a dollar sign ($). A few listings are also marked with a double cross (‡). This indicates the market should be considered only by serious teen writers. Competition is likely to be tough because you will be competing against adults, the market receives many more submissions than it can use, or it has an unusual focus that may not be understood or appreciated by young writers.

The chart and sample market listing on pages 168-169 will help explain the information contained within each section. You may want to review the sections "What's new in this edition" and "More about the listings" in Chapter 1, plus the advice in Chapter 2, "Study and compare the opportunities" before reviewing these listings.

✔* **THE ACORN**, 1530 7th St., Rock Island, IL 61201. For young people in grades K-12, published six times a year.

Publishes: Fiction, nonfiction, articles on any subject of interest to young people. Uses 4″ × 5″ black ink drawings on any subject. Uses material from adult authors, as well as young authors, but work must be slanted to students in grades K-12.

Submission Info: Handwritten material OK if readable. Prefers standard format. Maximum length for fiction and nonfiction 500 words; 200-word limit for articles; poetry up to 32 lines. *Always* put author's name, address, age or grade on manuscript. Submissions will *not* be returned without SASE. Reports in one week. Pays in copies. Guidelines available for SASE. Sample copy $2.

Editor's Remarks: "Just be yourself. Write your feelings; dare to be different. You never know when what you have to say might be of help and encouragement to other young authors."

Subscription Rates: One year $10 (six issues: February, April, June, August, October, December).

✔ **AIM – AMERICA'S INTERCULTURAL MAGAZINE**, P.O. Box 20554, Chicago, IL 60620-0554. Quarterly publication for high school, college, general public.

Publishes: Some poetry on themes dealing with social issues. However, *no* religious material.

Submission Info: Use standard format; include SASE. Reports in two months. Payment $25. Sample copy $4.

Editor's Remarks: "To purge racism from the human bloodstream — that is our objective. To do it through the written word. We want to show that people from different ethnic and racial backgrounds are more alike than they are different. They all strive for the same things — education, jobs, good health, etc."

Subscription Rates: One year $10.

✔* **AMERICAN GIRL MAGAZINE**, 8400 Fairway Place, Middleton, WI 53562. Full-color magazine published bimonthly by Pleasant Company.

Publishes: Children should submit poems, tips, suggestions, and responses to polls and questions in *American Girl* magazine.

Submission Info: Guidelines available for adult submissions.

See sample issues for more information on submissions from young people. Send SASE for guidelines. See guidelines on how to obtain a sample copy, or purchase copies at bookstores.

Editor's Remarks: "The mission of Pleasant Company is to educate and entertain children with high-quality products and experiences that reinforce positive social and moral values."

Subscription Rates: Single issue $3.95. One year (six issues) $19.95.

[Author's note: For best chance at having work accepted, read one or more current copies and respond to requests for specific material or topics.]

✔* **THE APPRENTICE WRITER**, % Gary Fincke, P.O. Box 1836, Susquehanna University, Selinsgrove, PA 17870-1001. Published annually in September, featuring student writing and artwork; distributed to high schools and colleges throughout the Middle Atlantic states.

Publishes: Poetry, short stories, essays, plays, journalism (features/interviews), black-and-white artwork and photography. Considers submissions by high school students grades 9-12 from the Middle Atlantic Region and nearby states.

Submission Info: Manuscripts must be typed and double-spaced. Writer's name, address, and appropriate teacher must appear on each page of submission. Length limit 30 pages. Reports only on acceptances. Does not return submissions except art and photography with SASE. Annual submission deadline is March 15. Reports on acceptances by May 1. Send SASE for guidelines.

Editor's Remarks: "Eleventh issue published in 1993."

✔*$ **AUTHORSHIP**, National Writer's Club, 1450 S. Havana, Suite 424, Aurora, CO 80012. Accepts submissions from National Writer's Club members only; students welcomed as members. Published bimonthly.

Publishes: Articles on writing only. No fiction or poetry.

Submission Info: Use standard typed format. Maximum length 600 words. Payment in copies and credit for professional membership in the National Writer's Club. Submissions will not be returned without SASE. Reporting time one month for unsuitable materials; if it's held longer, we are considering it for publication.

Editor's Remarks: "We would like to see more young people as writers and members."

Subscription Rates: Membership includes subscription. For schools or institutions, one year $18.

[Author's note: NWC has a lot to offer serious young writers; discount membership fee available to students.]

* BOODLE: BY KIDS, FOR KIDS, P.O. Box 1049, Portland, IN 47371. (210) 726-8141. Published quarterly. (Formerly called *Caboodle: By Kids, For Kids*.) Ninety-five percent of magazine written by children. Audience children ages 6-12.

Publishes: Student-produced stories, articles, poems, mazes and puzzles. Readers are invited to write and illustrate their own ideas and send them to the editors. Uses about twelve short stories and twenty to thirty poems per issue. Seldom publishes sad or depressing stories about death or serious illness. Especially likes humor and offbeat stories and poems.

Submission Info: Never devotes more than two pages to any one story, so long stories are not acceptable. Handwritten material OK, if legible. Please include full name, grade when written, current grade, name of school, and a statement from parent or teacher that the work is original. Send SASE for reply, or if you wish your material returned. Guidelines available for SASE. Sample copies $2.50. Payment is two free copies of issue. Reports in two months.

Editor's Remarks: "Young writers and artists should read *Boodle* to see what kind of material is published, but do not try to write the same type of material you read. Try to think of something different. What kind of story would you like to read, but didn't find? The best way to get your story or poem published is to make the editor smile or laugh when she reads it."

Subscription Rates: One year (four quarterly issues) $10.

[Author's note: I have received many notes from young writers who have been happily published in *Boodle*.]

‡✓ BUSINES$ KIDS, 1300 I St. NW, Suite 1080 East,

Washington, DC 20005. Quarterly newsletter for entrepreneurs ages 10-20.

Publishes: Mainly interested in profiles, with photos, of teens who own their own business.

Submission Info: Use standard, typewritten format. Preferred length 500-1,000 words. Detailed guidelines and sample copy available for 9″ × 12″ SASE (four first-class stamps).

Editor's Remarks: "We cover stories about young entrepreneurs, how teens and preteens can become entrepreneurs, and useful information for effective business operation and management."

[**Author's note:** Specialty market but suitable for young writers who like to do profiles, who are involved in money-making businesses, or who know someone who is.]

‡✔ **CALLIOPE**, 7 School St., Peterborough, NH 03458. World history magazine for young people ages 8-14, published ten times per year. Each issue focuses on particular theme.

Publishes: Feature-length material relating to an upcoming theme; authentic historical and biographical fiction, adventure, retold legends, etc., relating to theme. Supplemental nonfiction directly and indirectly related to theme. Activities including crafts, recipes, woodworking projects, etc., that can be done either alone or with adult supervision. Poetry, puzzles and games. No word-finds. Uses crosswords and other word puzzles using the vocabulary of the issue's theme. Also mazes and picture puzzles.

Submission Info: Query first; see current guidelines and theme sheet for details. All submissions must relate to an upcoming issue's theme. Theme lists and writers' guidelines available for SASE. Pay varies depending on type of material accepted. Sample copy $3.95 plus 7½″ × 10½″ (or larger) self-addressed envelope with $1.05 postage.

Editor's Remarks: "Unfortunately, we do not have enough space to regularly publish student work other than letters, drawings and short poems. We occasionally have contests that involve creative writing; keep an eye out for them. All submissions for feature material, from students and adults alike, are evaluated equally."

Subscription Rates: One year $22.95. Also available on some newsstands.

[**Author's note:** This is a good market for nonfiction writers who really enjoy researching history; but you *must* query first and follow the editorial procedure exactly. The only reason *Calliope* is marked with a double cross (‡) is because it does regularly publish some student work.]

‡✔ **CANADIAN AUTHOR**, 275 Slater St., Suite 500, Ottawa, ON K1P 5H9, CANADA. Quarterly magazine dedicated to bringing news of Canadian writers, editors and publishers to developing freelance writers.

Publishes: Articles of interest to and about writers and the professional writing business; interested in sharing hints to beginning writers from professionals. See guidelines for specifics regarding submissions, by Canadian authors only, of fiction and poetry.

Submission Info: Query first about article and profile ideas. Use standard format for all submissions. Include SASE or IRCs for foreign submissions. Usually buys First North American Serial Rights. Payment rates and additional submission information on guidelines available for SASE (in Canada) or self-addressed envelope with IRC.

Editor's Remarks: "Above all, read and study a *recent* issue of *Canadian Author*!"

[**Author's note:** Notice that writers must query with ideas first.]

✔* **CHALK TALK**, 1550 Mills Rd., RR2, Sidney, BC V8L 3S1, CANADA. Magazine written for children by children ages 5-14, to encourage them to learn to love reading and writing.

Publishes: Original artwork, fiction, nonfiction, poetry, crafts, puzzles and activities. Stories or poems that resolve conflict with violence are not suitable.

Submission Info: Any format acceptable. Prefers drawings done in black ink. Include SASE for reply. Guidelines available in magazine. Offers, on request, ten free copies of issue containing published work.

Editor's Remarks: "All submissions are welcome regardless of 'talent' and ability. Submissions are chosen for originality, and grammar and spelling are edited. Chances of being published are excellent for *short* stories, poems or drawings. Only one long story per month accepted."

Subscription Rates: One year $16.95 in Canada; $20 for foreign subscriptions. Available to Canadian schools. *Chalk Talk* Club membership $5 each with minimum of eight memberships to one address.

✔* **CHICKADEE MAGAZINE,** 56 The Esplanade, Suite 306, Toronto, ON M5E 1A7, CANADA. Science and nature magazine for ages 3-9, published ten times per year.

Publishes: Readers' artwork and writing in response to requests in the "Chirp" section of magazine. Publishes drawings on a specific topic, a letter with photo from readers, and a "chuckle" submitted by a child. *Very* occasionally, publishes short poems by readers in "Chirp."

Submission Info: All materials submitted to "Chirp" become the property of The Young Naturalist Foundation. No payment made for submissions.

Subscription Rates: One year (ten issues) $14.95 in U.S. currency. Mail subscription requests to 255 Great Arrow Avenue, Buffalo, NY 14207-3082. In Canada, call (416) 946-0406.

✔* **CHILD LIFE,** 1100 Waterway Blvd., P.O. Box 567, Indianapolis, IN 46202. Publication for children 9-11 from the Children's Better Health Institute. Stresses health-related themes or ideas including nutrition, safety, exercise and proper health habits.

Publishes: From readers: original poetry, original stories, and favorite jokes and riddles.

Submission Info: Submissions do not have to be health-related. Tries to publish one original story (up to 500 words) in each issue. Please write your name, age, school and complete address on each submission. Jokes and riddles can be sent on postcards. Material cannot be returned. No payment for published reader material. Send SASE for special guidelines for young writers. Sample copies $1.25.

Editor's Remarks: "We usually select material sent in by children in the 9-11 age group."

Subscription Rates: One year $14.95. Special rate of $11.95 usually offered in every issue.

* CHILDREN'S DIGEST, 1100 Waterway Blvd., P.O. Box 567, Indianapolis, IN 46202. Publication for preteens from the Children's Better Health Institute. Stresses health-related themes or ideas including nutrition, safety, exercise and proper health habits.

Publishes: From readers: original fiction, nonfiction and poetry, favorite jokes and riddles. Material need not be health-related. Stories printed occasionally.

Submission Info: If possible, please type stories. Put your name, age, school and complete address on each page. Fiction and nonfiction stories may be up to 300 words. Material cannot be returned. Jokes and riddles can be sent on postcards. No payment for published reader material. Send SASE for special guidelines for young writers. Sample copies $1.25.

Editor's Remarks: "We usually select material sent in by children in the 8-13 age group. If you're older than 13, it would be best to find another market for your work. We feel that it is unfair for us to judge the work of young children against the work of teenagers."

Subscription Rates: One year $14.95. Special rate of $11.95 is usually offered in every issue.

* CHILDREN'S PLAYMATE, 1100 Waterway Blvd., P.O. Box 567, Indianapolis, IN 46206. Publication for children 6 to 8 from the Children's Better Health Institute. Stresses health-related themes or ideas including nutrition, safety, exercise and proper health habits.

Publishes: From readers: original poems, original artwork, favorite jokes and riddles. Does not publish any stories written by readers.

Submission Info: Poetry must be original. Artwork must be drawn by the reader. Jokes and riddles can be favorite ones readers have heard. Jokes and riddles can be sent on postcards. Sorry, no material can be returned. No payment for published reader material. Send SASE for guidelines. Sample copies $1.25. Submissions limited to young people ages 6-8.

Subscription Rates: One year $14.95. Special rate of $11.95 is usually offered in every issue.

‡ **COBBLESTONE,** 7 School St., Peterborough, NH 03458. American history magazine for young people, published ten times per year. Each issue focuses on particular theme.

Publishes: Feature-length material related to an upcoming theme; authentic historical and biographical fiction, adventure, retold legends, etc., relating to theme. Supplemental nonfiction directly or indirectly related to theme. Activities including crafts, recipes, woodworking projects, etc., that can be done either alone or with adult supervision. Poetry, puzzles and games. No word-finds. Uses crosswords and other word puzzles using the vocabulary of the issue's theme. Also mazes and picture puzzles.

Submission Info: All submissions must relate to an upcoming issue's theme. Theme lists and writers' guidelines available for SASE. Pay varies depending on type of material accepted. Sample copy $3.95 plus $7\frac{1}{2}'' \times 10\frac{1}{2}''$ (or larger) self-addressed envelope with $1.05 postage.

Editor's Remarks: "Unfortunately, we do not have enough space to regularly publish students' work other than the letters, drawings and short poems sent to *Cobblestone* for 'Dear Ebenezer.' We occasionally have contests that involve creative writing. Keep an eye out for these contests. All submissions for feature material, from students and adults alike, are evaluated equally."

Subscription Rates: One year $22.95. Also available on some newsstands.

[**Author's note:** This is a good market for nonfiction writers who really enjoy researching history; but you *must* query first and follow the editorial procedure exactly. The only reason *Cobblestone* is marked with a double cross (‡) is because it does publish student work.]

‡✔ **THE COLUMBUS JOURNAL,** P.O. Box 12506, Columbus, OH 43212. Prefers to be contacted via CompuServe: Erin

McCahan-Ashby 75570,2561. Monthly newsletter serving adults 50 and older in central Ohio.

Publishes: Articles on politics, economics, law, travel, sport, marriage and dating, widowhood, lifestyles, religion, hobbies, crime and safety, personality profiles, local news, world news and other topics. Articles need not deal specifically with central Ohio, provided they are of general interest to the 50+ generation.

Submission Info: Word length 500-2,500; will also accept articles of 100-400 words but will accept no fewer than four short pieces at a time. Pays $40 on acceptance for articles or $40 for four shorts. Buys one-time or second rights. Reports in two weeks on queries, sooner for online queries. Reports in two to four weeks on manuscripts. Query first, through e-mail only. No unsolicited manuscripts. Include tearsheets and credentials with query. Don't send résumés. Include mailing address with manuscripts. Manuscripts not returned without SASE. No additional guidelines available.

Editor's Remarks: "Age of author is irrelevant. I started writing as a young child myself. However, remember that our readership is intelligent, active, informed and aging, NOT ancient. Writers should not use the term 'senior citizen' in articles, and should not gear articles toward the very aged."

[**Author's note:** Note that this editor will consider work from young writers, but as with any manuscript she accepts, it *must* be relevant to her readers and meet all editorial guidelines. What type of article do you think would be suitable here?]

*$ COMPUSERVE INFORMATION SERVICES, P.O. Box 20212, 5000 Arlington Centre Blvd., Columbus, OH 43220. A computer information service featuring a variety of special-interest forums open to member subscribers.

Publishes: A variety of publishing opportunities exist on each of the various forums. Some where young writers are most welcome are: Journalism Forum (GO JFORUM); Computer Art & Graphics Forums (GO GRAPHICS); Literary Forum (GO LITFORUM); Motor Sports Forum (GO RACING); Outdoors Forum (GO OUT-DOORS); Pets/Animals Forum (GO PETS); Photography Forum

(GO PHOTOFORUM); Students' Forum (GO STUFO); Comic Book Forum (GO COMIC).

Submission Info: See individual forum guidelines available online.

Editor's Remarks: "We'd love to have information from young writers in the Motor Sports Forum." (Response by Michael F. Hollander)

Subscription Rates: Call (800) 848-8990.

[**Author's note:** The response here is typical regarding young writers being welcome.]

‡✔ **THE COTERIE**, 2450 Grand Ave., Suite 144, Kansas City, MO 64108-2520. The Coterie is a theater located in the inner city area of Kansas City, that produces plays of interest to all people, with a special interest in young people and families.

Publishes: Considers new plays for production.

Submission Info: Query with synopsis and scene first.

Editor's Remarks: "General submissions are not limited, really. However, membership in our Young Playwrights Round-Table is limited to Kansas City youth."

[**Author's note:** Before submitting here, be sure to read the profile on Jeff Church, artistic director of The Coterie, that appears on page 160.]

* **CREATIVE KIDS**, Prufrock Press, P.O. Box 8813, Waco, TX 76714-8813. A full-size magazine by kids, for kids.

Publishes: Stories, prose, poetry, plays, photography, games and music from young people ages 5-18. Work must be original and submitted only to *Creative Kids* (no simultaneous submissions). Material must be nonracist, nonsexist and nonviolent.

Submission Info: Cover letter necessary. Include name, address, birthdate, school, school address, signature by parent or teacher authenticating originality and a photo (if available). Must include SASE for reply. Send SASE for detailed guidelines. Sample copy $3.

Editor's Remarks: "*Creative Kids* is the only award-winning, full-size magazine with all of its contents contributed by gifted, creative and talented youngsters."

Subscription Rates: One year $24. New-reader rate for one year $17.97. Schools and libraries may request a free sample copy by sending a request on school or library stationery.

* CREATIVE WITH WORDS, P.O. Box 223226, Carmel, CA 93922. Publishes anthologies, many for or by children.

Publishes: *CWW* is devoted to furthering: (1) folk/artistic tales and such; (2) creative writing by children (poetry, prose and language artwork); (3) creative writing in special-interest groups (senior citizens, handicapped, general family). Particularly interested in prose, language arts work, fillers, puzzles and poems from young people.

Submission Info: Submissions from young writers must be their own work and not edited, corrected or rewritten by an adult. Will work with individual young writers if editing and corrections are necessary. Do not send personal photo unless requested. Use standard format for preparing manuscripts. Poetry must be 20 lines or less. Prose should not exceed 1,000 words. Shorter poems and articles always welcome. Do not send previously published material. Copyright reverts to author after publication. No payment is made to contributors, but they do receive a 20 percent cost reduction on publication in which their work appears. No free copies in payment. Send SASE for return of manuscript and/or correspondence. Send SASE for current guidelines. Address submissions to B. Geltrich.

Editor's Remarks: "*CWW* is an educational publication, which means that it serves both the academic and non-academic communities of the world. The editors organize one annual poetry contest (only for those 19 and *older*), offer feedback on manuscripts submitted, and publish a wide range of themes relating to human studies and the environment that influences human behaviors. *CWW* also critically analyzes manuscripts for minimal charge."

Subscription Rates: Discontinued taking subscriptions.

‡✓ CRUSADER MAGAZINE, P.O. Box 7259, Grand Rapids, MI 49510. Christian magazine for boys age 9-14; official publication of the Cadet Corp.

Publishes: Sports articles up to 1,500 words, accompanying black-and-white photos appreciated; crafts and hobby articles; articles about camping and nature (how-to or "God in nature" themes); fast-moving fiction stories of 1,000-1,300 words that appeal to a boy's sense of adventure or sense of humor. Avoid "preachiness" and simplistic answers to complicated problems. Avoid long dialogue and little action. Also publishes boy-oriented cartoons. All submissions must relate to upcoming theme.

Submission Info: Use standard format, include name and address in upper left corner along with number of words and statement regarding terms of sale (all rights, first rights or second rights). Enclose SASE for return of submission. Payment for manuscripts $.03 per word and up (first rights with no major editing). Cartoons $5 and up for single gags; $15 and up for full-page panels. Puzzle rates vary. Photos $5 for each one used with an article. Send SASE for guidelines and theme sheet.

Editor's Remarks: "A writer desiring to sell fiction to *Crusader* should request a list of themes."

[**Author's note:** This is the *same* information supplied to adult writers.]

‡✔ **DIARIST'S JOURNAL,** 102 W. Water St., Lansford, PA 18232. Quarterly publication featuring excerpts from people's diaries and other information about diary-keeping.

Publishes: Dated diary excerpts preferred, as opposed to essays, dissertations, and other types of writing that are not specifically diary entries. Also uses articles about diaries, diary-keeping, and reviews of books about diaries.

Submission Info: Retype excerpts (double-spaced). Preferred length from one to three pages. Do not send original diary material. Unless requested otherwise, includes author's name and location with published material. Pictures welcome. Send SASE for return of material. Payment in copies only. Sample copy $3.

Subscription Rates: One year $12.

[**Author's note:** This is a *very small, specialized publication.*]

✔$ **DIGITAL PUBLISHING ROUNDTABLE,** located on GEnie, page 1395, option #8. New category in the

GENIELAMP section (as of April 22, 1993). Official online service for the Digital Publishing Association.

Publishes: Online library offers online magazines, newsletters, short stories, poetry, informational text files and other text-oriented articles.

Submission Info: See appropriate online message area and libraries for details. Or download the latest copy of GEnieLamp (Computing on GEnie Newsletter) on page 515.

Editor's Remarks: "The Digital Publishing RoundTable is for people who are interested in pursuing publication of their work electronically, whether on GEnie or via disk-based media. In the DigiPub bulletin board you can converse with people in the digital publishing industry, meet editors from some of the top electronic publications, and get hints and tips on how to go about publishing your own digital online book."

Subscription Rates: Must be a member of GEnie to access, no extra charge to join roundtable.

[**Author's note:** Producing your own online book is a form of self-publishing (see Chapter 1, page 11). It also appears that other electronic markets available through this association may be a mixture of vanity/subsidy presses as well as more traditional publishing ventures. It is listed *as an example of what may be found online*. Consult with a knowledgeable adult and proceed with caution.]

✒* **DIRT**, 5900 Wilshire Blvd., Suite 720, Los Angeles, CA 90036. Irreverent magazine for teenage boys, currently (early 1993) published quarterly.

Publishes: Band reviews, book reviews, short articles on anything topical.

Submission Info: Any format OK. SASE appreciated. Send for writers' guidelines. Sample copies not available.

Editor's Remarks: "Anything, basically."

Subscription Rates: Subscription not available. Packaged with *Sassy* magazine; also available at Marvel Comics outlets and Tower Record stores.

[**Author's note:** *Dirt* has the wackiest writers' guidelines I've ever seen!]

‡ **FACES**, 7 School St., Peterborough, NH 03458. Anthropology magazine for young people, published nine times per year.

Publishes: Variety of feature articles and in-depth, personal accounts relating to themes. Word length: about 800. Also uses supplemental nonfiction, 300-600 words. Includes subjects directly and indirectly related to themes. Some fiction, activities, photos, poetry, puzzles and games with a connection to an upcoming theme.

Submission Info: Operates on a by-assignment basis, but welcomes ideas and suggestions in outline form. Ideas should be submitted at least six months prior to the publication date of related theme's issue. Pays on individual basis. Guidelines with theme list available for SASE. Sample copy $3.95 plus 7½" × 10½" (or larger) self-addressed envelope with $.98 postage.

Editor's Remarks: "Unfortunately, we do not have enough space to regularly publish student work other than the letters, drawings and short poems on the 'Letters Page.' We occasionally have contests that involve creative writing. Keep an eye out for them. All submissions for feature material, from students and adults alike, are evaluated equally."

Subscription Rates: One year $21.95.

[Author's note: This is a good market for nonfiction writers who really enjoy researching history; but you *must* query first and follow the editorial procedure exactly. The only reason *Faces* is marked with a double cross (‡) is because it does regularly publish some student work.]

* **FLYING PENCIL PRESS**, P.O. Box 7667, Elgin, IL 60121. Independent publishing house dedicated to the writing and artwork of children ages 8-14. New theme each issue.

Publishes: Anthologies of children's work (fiction, nonfiction, poems, art and cartoons) in quality paperback books.

Submission Info: Prefers typed manuscripts but will accept handwritten material if clear and readable. Artwork, illustrations and cartoons should be on unlined white paper. Manuscripts must be angled to an upcoming theme. Material *must* be the original work of submitting author or artist. Submissions will not be returned without SASE. Be sure to keep a copy of your material in case original is lost in handling or mailing. Replies by mail in four to six weeks if your work is accepted. Payment may be offered. Guidelines and sheet explaining upcoming themes available for SASE.

Editor's Remarks: "We are looking for original, honest, imaginative, bright work. Be sure to send material appropriate to a current theme. We hope to hear from you soon."

Subscription Rates: Send SASE for information on purchasing past editions. All proceeds go to publish future editions.

[**Author's note:** If material you submitted to *Flying Pencil Press* before April 1993 was returned to you *unopened*, you may resubmit the material. According to the editor, the mistake was due to a post office filing error.]

‡ **FUTURIFIC MAGAZINE**, 150 Haven Ave., New York, NY 10032. Published twelve times a year by Futurific, Inc., a nonprofit educational organization dedicated to finding a better understanding of the future.

Publishes: Material analyzing any issue in current events. All material must show what *improvements* are coming in the new future. No gloom-and-doom stories, and do not tell readers how they should live their lives. Wants material that tells what *will* happen.

Submission Info: Buys one-time rights. Payment negotiated. Material will not be returned without SASE. Presently only black-and-white photos and artwork are used. Sample copies $5.

Editor's Remarks: "We've had seventeen years of accurate forecasting, reporting solutions not problems."

Subscription Rates: One year for individuals $60; institutions $120.

[**Author's note:** Be sure you understand the special focus of this magazine before submitting material.]

*$ **GENIE**, 401 N. Washington St., Rockville, MD 20850. The General Electric Network for Information Exchange, a computer information service featuring a variety of special interest roundtables open to member subscribers.

Publishes: Many special interest roundtables offer opportunities for young writers to share their work in online publications and libraries. Some where young writers are most active or welcome: GENEALOGY RT, page 540; HOBBY RT, page 180; TELEJOKE RT, page 230; MAGGIE-MAE'S PET-NET & CO RT, page 295; PHOTOGRAPHY RT, page 660; SCIENCE FICTION AND FANTASY RT, page 470.

Submission Info: Review accessing and uploading details in your user's manual. See individual roundtable guidelines available online.

Editor's Remarks: "GEnie is a world of instantaneous tele-communications—across the continent or around the world; a world in which a host of electronic services put you in instant contact with thousands of other computer users."

Subscription Rates: Call (800) 638-9636.

[**Author's note:** See the separate listings for WRITERS.INK, the Electronic Writers Association.]

✒* THE GOLDFINCH: IOWA HISTORY FOR YOUNG PEOPLE, State Historical Society of Iowa, 402 Iowa Ave., Iowa City, IA 52240. Award-winning quarterly history magazine for 4th-7th graders, focused on Iowa, Midwestern and U.S. history. Each issue devoted to one theme in Iowa history.

Publishes: Special section called "History Makers" features activities, photographs, artwork, class projects and essays created by young people. Must relate to the issue's theme.

Submission Info: Submissions should include age, grade, school. Feel free to include photos. Include SASE with submission. Pays in copies. Send for free writers' guidelines and list of upcoming themes. Sample copy $4.

Editor's Remarks: "We rarely publish fiction, but would do so if the story related directly to the issue theme."

Subscription Rates: One year (four issues) $10.

‡ GREEN'S MAGAZINE, P.O. Box 3236, Regina, Saskatchewan S4P 3H1, CANADA. Quarterly literary magazine for general audience, including libraries and many writers.

Publishes: See writer's guidelines for specifics. Material targeted to a general audience. Study sample copy.

Submission Info: Send complete manuscripts with SASE or

self-addressed envelope (SAE) with adequate IRC. Send cover letter and biographical information with manuscripts. Buys first rights, but can be reassigned to authors on written request with SASE or SAE plus IRC. Do not send multiple submissions. Reports in eight weeks. Payment in two copies. Send SASE or SAE with IRC to receive writer's guidelines. Sample copy $4.

Editor's Remarks: "We do not go out of our way to publish young writers, but report happily that we have published many, including pre-teens."

Subscription Rates: One year (four issues) $12. Single issues $4 each.

‡✓ **GUIDE MAGAZINE,** 55 West Oak Ridge Dr., Hagerstown, MD 21740. Weekly Christian publication for young people ages 10-14; aim is to foster a greater sense of self-worth, assurance, and a concern for others in its readers.

Publishes: Devotional, adventure, personal growth and Christian humor stories. Present stories from a young person's viewpoint, written in the active voice, concisely and with clarity. Avoid stories with violence, hunting, etc. Uses very little poetry.

Submission Info: Use standard format; be sure to include name, address, phone and Social Security number in upper left-hand corner of first page. Include SASE with submissions and requests for guidelines and sample copy. Pays on acceptance; complimentary copies sent when published. Reports in one week. Considers first rights, reprints and simultaneous submissions.

Editor's Remarks: "When writing for *Guide*, please don't preach or use adult sentiments. (This doesn't mean kids don't have important issues to address. It just means there are effective and ineffective ways to deal with their problems.) In general, *Guide* is interested in creative approaches to topics that will provide young people with ideas and tools to help enrich their lives in Christ."

Subscription Rates: One year (52 issues) $34.97. Higher outside U.S. Send check or money order to above address or call (800) 765-6955.

[**Author's note:** These are the same guidelines given to adult writers.]

‡✓* **HELIOCENTRIC NET MAGAZINE & NEWS-LETTER**, P.O. Box 68817, Seattle, WA 98168-0817. Full-size quarterly, small press magazine; plus newsletter for new and developing writers, especially those interested in writing science fiction, fantasy or "creepy" stories.

Publishes: Various types of fiction in the tradition of *Night Gallery, Twilight Zone, Tales from the Crypt, Tales from the Darkside, Amazing Stories*, etc. Short essays or articles (including personal writing experiences) on writing, editing, publishing, fiction genres, and film, book or small press magazine reviews. Also considers poetry and black-and-white art. Pornography, explicit violence or language, and racism not acceptable.

Submission Info: Use standard format. Maximum length for magazine fiction 2,500 words; 1,200 words for newsletter. Poetry must be on genre-related themes and no longer than 15 lines; five poems per submission allowed. Black-and-white artwork up to 8½" × 11"; *non-explicit* and *no x-rated material*. Maximum length for nonfiction magazine articles and interviews is 1,200 words; letters and reviews 150 words; events and miscellaneous items 50 words. Word length for newsletter nonfiction is half that allowed for magazine. All submissions *must* include SASE or won't be considered. Responds in three to five weeks; contract sent to accepted contributors. Payment is one copy of magazine on publication; three copies of newsletter. Send SASE for guidelines. Sample copy of magazine $2.50; $3.75 in Canada. Send two first-class stamps for sample newsletter; $1 in Canada.

Editor's Remarks: "*Heliocentric Net* encourages new and developing writers and artists, and we do our best to fully and quickly communicate with potential contributors. If we cannot use your work (and this reflects *only* our space and content needs, *not* the ultimate publishability of your work) we'll offer you our reasons, suggestions and comments, and, if possible, alternate markets to attempt. *H-Net* has published several first-time writers, including two high school students and a few college students. We will help with revisions and streamlining your work if we would like to see it again."

Subscription Rates: One year (four issues) $9 for magazine;

$2.50 for newsletter. In Canada, one year $13 for magazine; $3.75 for newsletter.

* HIGHLIGHTS FOR CHILDREN, 803 Church St., Honesdale, PA 18431. Published monthly for youngsters ages 2-12.

Publishes: Poems, drawings and stories from readers. Also runs two unfinished stories a year, to which readers submit their creative endings. For writers 16 or older, also reviews submissions of short stories, factual features, puzzles, party plans, crafts, finger plays and action plays. Seldom buys verse.

Submission Info: For writers up to age 15, drawings may be in color or black and white. Prose may be no more than two double-spaced typed pages or three double-spaced handwritten pages. Acknowledges all material submitted. However, material is not returned; *do not enclose SASE.* No payment made for contributions from writers 15 or under. For writers 16 and older, consult regular freelance guidelines available free. Fiction should not be more than 800 words; pays $.08 and up per word. Science and factual articles within 800 words bring $75 and up. Other material brings $25 and up. Those 16 and older should send complete manuscript with SASE. All submissions need to include name, age and complete home address. Personal photo unnecessary.

Subscription Rates: One year $19.95. Three years $49.95. Write: *Highlights for Children*, 2300 West Fifth Avenue, P.O. Box 269, Columbus, OH 43216.

[**Author's note:** Be sure to read the foreword written by Kent Brown, editor of *Highlights*.]

‡✔ HOME EDUCATION MAGAZINE, P.O. Box 1083, Tonasket, WA 98855. Bimonthly (64 pages) magazine for home schooling families.

Publishes: Nonfiction articles, interviews and essays about home-based education. Regular column, called "Higher Education," features articles about how home-schooled youngsters have furthered their education by going on to college, locating apprenticeships or finding jobs. Also uses black-and-white and color photos of children and families in all kinds of situations, not necessarily those traditionally thought of as "educational." Artwork and cartoons will be considered, but we do not publish poetry or fiction.

Submission Info: Accepts submissions in any format. Prefers articles between 1,000 and 2,500 words. If your submission is handwritten, take care to write as neatly as possible. Include name and address on each page of all articles and on photos, artwork and other submissions. Guidelines available for SASE. Sample copy $3.50. Purchases First North American Serial Rights. Pays $.45 per column inch for articles, $5 each for inside black-and-white photos (send normal size prints, not enlargements), and $25 for color cover photos (send transparencies or slides). Rates vary for other material; write for specific information. Include SASE for reply or return of submissions. Cannot acknowledge submissions not accompanied by SASE.

Editor's Remarks: "We are particularly interested in articles describing young writers' homeschooling experiences."

Subscription Rates: One year (6 issues) $24. Foreign countries write for rates. Available in most public libraries. Free twenty-four-page catalog available.

[**Author's note:** Not a suitable market for young writers who attend public or private schools.]

✔* **HOW ON EARTH!** *Teens supporting compassionate, ecologically sound living*, P.O. Box 3347, West Chester, PA 19381. *HOE!* is a nonprofit, all-volunteer quarterly vegetarian newsletter for and by teenagers concerned about environmental, animal and global issues. Geared toward youth ages 12-20. Youth are also involved in all aspects of planning, development and production.

Publishes: Research articles, poetry, creative writing and essays concerning ecology, ethics, animal and global issues, health, vegetarianism, vegetarian lifestyle and activism. Original artwork and photographs accepted. Food articles and vegetarian recipes suitable for young people encouraged, as are articles containing practical information for compassionate, ecologically sound living. Authors must be age 20 or younger.

Submission Info: Accepts typed or handwritten material, if legible. Send SASE for writers' guidelines. Sample copy $3. Payment not offered at this time.

Editor's Remarks: "We encourage young writers, artists and activists interested in environmental, animal and global issues to get involved with *HOW ON EARTH!* We also welcome young people with other skills who want to volunteer. All material must be original, factual and preferably presented in a positive, educational manner. *HOW ON EARTH!* welcomes ideas, input and participation from its readers in every way possible."

Subscription Rates: One year (4 issues) $12.

✔* **HUMPTY DUMPTY'S MAGAZINE**, 1100 Waterway Blvd., P.O. Box 567, Indianapolis, IN 46202. Published by the Children's Better Health Institute for preschool level children ages 4-6.

Publishes: Black and white or color drawings by readers ages 4-6.

Submission Info: No payment for published reader materials. Editors advise readers to keep copies of their contributions, because unused material cannot be returned. Publisher owns all rights to material printed.

Editor's Remarks: "We cannot promise to publish what you send, because we receive many, many letters from children all over the world. We do promise to read and consider all the material sent to us, though! We are sorry, but because of the large amount of mail, we cannot write to each of you personally."

Subscription Rates: One year (eight issues) $13.95 in U.S. currency. Subscription office: P.O. Box 7133, Red Oak, IA 51591-0133.

✔* **INK BLOT**, 7200 Burmeister, Saginaw, MI 48609. Monthly newsletter designed to provide a new outlet for young writers and artists; distributed to local schools, libraries and hospital waiting rooms.

Publishes: Nonfiction essays, short stories, poetry, acrostics. Will consider other short manuscripts and black-and-white artwork. Especially in need of short fillers. No photos.

Submission Info: Handwritten is accepted; typed material preferred. Students should include age, grade and school name. Short fillers should be 25-75 words long. Poetry limited to 30 lines. Maximum length for essays and stories 500 words. No submissions returned, however contributors retain copyright. If you send an SASE, you will receive a free copy of the newsletter containing your published work. Guidelines available for SASE. Sample copy $1 plus SASE.

Editor's Remarks: "We like to receive material written from your heart. Write your feelings into words. Remember to send your best work. Double-check for grammar, spelling and writing errors before mailing. We want to promote a positive outlook to our readers. We do not want negative or derogatory material."

Subscription Rates: No subscriptions available. Monthly copies may be obtained for $1 each plus SASE.

[**Author's note:** Be sure to read the profiles of editor Margaret Larkin on page 142 and assistant editor Vicki May Larkin on page 111.]

✔* **IOWA WOMAN MAGAZINE**, P.O. Box 680, Iowa City, IA 52244. Quarterly magazine featuring fiction, poetry, essays, interviews, articles, historical pieces and visual art by women everywhere for readers of both genders anywhere. Published since 1980 by a nonprofit educational organization.

Publishes: Work by younger women in any genre, and for specific departments "Under 21" (generally essays or personal writing) or "New Writer" (never before published; any genre).

Submission Info: Use standard format; enclose SASE. Send SASE for submission guidelines prior to sending work. Please indicate if you are a younger writer in cover letter. Payment terms (as of 1992-93) are $5 per published page, plus $20 bonus if writer is a current or former Iowa resident; two copies of issue containing your work; discounts on advertising and extra copies. Payment terms subject to modification after mid-1993 due to Iowa writer incentive project. Reports in three months. Sample copy $6.

Editor's Remarks: "We rarely get submissions from young women; we're interested in them, and we make special considerations to help and encourage young writers. Recent writing by younger women includes essays about teen pregnancy choices, a visit to New York City with an aunt, a reflective look at mother/ daughter relationships and their differing approaches to being Chinese American. Recent artwork includes illustrations for fiction by two third-graders. Would love to have young women's writings about rural life, rural experiences, Midwest living."

Subscription Rates: One year (four issues) $18.

✓* JACK AND JILL, 1100 Waterway Blvd., P.O. Box 567, Indianapolis, IN 46202. Publication for children 7-10 from the Children's Better Health Institute. Stresses health-related themes or ideas including nutrition, safety, exercise and proper health habits.

Publishes: From readers: original poetry and favorite jokes and riddles. Occasionally publishes original stories (500 words or less) and original drawings.

Submission Info: Submissions do not have to be health-related. Please write your name, age, school and complete address on each submission. Jokes and riddles can be sent on postcards. Material cannot be returned. No payment for published reader material. Send SASE for guidelines for young writers. Sample copies $1.25.

Editor's Remarks: "We usually select material sent in by children in the 7-10 age group."

Subscription Rates: One year $14.95. Special rate of $11.95 is usually offered in every issue.

✓* KIDS & COMPUTERS, 200 Oakview Rd., High Point, NC 27265. May also contact via e-mail to Peter Scisco, on GEnie: COMPUTE.SCIS; on CompuServe: 75300,2101; on America Online: Scisco.

Publishes: Reviews from writers 18 and under, such as software reviews. No fiction. Also publishes tips and activities.

Submission Info: Submit or query by regular mail or query using e-mail. Offers some payment for material published. More detailed guidelines geared to mature writers available in several forum and roundtable libraries. For instance, see the file K&CGUIDE.TXT on the Writers.Ink library.

Editor's Remarks: "I have been wanting to feature the work of young people in the magazine in some way, but have never been able to work it all out. They are welcome to contribute ideas."

✔* **KID'S KORNER NEWSLETTER**, P.O. Box 413, Joaquin, TX 75954. Newsletter written for kids and by kids under age 18. Marcella Simmons, editor.

Publishes: Fiction and nonfiction written by kids, for kids under age 18. Also artwork on any theme.

Submission Info: Handwritten material accepted. Manuscript length for fiction 100-2,000 words; for nonfiction 50-500 words. Sample copy $1.

Editor's Remarks: "Writing is not easy but requires lots of time, patience and willpower. If you have these three ingredients, writing is a cinch!"

Subscription Rates: One year $10.

✔* **KIDS N' SIBS**, 191 Whittier Rd., Rochester, NY 14624. May also reach via CompuServe e-mail: Elizabeth Fogg 75260, 1730. Free newsletter focusing on sharing the views and experiences of disabled children and siblings.

Publishes: Anything as long as it's in good taste and relates to newsletter's theme. Prefers submissions made by those 18 and under, but will publish stories by older writers if they are personal accounts of their childhoods and what it was like as a disabled child or sibling of one. Also interested in information on different disabilities and diseases.

Submission Info: Submissions longer than one column or page will be used, with author's permission, as a series. No guidelines available. May contact Fogg by regular or e-mail. Send SASE for free sample. No payment. Contributors receive free copy with published piece.

Editor's Remarks: "This newsletter is for anyone with an interest in disabilities and handicaps. Feel free to write for us or just subscribe! Currently there aren't any 'rewards' for submitting an article because there isn't any charge for subscription."

Subscription Rates: Free, may charge for subscriptions in future.

✒* **KOPPER BEAR PRESS**, P.O. Box 19454, Boulder, CO 80303. May also reach via CompuServe: Howard S. Bashinski 70732,2505. New book publisher dedicated to helping exceptional authors between ages 13-21 get published in high-quality format.

Publishes: Fiction, nonfiction, poetry, short stories, novels, novellas, essays, etc., from young people ages 13-21. Is very interested in publishing novels written by young people.

Submission Info: Will accept typed or handwritten work, but be sure you keep a copy as submissions are not returned. For additional information e-mail to the above CompuServe number.

Editor's Remarks: "We want to read *everything*! We promise a thorough reading of everything we receive, and usually provide feedback, if requested."

[**Author's note:** This was a brand-new market beginning April 1993. *It is not a vanity or subsidy press.*]

* **LIFEPRINTS**, P.O. Box 5181, Salem, OR 97304, (503) 581-4224. Published four times annually by Blindskills, Inc., a nonprofit organization for visually impaired adults and youth. Available in large print and braille. International readership.

Publishes: Career, sports and leisure articles, topics of interest to students, fashion, study skills, social skills, book reviews, notices about technology and other aids available to visually impaired persons, and personal experience pieces by visually impaired adults and youth.

Submission Info: *Must* be written by visually impaired individuals. Send SASE for guidelines and study a sample copy in either large print or braille. Visually impaired adults write on a volunteer basis. Visually impaired students who submit articles that are published receive a small honorarium from monies donated for that purpose. Sample copy $3; specify format desired. Brochure available for SASE to all persons interested in learning more about *Lifeprints*.

Editor's Remarks: "Our emphasis is on experiental articles and methods used by successful visually impaired students and adults. We welcome submissions from middle and high school, as well as college youth. *Lifeprints* is a role model publication that, by example, inspires its readers to realize their vocational and life potential. We now have printed guidelines. However, it is best to study a sample issue."

Subscription Rates: Subscription/donation of $15 is suggested annually.

[**Author's note:** This a good example of a magazine with a narrow focus. Note that submissions are restricted to those who *are* visually impaired.]

* LISTEN, CELEBRATING POSITIVE CHOICES,

P.O. Box 7000, Boise, ID 83707. A monthly publication for teens and young adults, encouraging the development of good habits and high ideals of physical and mental health.

Publishes: Special column for teens, called "Listening," using short, well-written, thought-provoking poems, stories and essays from teen writers. Also factual features or opinion essays with or without accompanying quality photos, narratives based on true-life incidents, poetry, puzzles and cartoons.

Submission Info: Submissions for "Listening" should include age, grade, school, etc.; no photos. Poetry limited to 20 lines; stories and essays 300-500 words. Address to "Listening" in care of *Listen* magazine. Include SASE. Send for free writers' guidelines and tip sheet. Samples available for $1 and large manila envelope with SASE. No payment for "Listening," but contributors will receive a free *Listen* T-shirt. Varying rates for other material.

Subscription Rates: One year (12 monthly issues) $24.95. Higher outside U.S. Also available in many school libraries.

* THE MCGUFFEY WRITER, 5128 Westgate Dr., Ox-

ford, OH 45056. Magazine of children's writing published three times a year for nationwide audience.

Publishes: Short stories, essays, poems and songs. Also black-and-white artwork. Open to students K-12.

Submission Info: Manuscripts acknowledged but not returned. Please enclose SASE. Students must list name, grade level, school and address on *every* submitted page. Do not include photo. A teacher, supervisor or responsible adult must sign the initial page for verification. Typed or handwritten submissions are equally welcome as long as they are readable; however, the child's original copy is preferred. Due to limited space, excerpts may be taken from work longer than six double-spaced typewritten pages. Guidelines available at the above address. Sample copy $3.

Subscription Rates: One-year subscription (three issues — Fall, Winter, Spring) $7.50. Institutional rates (for three yearly subscriptions sent to a single address) $15. One-year patron subscription (helps to defray costs) $25. Patrons are listed on the inside of Spring issue.

* MERLYN'S PEN: THE NATIONAL MAGAZINE OF STUDENT WRITING, GRADES 7-10, P.O. Box 1058, East Greenwich, RI 02818, (401) 885-5175. Magazine written by students in grades 7-10. Four issues a year.

Publishes: Stories, plays, poems, essays on important issues, review letters, word games, opinions, critiques of writing in magazine, and art by students in grades 7-10. Also considers puzzles. Letters to the editor welcome.

Submission Info: A statement of originality must be signed for each accepted piece. Authors and artists receive three complimentary issues that contain their work and a small gift. Guidelines must be followed exactly. Response within twelve weeks. All submissions (art and literature) *must* include a large SASE; a cover sheet with author's name, grade, age, home address, home phone number, school name, school address, school phone and supervising teacher's name. Manuscripts must be typed, double-spaced, with extra-wide margins. No personal photos necessary.

Editor's Remarks: "We find that young fiction writers who are successful in *Merlyn's Pen* choose subjects, characters and plots that come from personal experience. For example, they set stories in places they know (school, home, vacation spots, etc.), write about characters their own age, and choose conflicts that they've handled themselves (peer pressure, parents, growing up, sports, etc.). Writing about anything else is bound to be nonspecific, unclear, and therefore unconvincing and unpublishable. More advanced writers can disregard this advice!"

Subscription Rates: For one year (four issues during school year) $18.95 each for one to ten subscriptions; $9.95 each for eleven to twenty subscriptions; $6.95 each for twenty-one or more subscriptions. Two-year individual subscriptions $29.95.

[Author's note: See the profile of editor Jim Stahl on page 154 and young writer Matthew Cheney on page 120.]

✓* MERLYN'S PEN: THE NATIONAL MAGAZINE OF STUDENT WRITING, "SENIOR EDITION," GRADES 9-12, P.O. Box 1058, East Greenwich, RI 02818, (401) 885-5175. Magazine written by students in grades 9-12. Four issues a year.

Publishes: Stories, plays, poems, essays on important issues, review letters, word games, opinions, critiques of writing in magazine, and art by students in grades 9-12. Also considers puzzles. Letters to the editor welcome.

Submission Info: A statement of originality must be signed for each accepted piece. Authors and artists receive three complimentary issues that contain their work and a small gift. Guidelines must be followed exactly. Response within twelve weeks. All submissions (art and literature) *must* include a large SASE; a cover sheet with author's name, grade, age, home address, home phone number, school name, school address, school phone and supervising teacher's name. Manuscripts must be typed, double-spaced, with extra-wide margins. No personal photos necessary.

Editor's Remarks: "We find that young fiction writers who are successful in *Merlyn's Pen* choose subjects, characters and plots that come from personal experience. For example, they set stories in places they know (school, home, vacation spots, etc.) write about characters their own age, and choose conflicts that they've handled themselves (peer pressure, parents, growing up, sports, etc.). Writing about anything else is bound to be nonspecific, unclear, and therefore unconvincing and unpublishable. More advanced writers can disregard this advice!"

Subscription Rates: For one year (four issues during school year) $18.95 each for one to ten subscriptions; $9.95 each for eleven to twenty subscriptions; $6.95 each for twenty-one or more subscriptions. Two-year individual subscriptions $29.95.

‡✓* NATIONAL GEOGRAPHIC WORLD, 1145 17th and M St. NW, Washington, DC 20036-4688. Published monthly

by the National Geographic Society for junior members ages 8-14.

Publishes: Artwork, photos and poems for "Mailbag" feature and "Junior Member Express" pages. Occasionally prints letters or excerpts from them. Does *not* publish essays or stories.

Submission Info: No payment for submissions. Material becomes the property of *National Geographic WORLD* and will not be returned. Check issues and features for addresses. They vary monthly.

Editor's Remarks: "The mission of *National Geographic WORLD* is to inspire in young readers curiosity about our world and beyond, and to encourage geographic awareness. As the official journal of junior membership, [its mission] is to provide junior members privileged access to the benefits of membership in, and the unique resources of, the National Geographic Society."

Subscription Rates: One year $12.95 in U.S.; $19.20 in Canada; $20.75 in other countries. Make checks payable to *WORLD*; mail to National Geographic Society, P.O. Box 2330, Washington, DC 20077-9955.

[**Author's note:** This is a good example of a market that offers young writers a special opportunity yet is also a tough market because of the high volume of submissions it receives.]

✔* **NEW ERA MAGAZINE**, 50 East North Temple St., Salt Lake City, UT 84109. Official monthly publication for youth (ages 12-18) of the Church of Jesus Christ of Latter-day Saints.

Publishes: All types of writing—fiction, articles, poetry. Also seeks color or black-and-white slides or prints. Also uses short, humorous anecdotes about Mormon life, ideas for Mormons (refer to magazine for format) and material for FYI ("For Your Information") section, which features news of young Latter-day Saints from around the world. Considers submissions of artwork only for annual contest, unless portfolio has been shown to art director. All material must uphold Church standards (example: modesty in dress). Written material must have an LDS (Mormon) point of view.

Submission Info: Use standard format, include SASE. Except for short pieces, best to query by letter, showing an example of your proposed writing style. Preferred length 150-2,000 words. Reports in six to eight weeks. Submit seasonal material six months to one year in advance. Payment on acceptance. Send SASE for detailed guidelines and story idea sheets. Sample copy $1.

Editor's Remarks: "We're after material that shows how the Church of Jesus Christ of Latter-day Saints is relevant in the lives of young people today. It should capture the excitement of being a young Latter-day Saint. We have a special interest in personal experience; personality profiles; activities involving LDS youth; and in the experiences of young Latter-day Saints in other countries. Please don't send general library research or formula pieces without the *New Era* slant."

Subscription Rates: One year $8.

‡✔ **ODYSSEY**, 7 School St., Peterborough, NH 03458. Magazine focusing on science for young people.

Publishes: Feature-length material related to an upcoming theme. Authentic historical and biographical fiction, adventure, retold legends, etc., relating to theme. Supplemental nonfiction directly or indirectly related to theme. Activities including crafts, recipes, woodworking projects, etc., that can be done either alone or with adult supervision. Poetry, puzzles and games. No word-finds. Uses crosswords and other word puzzles using the vocabulary of the issue's theme. Also mazes and picture puzzles.

Submission Info: Query first; see current guidelines and theme sheet for details. All submissions must relate to an upcoming issue's theme. Theme lists and writers' guidelines available for SASE. Pay varies depending on type of material accepted. Sample copy $3.95 plus 7½″ × 10½″ (or larger) self-addressed envelope with $1.05 postage.

Editor's Remarks: "Unfortunately, we do not have enough space to regularly publish student work other than letters, drawings and short poems. We occasionally have contests that involve creative writing; keep an eye out for them. All submissions for feature material, from students and adults alike, are evaluated equally."

Subscription Rates: One year $22.95. Also available on some newsstands.

[**Author's note:** This is a good market for nonfiction writers who really enjoy research; but you *must* query first and follow the editorial procedure exactly. The only reason *Odyssey* is marked with a double cross (‡) is because it does regularly publish some student work.]

‡* OUR FAMILY, P.O. Box 249, Battleford, Saskatchewan, S0M 0E0, CANADA. Monthly magazine published for Catholic families, most of whom have children in grade school, high school or college.

Publishes: Nonfiction related to the following areas: people at home; people in relation to God; people at recreation; people at work; people in the world; biography (profiles of Christians whose Christian values have had a positive effect on their contemporaries); and inspirational articles. Also spiritual reflection; humorous anecdotes; poetry on human/spiritual themes; cartoons (family-type); photos. *No fiction.*

Submission Info: Send for theme list and detailed guidelines for nonfiction and photos by enclosing SAE and $.48 (Canadian currency) or IRC. (Average cost to return manuscript: $1.08 in Canadian currency.) Sample copy $2.50

Editor's Remarks: "The majority of our readers are adults. If young people write for us, they must understand that they are writing and competing in an adult market. Because our publication stresses the personal experience approach, young people could find a slot in our publication by focusing on teenage concerns. We make no age distinctions. If a particular article/poem/filler effectively reaches a certain segment of the family, we are pleased to purchase it for publication in our magazine."

✔* OUR LITERATE LEGACY, *Bonding Times*, P.O. Box 736, Dept MG, Lake Hamilton, FL 33851. *Bonding Times* is a quarterly publication for Christian families. The section "Our Literate Legacy" showcases children's work, opinions, talents.

Publishes: Most types of written work by children 18 and under: poems, fiction, exegetical reports [interpretations of passages from the Bible], book reviews, field trip reports, letters to the editor, journalism pieces, science project lab reports. Anything that you are already writing for your school subjects or in your personal life will be considered. Artwork also considered.

Submission Info: All submissions should be typed. Each piece must include name, age, address, school (home, private or public), and signatures of both student and parent stating that work is original and granting *The Bonding Place* permission to publish, market and distribute accepted work per stated compensation. Work becomes the property of *The Bonding Place*. Payment is $.02 per word published. Payment for artwork is $1-$10 depending on size, detail and reproducibility. Detailed guidelines and additional information available for SASE.

Editor's Remarks: "We are looking for exceptional work that children are already accomplishing. All work must be written from a Christian world view. This is a Christian, pro-family publication. Any work written with an anti-Biblical perspective will not be published."

Subscription Rates: One-year subscription provided free of charge. Donations to help with postage are appreciated but not required. Send your subscription request, name and address on a postcard. Inquire for details regarding bulk mailings for home-schooling support group members and churches.

[**Author's note:** Be sure to see the profile of editor Jill Bond on page 146.]

‡✔* **PIKESTAFF FORUM,** P.O. Box 127, Normal, IL 61761. Annual publication that, though intended for adults, has a regular department featuring writing and art from young people ages 7-17. May begin publishing twice a year in future.

Publishes: Original poetry, short fiction and black-and-white artwork of young people ages 7-17, in special "Young Writers" department. Though currently only published once a year (which means a long wait for young writers if their work is among the earliest selected for an issue), work is presented in handsome layout and design, and gets nationwide exposure. Wants only work by young people who do their own submitting. Does *not* want teachers sending assignments. Does not publish personal essays, autobiography or family history. Otherwise, no restrictions on topic, subject matter or style.

Submission Info: Use standard typed format. Handwriting acceptable if clear and legible. Fiction should not exceed 750 words. Prefers poems less than 30 lines in length. Put author's name, address and age at the time the piece was written on every page. Include SASE. Do not send photographs or work that requires halftoning. Tries to respond promptly to submissions. Authors receive three free copies of issue in which their work appears, and may purchase additional copies at 50 percent discount. Detailed guidelines available upon request. Sample copy $2.

Editor's Remarks: "Our aims in publishing young writers are twofold: (1) to put excellent writing by young people before the general public, and (2) to encourage young people in developing their self-confidence and powers of literary expression. If a work is rejected, we usually include some friendly comment as to the reasons for our decision, with perhaps suggestions for improvement. We are highly selective, publishing in the neighborhood of 3 percent of works submitted for consideration. Submitters should be aware of this."

‡✔ **POETRY CANADA**, P.O. Box 1061, Kingston, ON K7L 4Y5, CANADA. Quarterly poetry publication.

Publishes: Poetry.

Submission Info: Submit 8-10 poems in standard typed form. Include cover letter, SASE (or IRCs if submitting from the U.S.). Make sure writer's name appears on every page submitted for publication.

Editor's Remarks: "We seek to publish the best poetry in all genres."

Subscription Rates: One year (four issues) $17.12; two years $28.35.

[**Author's note:** This publication is suitable for serious teen writers only.]

‡✔ **ROOM OF ONE'S OWN**, P.O. Box 46160, Station D, Vancouver, BC V6J 5G5, CANADA. Feminist quarterly of literature and criticism.

Publishes: Writing by and about women. Poetry, short fiction (2,000 to 3,000 words) and reviews of current books. Also graphic images for cover and interior art. Limited amount of non-Canadian manuscripts accepted.

Submission Info: Use standard format. Submissions must include SASE. Outside Canada, send three IRCs. Purchases First North American Serial Rights. Contributors paid honorarium and two copies of issue containing their work.

Editor's Remarks: "*Room of One's Own* is the longest published feminist literary journal in Canada. It is run by a volunteer editorial collective and serves as a forum in which women can share and express their unique perspective on themselves, each other and the world. The best way to find out what kind of work we are looking for is to read recent back issues."

Subscription Rates: In Canada $20 year, $35 two years. Outside Canada $30 year, $45 two years. Institutions add $5.

✓* **SAVANNAH PARENT**, 31 W. Congress St., Suite 203, Savannah, GA 31401. Family, newspaper-style magazine with special section featuring submissions by Savannah children ages 4-12.

Publishes: Short poems and illustrations. Other short creative writing used as space permits. Seasonal submissions encouraged. Open only to Savannah children ages 4-12.

Submission Info: Submissions may be handwritten or typed. Maximum length approximately four paragraphs. Note: no rejection slips sent. Submissions are held and used as space permits. Each contributor receives an attractive parchment certificate suitable for framing. SASE needed for work to be returned. However, it is usually returned along with the certificate and a copy of the paper in which the work appears. Guidelines and a sample copy available for $1 to cover postage and handling.

Editor's Remarks: "The children's 'Creative Expressions' page appears in the centerfold of each issue of *Savannah Parent*, and it is highlighted with spot color. The choice spot selected for the 'Creative Expressions' page reflects the integral part of the publication the editor considers this page to be. It is intended to provide a forum for local children to share their creative endeavors, while experiencing the excitement of seeing their work and names in print."

Subscription Rates: One year (ten issues) $12. One year grandparents' rate $10. Group rates available.

[Author's note: Be sure to see the profile of editor Maxine Pinson on page 149. Don't live in Savannah? Look for similar opportunities in your own area.]

SHOFAR, 43 Northcote Dr., Melville, NY 11747. Published October through May for Jewish children ages 8-13. Managing editor: Gerald H. Grayson.

Publishes: Nonfiction, fiction (500-700 words), poetry, photos, puzzles, games, cartoons. (Artwork on assignment only.) *All material must be on a Jewish theme.* Special holiday issues. Black-and-white or color prints purchased with manuscripts for an additional fee.

Submission Info: Complete manuscripts preferred. Queries welcome. Submit holiday pieces at least four months in advance. Will consider photocopied and simultaneous submissions. Buys First North American Serial Rights or first serial rights. Pays on publication: $.07 per word plus five copies. Send 9″ × 12″ SASE with $.98 postage for free sample copy.

Editor's Remarks: "All material must be on a Jewish theme."

* SKIPPING STONES, P.O. Box 3939, Eugene, OR 97403. International nonprofit quarterly children's magazine featuring writing and art by children 7-18. Writing may be submitted in *any* language and from any country.

Publishes: Original artwork, photos, poems, stories, magic tricks, recipes, science experiments, songs, games, movie and book reviews; writings about your background, culture, religion, interests and experiences, etc. May send questions for other readers to answer or ask your pen pal to send a letter. Submissions welcome in *all* languages. (Work published in the language submitted, with English translation.)

Submission Info: Prefers original work (keep your own copy). Short pieces preferred. Include your age and a description of your background. Can be typed, handwritten or handprinted. Free copy of the issue in which your work appears. Material not copyrighted for exclusive use. Reproduction for educational use encouraged.

Guidelines available, please enclose SASE or SAE with IRC if possible. Sample copy $4. (Enclose SASE with submissions if possible.) Address submissions to Arun Toké, editor.

Editor's Remarks: "*Skipping Stones* is a place for young people of diverse backgrounds to share their experiences and expressions. Our goal is to reach children around the world, in economically disadvantaged as well as privileged families, including underrepresented and special populations within North America. We invite you to suggest ways your organization might network with *Skipping Stones*, perhaps through sharing insights on possible submission of material, outreach, or ideas on the contents or format. In turn, if your group supports projects relevant to children, send this information to us and we will do our best to let our readers know about your work."

Subscription Rates: In the U.S.: one year $15; two years $28. Foreign: one year $20 in U.S. funds. Third World libraries and schools, or low-income U.S. families, may purchase one-year subscriptions for $10. Free subscriptions available when situation warrants. Contact editorial office for information.

[**Author's note:** Be sure to see the profile of editor Arun Toké on page 135.]

✔* **SKYLARK**, Purdue University Calumet, 2200 169th St., Hammond, IN 46323. *Skylark* magazine annually reserves fifteen to twenty pages out of one hundred for the works of young writers 8-18 years old.

Publishes: Prose, poetry and graphics from young writers that shows an original bent and has a positive impact. Material illustrated by author welcome.

Submission Info: Manuscripts must be typed, double-spaced and mailed *flat* with SASE. Poetry 18 lines or less. Prose 1,500 words or less. Graphics should be suitable for 8½″ × 11″ page, may include black-and-white photos or ink sketches on white paper. No color, light pencil or lined paper. Payment one free copy on publication. Entries from schools earn the teacher one free copy, too. Schools are credited in issue where student's work is published. Teachers encouraged to submit portfolios. Reporting time four months. Guidelines available for SASE. Sample copy $4 post-paid.

Editor's Remarks: "Our best advice to a young writer: Go with your own feelings and state them as clearly as you can. We look for the spontaneous rather than the correct. If we feel you have a good point, we'll be willing to work with you to improve your presentation."

Additional Editor's Remarks to Parents/Teachers: "In the Young Writer's section, we concentrate on work by young writers. But if their work is applicable in other sections (e.g., special theme), it will be placed there. However, *Skylark* is a magazine for adults, so much of its contents will include adult themes and perhaps some adult language. Parents and teachers who may not like controversial or mature material in the same book with work by young writers should keep this in mind."

* SNAKE RIVER REFLECTIONS, 1863 Bitterroot Dr., Twin Falls, ID 83301-3561. Formerly called *Writing Pursuits*. Bill White, editor. Published monthly except September and December. Target audience includes writers of all ages.

Publishes: Tips for writers, poetry, short stories, notices of contests and publications, cartoons on writing topics, news of writing events, credits of subscribers, and news of writing chapters.

Submission Info: Short articles one page or less are preferred. Limit poems to 30 lines. Cover letter optional. Include SASE with all inquiries and submissions. Rights revert to author after publication. Payment in copies only. Response in two weeks. Material returned only if SASE included. No simultaneous submissions accepted. Sample copy available for SASE with $.29 postage.

Subscription Rates: One year (ten issues) $6.

✔* SPARK!, 1507 Dana Ave., Cincinnati, OH 45207. Full-color magazine devoted to nurturing creativity, literary and artistic growth in children ages 6-12.

Publishes: Accepts art and writing submissions for possible publication in "Show and Tell" column, in which kids' original work is shared.

Submission Info: Use standard format; will accept handwritten and hand-drawn work. Include SASE if writer/artist wants work returned. Drawings should be mailed flat, not folded. Payment two free copies of issue in which work appears. Details for young writers available in magazine. (More mature young writers may want to send SASE for adult writers' guidelines.) Sample copy $3, address request to "Back Issues Manager" at above address.

Subscription Rates: One year (nine issues) $21.95. Send check or money order to *SPARK!*, P.O. Box 5028, Harlan, IA 51593-4528.

* SPRING TIDES, Savannah Country Day Lower School, 824 Stillwood Dr., Savannah, GA 31419. Literary magazine written and illustrated by children ages 5-12.

Publishes: Stories and poems with or without illustrations. Illustrations may be black and white or color.

Submission Info: Any child, ages 5-12, may submit material. Limit stories to 1,200 words and poems to 20 lines. No simultaneous submissions. All work must be accompanied by SASE. Label each work with child's name, birth date, grade, school, home and school address. Also include a statement signed by the child's parent or teacher attesting to the work's originality. All material should be carefully proofread and typed. All material must be original and created by the person submitting it. Payment a free copy of the issue in which the work appears. Send SASE for guidelines. Sample copy $5.

Subscription Rates: Per copy price $5, plus $1.25 postage and handling. Georgia residents add 6 percent sales tax. Order from above address.

[**Author's note:** *Savannah Parent* editor Maxine Pinson (see page 149) was one of the founders of this student literary magazine.]

* STONE SOUP, THE MAGAZINE BY CHILDREN, Children's Art Foundation, P.O. Box 83, Santa Cruz, CA 95063, (800) 447-4569. Founded in 1973. Each issue includes an activity guide with projects designed to sharpen reading and writing skills. Five issues published yearly.

Publishes: Stories, poems, personal experience, book reviews and art by children though age 13.

Submission Info: Writing need not be typed or copied over. Stories may be any length. Children interested in reviewing books should write the editor, Ms. Gerry Mandel, stating their name, age, address, interests, and the kinds of books they like to read. Children interested in illustrating stories should send two samples of their artwork along with their name, age, address, and a description of the kinds of stories they want to illustrate. Reports in four weeks. CAF reserves all rights. Authors of stories and poems receive $10, book reviewers receive $15, and illustrators receive $8 per illustration. All published contributors receive a certificate, plus discounts on subscriptions and single copies. Guidelines available at no charge. Sample copies available for $2.

Editor's Remarks: "We can't emphasize enough our interest in your experiences. If something that happened to you or something you observed made a strong impression on you, try to turn that experience or observation into a good story or poem. We also look for vivid descriptions of people, places and emotions, and for realistic dialogue."

Subscription Rates: *Stone Soup* is mailed to members of the Children's Art Foundation. Rates are: One year (five issues) $23; two years $40; three years $55. Canada and Mexico add $5 per year. Other countries add $15 per year. All checks must be in U.S. funds drawn on a U.S. bank.

[**Author's note:** It's believed that *Stone Soup* has been published longer than any other literary magazine by and for creative young writers and artists. A profile of the editors appears in the 3rd edition of *Market Guide for Young Writers*.]

* **STRAIGHT**, 8121 Hamilton Ave., Cincinnati, OH 45231. Published quarterly for Christian teens ages 13-19. Distributed through churches, youth organizations and private subscriptions.

Publishes: Poetry, stories and articles from teens. Material must be religious/inspirational and must appeal to other teens.

Submission Info: Submit manuscript on speculation. Enclose SASE, birthday (day and year) and Social Security number. Reports in four to six weeks. Buys first and one-time rights; pays

$.03-$.05 per word. Samples automatically sent to contributors. Guidelines and sample issues available for SASE. Pays a flat fee for poetry.

Editor's Remarks: "Most teen work that I reject does not fit our editorial slant (religious/inspirational). A look at our guidelines or a sample copy will help teen writers in deciding what to submit. Also, I'd like to encourage teens to write about things they know, but not necessarily 'common' or general topics. We see scores of poems about rainbows and loneliness and friends, but hardly any about 'How I feel about working at McDonalds,' 'What happened when I tried something new . . . ,' or 'Why I believe in. . . .' Also a tacked-on moral does not make a religious story. Make your *characters* Christian, and the religious slant will take care of itself."

* TEEN POWER, P.O. Box 632, Glen Ellyn, IL 60138. Sunday School take-home paper for young teens ages 11-15; published quarterly in weekly parts.

Publishes: True, personal-experience stories of how God has worked in the life of a teen. Also poetry, nonfiction and puzzles.

Submission Info: Double-spaced, typed manuscripts only, 500-1,000 words. Always include SASE for return of manuscript or reply. Pays $.06-$.10 per word on acceptance. Reports in eight weeks. Send business-size envelope (#10) SASE for sample copy and writer's guidelines.

Editor's Remarks: "Our goal is to help teens apply biblical principles for Christian living to their everyday lives. Everything we publish must have a strong, evangelical Christian basis."

Subscription Rates: One year $7.50. Slightly higher in Canada.

✔ TEXAS HOME EDUCATORS NEWSLETTER, P.O. Box 43887, Austin, TX 78745-0018. Co-published bimonthly with *The Teaching Home* magazine.

Publishes: News, articles and information about homeschooling in Texas.

Submission Info: Use standard format. Maximum length is 750 words. Pays $.02 per word published.

Editor's Remarks: "Material *must* relate to homeschooling in Texas."

[**Author's note:** This market limited to Texas residents involved with homeschooling.]

* THUMBPRINTS, 928 Gibbs, Caro, MI 48723. Monthly newsletter published by the Thumb Area Writer's Club.

Publishes: Poetry, short fiction, articles, essays, information, how-to, opinions, etc. Accepts general information but prefers manuscripts that relate to writing, publishing, or the writer's way of life. Also interested in short profiles of writers.

Submission Info: Material must be typed following standard formats. Will consider handwritten material only from writers 12 and under. Send SASE with submissions. Limit stories and articles to 1,000 words. Prefers items 500 words or less. Limit poems to 32 lines. Pays in copies. Sample issue $.75. You do not need to live in Michigan to submit material; however, the work of club members and subscribers will be given first consideration. Send SASE for yearly theme list for ideas.

Editor's Remarks: "We've published many young writers in the past."

Subscription Rates: One year for nonmembers $9.

[**Author's note:** Unlike the annual contest sponsored by TAWC, *Thumbprints* is *not* restricted to Michigan residents. Anyone may submit material.]

✔* TURTLE MAGAZINE, 1100 Waterway Blvd., P.O. Box 567, Indianapolis, IN 46202. Published by the Children's Better Health Institute for preschool level children ages 2-5.

Publishes: Black-and-white or colored drawings by readers ages 2-5.

Submission Info: No payment for reader materials. Editors advise readers to keep copies of their contributions, because unused material cannot be returned. Publisher owns all rights to material printed.

Editor's Remarks: "We cannot promise to publish what you send, because we receive many, many letters from children all over the world. We do promise to read and consider all the material sent to us, though! We are sorry, but because of the large amount of mail, we cannot write to each of you personally."

Subscription Rates: One year (eight issues) $13.95 in U.S. currency. Subscription office: P.O. Box 7133, Red Oak, IA 51591-0133.

✔* **U*S*KIDS**, 1100 Waterway Blvd., P.O. Box 567, Indianapolis, IN 46202. Publication for children 5-10 from the Children's Better Health Institute. Stresses health-related themes or ideas including nutrition, safety, exercise and proper health habits.

Publishes: From readers: original drawings and poetry for the "Best for the End" column.

Submission Info: Submissions do not have to be health-related. Please write your name, age, school and complete address on each submission. Material cannot be returned. No payment for published reader material. Send SASE for guidelines for young writers. Sample copies $1.25.

Editor's Remarks: "We usually select material sent in by children in the 5-10 age group."

Subscription Rates: One year $20.95. Special rate of $14.95 is usually offered in every issue.

VEGETARIAN JOURNAL, P.O. Box 1463, Baltimore, MD 21203. Publication of The Vegetarian Resource Group.

Publishes: Poetry that relates directly to the vegetarian aspects of health, nutrition, animal rights, ethics, environment or world hunger.

Submission Info: Send poem along with SASE to Poetry Editor at the above address. Pays in copies.

Editor's Remarks: "Poems should reflect your personal feelings about a subject, be humorous or convey factual information. Poems should be positive and *not* describe animal abuse in gory details."

‡✔ **WEST COAST LINE**, 2027 East Academic Annex, Simon Fraser University, Burnaby, BC V5A 1S6, CANADA. Focuses on contemporary writers who are experimenting with, or expand-

ing the boundaries of, conventional forms of poetry, fiction and criticism.

Publishes: Poetry: poems in extended forms; excerpts from works in progress; experimental and innovative poems. Fiction: short stories; excerpts from novels in progress; experimental and innovative writing. Nonfiction: critical and theoretical essays on contemporary and modernist writing; interviews; statements of poetics; reviews. Other work: bibliographies; edited letters and manuscripts; translations into English of innovative contemporary writing.

Submission Info: Must be typed; use standard format; MLA format. Prefers printed manuscript and computer disk copy. Maximum lengths: poetry to 400 lines; fiction to 7,000 words; nonfiction and "other" not indicated. Recommends that potential contributors query before submitting manuscripts. SASE required for return of manuscript. Pays $3-$4 per page after publication; copyright reverts to writer after publication. Responds in four months. Send SASE for guidelines. Sample copy $10.

Editor's Remarks: "Our editorial slant shows a special concern for contemporary writers who are experimenting with or expanding the boundaries of conventional forms of poetry, fiction and criticism; also interested in criticism and scholarship on Canadian and American modernist writers who are important sources for current writing."

Subscription Rates: One year (3 issues) $20. One year for institutions $26. U.S. subscribers pay in U.S. funds. Single copy $10.

[**Author's note:** Only mature young writers (high school or college age) should consider this market.]

‡✓ **WHITE WALL REVIEW**, % Oakham House, 63 Gould St., Toronto, ON M5B 1E9, CANADA. Annual journal of poetry, short stories and photographs that draws submissions from all over the world.

Publishes: Poetry, short stories, photography. No particular content preference, however, does not accept work that is gratuitously violent, vulgar or in bad taste.

Submission Info: Manuscripts must be typed. Include a short biography and SASE with submissions. No poem should be more than five pages long. Maximum of ten poems may be submitted at one time. Limit short stories to 3,000 words. Accepts black-and-white, unmounted photography in 8½″ × 11″ size. No slides. Reviews submissions from September to first Friday of December each year. Pays with one free copy. All those submitting work receive a written comment by April, whether work is accepted or not. Sample copy $8.

Editor's Remarks: "The *Review* publishes work from all over the world and can be found in library and personal collections across Canada and the United States."

✒* **WHOLE NOTES**, P.O. Box 1374, Las Cruces, NM 88004. Special issue of writing by young people published in even-numbered years. Seeks to recognize outstanding work from across the country. Publishes: Poems, especially free verse, by young people up to and including age 21. All poetic forms considered, including haiku, riddles, sonnets, long poems, prose poems and free verse. Some black-and-white drawings are used. Special young writers' issue published in December of even-numbered years.

Submission Info: Typed poems preferred. We will read neat handwriting, if necessary. Drawings must be in black ink, ready to print. Do not send original drawing; a clean photocopy is best. Be sure to include SASE so you receive a prompt reply. Prefers not to receive multiple or simultaneous submissions. Usually reports in two to three weeks. Pays with one free copy of issue containing published work. Send SASE for copy of writers' guidelines. Sample copy $3.

Editor's Remarks: "We look for poems that are clearly written, with fresh images. Poems about the natural world as well as the human one are welcomed. A surprise at the end is a delight, if it's not forced. We want the poem to come from your imagination."

Subscription Rates: One year (two issues) $6; two years $10.

✒*$ **WORLD PEN PALS**, 1694 Como Ave., St. Paul, MN 55108. Sponsored by International Institute of Minnesota (a United Way-affiliated agency). Promotes friendship through understanding, providing service for all nationalities.

Publishes: A letter-writing program that links more than 20,000 students ages 12-20 from 175 countries and territories around the world with students in the United States. Does not link students within the U.S. Small service fee. Short letters about pen pal experiences appear in newsletter.

Submission Info: Send SASE for details. Offers "Suggestions," a guideline sheet for letter writing, and a newsletter called *Pen Pal Post*, along with the name and address of your new pen pal.

Editor's Remarks: "It is fun for students to receive letters from another country. As pen pals correspond, they become good friends even though separated geographically and culturally. Their interest grows in other languages and customs. Some pen pals even visit one another after corresponding."

Subscription Rates: Fee is $3 for each pen pal requested. Groups of six or more may apply for a fee of $2.50 per person; names and addresses of pen pals will be sent to the group's leader.

[**Author's note:** Writing to a pen pal, especially one from another country, is an excellent way for young writers to hone their writing skills as they try to bring their personal experiences to life.]

✔ **THE WRITER'S COMPANION,** 1406 Abbey Dr., Norman, OK 73071. Newsletter focusing on writing, and pen pal exchange for writers, published bimonthly. Kira Sampson, editor.

Publishes: Articles about writing, literary biographies and other related material. "The Poet's Page" features four to six poems by a single poet. "My Favorite Poem" column features your favorite poem and why you like it.

Submission Info: Typed or neatly printed copy only. Maximum length for articles 800 words. Maximum length for literary biographies (poet or writer featured during his/her birth month) 500-700 words. Maximum length for "My Favorite Poem" essay 150 words. Payment in copies. Reports in two to four weeks. Send SASE for writer's guidelines, additional information and pen pal questionnaire. Sample copy $3.

Editor's Remarks: "Writing is a lonely process; TWC's goal is to provide writers with a way to connect with others who have the same interests and aspirations."

Subscription Rates: One year (six issues) $8.

✔ **THE WRITER'S HAVEN NEWSLETTER**, P.O. Box 413, Joaquin, TX 75954. Publication that focuses on writing for writers of all ages. Marcella Simmons, editor.

Publishes: Articles, poems and how-tos about the writing life. No fiction accepted at this time.

Submission Info: No handwritten material accepted for manuscripts longer than 3,000 words. Sample copy $2.

Editor's Remarks: "Writing is not easy, but requires lots of time, patience and willpower. If you have these three ingredients, writing is a cinch!"

Subscription Rates: One year $12.

✔*$ **WRITERS' INK NEWSLETTER**, GEnie mail address: INKNEWS$. Periodic publication by the members of the Writer's Ink RoundTable on GEnie.

Publishes: Quality short stories and poems written by members of WINK. (Note: There is no additional cost to become a member of WINK. Normal GEnie charges apply.) Issues usually relate to a single topic announced online.

Submission Info: See directions in WINK RoundTable or libraries. Or e-mail to INKNEWS$.

Editor's Remarks: "It is our goal to produce an informative, useful and entertaining newsletter, and to showcase some of the talent that is so evident on GEnie. The newsletter also serves as an introduction to Writers' Ink (WINK); portions of it are uploaded to the GEnie Info Library, where new GEnie members can practice uploading and downloading at no charge, and find information on roundtables that may be of interest to them."

Subscription Rates: To join, see information in Chapter 4 or call (800) 638-9636 for GEnie member information.

✔*$ **WRITERS' INK ROUNDTABLE**, GEnie page 440. An electronic association of writers. No extra charge to join or take part in WINK, just basic GEnie subscriber fee.

Publishes: Separate category specifically for students and young writers. Topics have included: Story Exchange for Young

Writers, Young Writer's Round-Robin Story, Humorous Short Story Exchange and more. Also serves as home or host for a number of online magazines, traditional and electronic book publishers, newsletters, etc. Members may upload their manuscripts (any genre) to the library section. For instance, *STANZA* (WINK library file #3760; uploaded by R.MACMICHAEL) features teen poets. Young writers also welcome in all but the adult category (access barred to anyone under 21) and the Professional's Corner.

Submission Info: Must be a GEnie subscriber or have access to family membership. See your user's manual to learn basics of uploading files.

Editor's Remarks: "Have you ever wished you could meet and talk with some professional writers, perhaps ask them a question or two? Maybe you'd like a critique of one of your short stories, or advice on solving a writing problem. Perhaps you're looking for a way to share your work online. Even though most of our members are adults, we welcome and encourage participation by interested young writers. Though you may participate in most of our categories, young writers on WINK also have their own young writers category where they can chat with their peers and share their manuscripts."

Subscription Rates: Call (800) 638-9636.

[**Author's note:** Read the profile of WINK member Tanya Beaty on page 129.]

✒* WRITERS' OPEN FORUM, P.O. Box 516, Tracyton, WA 98393. Publication that brings writers together to exchange ideas and improve their skills and marketability.

Publishes: "Writer to Writer" column features tips, ideas, questions and answers regarding writing. Short stories, any subject or genre; prefers stories with a protagonist the reader can care about, a problem to resolve, complications along the way, and a resolution resulting from the protagonist's action. Open also to articles on any subject *except* writing-related. Prefers articles with an opening hook, the intention clearly stated, examples or facts to back up the idea and an effective ending. No poetry accepted at present time. Will consider writer-related cartoons.

Submission Info: Use standard format. Be sure to number

pages, include accurate word count, and write "End" at bottom of last page. Include SASE for return of material. Cover letter required; include a brief statement explaining your story or article's purpose or proposed market, and a brief note about yourself. Young writers should note their age. Payment $5 upon publication, two copies of publication, and all critiques sent in by readers. Submission guidelines and guidelines for critiquing other readers' work available for SASE. Sample copy $3.

Editor's Remarks: "Our writers have included high school students and retirees, truck drivers and psychologists. We all gain when we help each other by learning how to critique, offering our critiques to other writers, and bravely submitting our writing for other writers to review. Not all stories submitted will be published, but all submissions that follow our guidelines receive a personal reply."

Subscription Rates: One year (six issues) $14; $24 in U.S. funds for foreign destinations.

✔* **THE WRITERS' SLATE**, P.O. Box 734, Garden City, KS 67846. Journal published three times per year featuring work from students in grades K-12. (One issue for contest winners.)

Publishes: Original poetry and prose from students enrolled in grades K-12. Bold, black-and-white student artwork may accompany manuscript.

Submission Info: Typed manuscripts appreciated, but not necessary. Submission dates are June 15 for fall issue; January 15 for spring issue. Sample copies available for $4.50 by writing to the address for subscriptions below.

Editor's Remarks: "The journal is published three times per year, with one issue given to the winners of our writing contest. There is no cost to submit manuscripts."

Subscription Rates: One year (three issues) for students $6; for teachers and other adults $8.95. Address subscription and sample copy requests to: The Writing Conference, Inc., P.O. Box 664, Ottawa, KS 66067.

✔* **WRITER'S VOICE**, 1630 Lake Dr., Haslett, MI 48840. Quarterly newsletter plus yearly anthologies. No age restriction.

Publishes: Poetry of varying styles and skill levels. No profanity (unless relevant to the poem) or pornography. Nonfiction articles relating to poetry, writing, etc. Some fiction accepted for anthologies but competition is stiff. Also accepts black ink illustrations.

Submission Info: Prefers poetry typed in the format author prefers to see it in print; limit is one 8½" × 11" page. Handwritten poetry acceptable if printed legibly. Nonfiction and fiction should *always* be typed; use standard format. Maximum length for nonfiction 1,000 words. Payment for newsletter articles upon publication. No cash payment for poetry. Prefers illustrations in 5½" × 7" format. Guidelines available for SASE. Sample anthologies $7 (postage paid); sample newsletter $4 (postage paid).

Editor's Remarks: "We encourage young writers to submit their work to us as we are always interested in showcasing new talent."

✔* **THE WRITING NOTEBOOK**, P.O. Box 1268, Eugene, OR 97440-1268. Nonprofit journal for educators and others interested in using computers in the classroom to enhance reading and writing instruction.

Publishes: Students poetry (any grade level). May be accompanied by black-and-white artwork.

Submission Info: Type or write out poems, or send on disk formatted for Macintosh computers.

Subscription Rates: One year $32.

✔* **WRITING RIGHT NEWSLETTER**, Elmwood Park Publishing, P.O. Box 35132, Elmwood Park, IL 60635. Monthly newsletter designed for beginning writers (any age), featuring writing-related information. John C. Biardo, editor.

Publishes: Feature articles, writing tips, book reviews, news of writing contests and markets, newsworthy information. Looking for informative articles pertaining to writing, researching, publicity and promotion. No poetry or personal success stories.

Submission Info: Use standard typewritten format. Preferred length 500-1,000 words. Pays in copies. Reports in one month. Send SASE for guidelines. Sample copy $4.

Editor's Remarks: "Most of our articles are accepted from the beginning writer, as well as from subscribers."

Subscription Rates: One year (twelve issues) $30 in U.S.; $42 in Canada. Subscribers receive free book, *Anyone Can Write A Best-Seller ... and Get It Published*, mailed with first issue.

✔* **YOUNG PLAYWRIGHTS ROUNDTABLE,** % The Coterie, 2450 Grand Ave., Suite 144, Kansas City, MO 64108-2520. Theater staff members help young writers plan and write plays. Membership limited to Kansas City youth. For more information, see the profile of Jeff Church on page 160.

✔* **YOUNG SALVATIONIST MAGAZINE,** % Captain Lesa Salyer, P.O. Box 269, Alexandria, VA 22313. Published monthly, except summer, for high school and early college-aged youth by The Salvation Army.

Publishes: Nonfiction articles that deal with real-life issues teenagers face and that present a Christian perspective. Fiction along same lines as nonfiction. Rarely uses fillers or poetry.

Submission Info: Use standard format. SASE required for return of material. Pays $.10 a word on acceptance. Reports in one month on unsolicited manuscripts. Sample issue, guidelines and theme list available for 8½" × 11" SASE with three first-class stamps.

Editor's Remarks: "Before sending your manuscript, please take time to request sample copy and theme lists. We like to work with new writers, but all material must fit our guidelines."

Subscription Rates: One year $4 (U.S. funds).

✔* **YOUTH! MAGAZINE,** P.O. Box 801, Nashville, TN 37202-0801. Published monthly by The United Methodist Publishing House for junior and senior high youth. Its purpose is to help teens live out the Christian faith in contemporary culture.

Publishes: Nonfiction from adults and youth. Uses fiction by teens only; may be adventure, romance, science fiction, fantasy, relationship stories or humor. Considers poetry by teens. Does not use puzzles or adult poetry. Art and photos by teens also encouraged.

Submission Info: Prefers submissions to be in standard format. Poetry submissions by teens must be addressed to "Express Mail" to be considered for publication. Queries preferred for nonfiction. Photos accompanying manuscripts must be clear and sharply focused; black-and-white photos must be of good contrast. Color transparencies preferred over photos. Reports in three weeks for queries; six months for unsolicited manuscripts. SASE required for return of manuscript. Pays $.05 per word for one-time publication rights. Detailed guidelines available for SASE. For sample copy and guidelines send a 9½" × 12" SASE (use five first-class stamps on return envelope).

Editor's Remarks: "Write to *teens* 'friend to friend.' Treat instructional pieces with humor and grace, not judgementally. Keep tone personal. Appreciate the wonders and joys of adolescent life. Use faith language in a natural manner."

Subscription Rates: One year $18. Single copy $2. Higher outside U.S. Send check or money order. Bulk subscriptions (three or more yearly subscriptions mailed to a single address) $15 each. A copy of *Youth!, too*, a teaching supplement, is free with bulk subscriptions. Address to: Cokesbury Subscriptions, P.O. Box 801, Nashville, TN 37202-0801.

‡✔* **YOUTH UPDATE,** 1615 Republic St., Cincinnati, OH 45210-1298. Monthly publication from St. Anthony Messenger Press to support the growth of teenagers (ages 14-18) in a life of faith by applying Catholic principles to topics of timely interest.

Publishes: One 2,300-word article per issue. No poetry, fiction or sermons.

Submission Info: *Query first*, include SASE. Send SASE for writers' guidelines and sample. Pays $.14 per word.

Editor's Remarks: "*Youth Update* has published adult-teen collaborations before with great success."

Subscription Rates: One year $10.

[**Author's note:** Note that this market uses only one article per issue and you *must* query first.]

Chapter Nine

Contest List

Many different types of contests are listed in this guide. Some are sponsored by various publishers, some by writing groups, and others by for-profit companies and not-for-profit associations. Contests are listed alphabetically, including those accessed through online computer services.

Each listing contains three sections of information that will help you understand (1) general information about the contest and its sponsor, (2) how entering the contest might benefit you, and (3) prizes awarded. There are also two optional sections. "Sponsor's Remarks" provides extra insight into the history or goals of the contest and advice for producing a winning entry. "Subscription Rates" have been included as an extra service for those interested in subscribing to a sponsor's publication.

New additions to this edition's contest listings are preceded by a checkmark (✔). Contests of special interest to young people are preceded by a star (*). Contests that require an entry fee are marked with a dollar sign ($). A few listings are also marked with a double cross (‡). This indicates that this contest should be considered only by serious teen writers, as competition is likely to be against adults or very difficult.

Contest listings were researched and chosen using the same criteria as that used for market listings. See details on page 170.

The following chart and sample contest listing will help explain the information contained within each section. You may want to review the sections "What's new in this edition" and "More about the listings" in Chapter 1, plus the advice in Chapter 2, "Study and compare the opportunities" before reviewing these listings.

CONTEST LISTING CHART

SEC.	YOU WILL FIND	PAY SPECIAL ATTENTION TO
1	Name of Contest. Mailing address for entries, forms, and complete list of rules. Brief description including who is eligible, frequency of contest. Name of sponsor.	Who sponsors this contest and the general theme of each contest. The goal of the contest.
2	General information about the contest. Deadlines for entries. Eligibility requirements. Entry fees, if any. How the contest is judged. Availability of rules and samples.	Any contest designed specifically for young people. Note any age limits. How to enter. Any restrictions.
3	Prizes awarded including cash, certificates, merchandise, and publication and display of winning entries.	The number of prizes awarded. How entries may be published or displayed. How often and how many times you may enter.
4	History of the contest, plus advice and tips for entering and winning, quoted directly from the sponsor or entry form.	Advice to help you submit a winning entry.
5	Subscription rates if sponsored by a publication. Subscription mailing address when it differs from contest entry address.	Included as an extra service for young people, parents and teachers.

SAMPLE CONTEST LISTING

1 _____ GUIDEPOSTS YOUTH WRITERS CON-TEST, 16 E. 34th St., New York, NY 10016. Sponsored annually by *Guideposts* magazine for high school juniors and seniors.

2 _____ **General Info:** Open to any high school junior or senior, or students in equivalent grades in other countries. Entrants must write a true first-person story about a personal experience. All manuscripts must be the student's original work and must be written in English. Use standard format. Maximum 1,200 words. Entries must include: home address, phone number, and name and address of entrant's school. Write for rules and current deadlines. Winners will be notified by mail prior to announcement in *Guideposts*. Prize-winning manuscripts become the property of *Guideposts*.

3 _____ **Prizes:** Eight cash awards totalling $20,000 in scholarships, plus seventeen honorable mentions. All winners and honorable mentions receive a portable electronic typewriter. Scholarships to the accredited colleges or schools of winners' choice will be: First prize $6,000; second $5,000; third $4,000; fourth through eighth $1,000. Prizes are not redeemable in cash, are non transferable, and must be used within five years after high school graduation.

4 _____ **Sponsor's Remarks:** "A winning story doesn't have to be complicated or filled with drama. It only has to come from the heart, and be an honest and straightforward account of an experience that touched you deeply or changed your ideas or outlook. Think of something that happened to you at home, at school or at a job: an exciting close call, or a tough personal decision that took moral courage. Then write about it as if you were telling a story to a friend. Don't be shy about revealing your innermost feelings."

5 _____ **Subscription Rates:** In the United States one year $9.95. In Canada one year $10.95. Sample copy for $.52 stamp.

* ACHIEVEMENT AWARDS IN WRITING, NCTE, 1111 Kenyon Rd., Urbana, IL 61801. The National Council of Teachers of English has sponsored this awards program for thirty-six years. Only writers who are nominated may enter.

General Info: To encourage high school students and to recognize some of the best student writers in the nation, the NCTE gives achievement awards in writing to more than eight hundred graduating seniors each year. Only students who are juniors in the contest's academic year may be nominated. High school juniors from public, private and parochial schools in the U.S. and Canada, and from American schools abroad, are eligible. Each high school selects its own nominee or nominees: one or more juniors agreed upon by the English department, not chosen by an individual teacher. A current official nomination blank for each nominee must be submitted to NCTE. Write for details.

Prizes: In 1993, 876 awards possible.

Sponsor's Remarks: "Because NCTE is a nonprofit educational association, it has no funds to award scholarships to winners. Their names and addresses, however, are printed in a booklet that is mailed in October to directors of admissions and freshman studies in 3,000 colleges, universities and junior colleges in the U.S. Accompanying each booklet is a letter in which NCTE recommends the winners for college admission and for financial assistance, if needed. Booklets are also sent to state supervisors of English, to NCTE affiliate organizations, and to the winners and their high school principals."

✔ AIM MAGAZINE'S SHORT STORY CONTEST, P.O. Box 20554, Chicago, IL 60620. Annual contest sponsored by quarterly publication for high school, college and general public.

General Info: No fee to enter. Stories judged by *AIM*'s editorial staff. Deadline is August 15.

Prizes: First prize—$100; second prize—$50. Winner published in the autumn issue.

Sponsor's Remarks: "To purge racism from the human bloodstream—that is our objective. To do it through the written word. We want to show that people from different ethnic and racial backgrounds are more alike than they are different. They all strive

for the same things — education, jobs, good health, etc."
Subscription Rates: One year $10.

✒* **AIR CANADA AWARD**, CAA, 275 Slater St., Suite 500, Ottawa, ON K1P 5H9, CANADA. Annual competition sponsored by Air Canada, administered by the Canadian Authors Association. Open to Canadian writers under 30; writers must be nominated to enter.

General Info: Award goes to the Canadian writer under age 30 (at April 30 in the year of the competition) deemed most promising. There are no restrictions as to the field of writing and a winner may be chosen for work in several fields. Writers may be renominated until they reach the age limit. Nominations are made through CAA branches or other writing organizations to the Canadian Authors Association. Nominee does not need to be a CAA member. Nominations must be postmarked no later than April 30. A trustee appointed by the awards chairperson reviews the entries and recommends a winner. The recommended approach to nominating a writer is to submit a one-page outline of why the writer shows promise along with samples of the writer's work or reviews of that work. Full-length works need not be sent; copies of a few pages are sufficient.

Prizes: The airline offers winner a trip for two to any destination on Air Canada's routes. Awards are presented each June at the Annual Awards Dinner.

Sponsor's Remarks: "It takes many years for a Canadian writer to achieve national (and, increasingly, international) recognition. But Air Canada believes the signs of greatness can usually be detected before the writer reaches 30. Past winners include Gordon Korman, Larry Krotz, Mary deMichele, Wayne Johnston, Evelyn Lau and Leslie Smith Dow. Give a promising young writer in your community this opportunity."

* **AMERICA & ME ESSAY CONTEST**, Farm Bureau Insurance, Lisa Fedewa, Contest Coordinator, P.O. Box 30400, Lansing, MI 48909. Yearly contest that encourages Michigan youth to explore their roles in America's future.

General Info: Open to any eighth-grade student in any Michigan school. Students must participate through their school systems. Interested students and schools should contact the main office or a Farm Bureau Insurance agent in their area for complete information and requirements. Each school may submit up to ten essays for judging. A first-, second- and third-place winner will be selected from each school. Each first-place essay is automatically entered into the statewide competition, from which the top essays are selected. Essays must relate to yearly theme and may be up to 500 words long. (Topic examples from recent years: "America & Me—How We Will Work Together," "How I Can Contribute to America's Future.") Schools must pre-register.

Prizes: First- through third-place winners in each school receive certificates. The first-place winner's name also appears on a plaque that hangs permanently in his or her school. The top ten statewide winners each receive a plaque and share a total of $5,500 in savings bonds. Individual prizes range from $1,000 to $500 in savings bonds. In addition, the top ten essays and selected excerpts from other essays are compiled into a booklet distributed to schools, government leaders and the general public.

Sponsor's Remarks: "This (1992-93) is the contest's twenty-fourth year. Since it was started in 1968, more than 140,000 students have participated. Average participation each year is now more than 10,000 students. The final ranking of the top ten winners is made by a panel of VIP judges that in the past has included Governors Engler, Blanchard and Milliken, and former President Gerald Ford."

Subscription Rates: Samples of the compiled essays are available through Farm Bureau at the above address.

[**Author's note:** This contest is restricted to Michigan youth.]

* THE AMERICAN BEEKEEPING FEDERATION ESSAY CONTEST, P.O. Box 1038, Jesup, GA 31545. Annual contest coordinated by the American Beekeeping Federation and state 4-H offices.

General Info: Contest is open to *active* 4-H club members only. Essays must be 750 to 1,000 words long, written on the designated subject only. All factual statements must be referenced; failure to do so will result in disqualification. Essays should be submitted to the state 4-H office. *Do not submit essays to the American Beekeeping Federation office.* Each state 4-H office is responsible for selecting the state's winner. State winners will be forwarded to the national level. Essays will be judged on accuracy, creativity, conciseness, logical development of the year's topic argument and scope of research. Contact your local or state 4-H office for details, topic for current contest and state deadlines. Contest information is also available from the ABF at the above address.

Prizes: Cash awards to top national winners: first place $250; second place $100; third place $50. Each state winner receives a book about honey bees, beekeeping or honey. All national entries become the property of the ABF, and may be published. No essays will be returned.

Sponsor's Remarks: "This national essay contest has been established to stimulate interest among our nation's youth in honey bees and the vital contributions they make to mankind's well-being."

* AMHAY MORGAN HORSE LITERARY CONTEST, P.O. Box 960, Shelburne, VT 05482-0960. Sponsored by the American Morgan Horse Association. Open to all young people under 22.

General Info: In either essay or poetry form (1,000 words or less), tell *in your own words* what the contest theme statement means to you. Essays and poetry will be judged on general style, originality, grammar, spelling and punctuation. No entry fee, but you must attach an official entry form to your poem or essay. Work submitted may be used for promotional purposes by AMHA. Participants must be under 22 as of December 1, the contest deadline. Write the AMHA for current theme and entry form.

Prizes: Cash awards of $50 will be presented to the winner in both the essay and poetry categories. One-year subscriptions to *The Morgan Horse* magazine will be awarded to the second- through fifth-place winners. Winning entries are published in "The Morganizer," a national youth newsletter for AMHA members.

Sponsor's Remarks: "Winning entries are often published in *The Morgan Horse*, a glossy magazine with an international circulation of 10,000."

*$ ARTS RECOGNITION & TALENT SEARCH, National Foundation for Advancement of the Arts, 300 Northeast Second Ave., Miami, FL 33132. Annual nonprofit program administered by the Miami-Dade Community College. Scholarship opportunities for high school students interested in dance, music, theater, visual arts and writing.

General Info: Contact your teacher, guidance counselor or principal for complete registration packet. The ARTS program is designed for high school seniors and other 17 to 18-year-olds with demonstrable artistic achievements in dance, music, theater, visual arts (including film and video) and writing. Application materials also sent to individuals upon request. Fee of $25 for each discipline or discipline category entered; more for late entry.

Prizes: Winners receive between $500 and $3,000 in cash. NFAA earmarks up to $400,000 in cash awards for ARTS applicants whose work has been judged outstanding by a national panel of experts. Selected candidates are also invited to Miami, Florida, for a week of live adjudications [judging] consisting of: auditions, master and technique classes, workshops, studio exercises and interviews. NFAA pays travel, lodging and meal expenses for the cash award candidates. Additional college scholarships and internships worth more than $3 million have also been made available to all ARTS participants, whether or not they were award winners.

Sponsor's Remarks: "ARTS is a unique program in that applicants are judged against a standard of excellence within each art discipline, *not* against each other. ARTS does not predetermine the number of awards to be made on any level or in any discipline."

* AYN RAND INSTITUTE COLLEGE SCHOLARSHIP, The Ayn Rand Institute, 4640 Admiralty Way #715, Marina del Rey, CA 90292. Annual essay contest for high school juniors and seniors.

General Info: The Institute wishes to encourage good writing skills and thinking about issues crucial to young people and, ultimately, to help students gain an in-depth understanding of the meaning and ideas in *The Fountainhead* (by Ayn Rand). Entrants write an essay based on one of three topics detailed on the contest sheet. Entrants must be in the last two years of secondary school.

Essays must be typed and may not exceed four double-spaced pages. Work must be solely that of the entrant. Essays will be judged on both style and content. Judges look for writing that is clear, articulate and logically organized. Annual deadline is April 15. Send SASE for current contest sheet and complete details. All entries become the property of The Ayn Rand Institute.

Prizes: First prize—$5,000. Five second prizes of $1,000. Ten third prizes of $500.

Sponsor's Remarks: "Since 1985, *The Fountainhead* Essay Contest has brought important issues such as independence and integrity to the attention of thousands of high school juniors and seniors. To date, more than 20,000 students have written essays on the meaning of *The Fountainhead* and competed for $120,000 in cash awards."

* BAKER'S PLAYS HIGH SCHOOL PLAYWRITING CONTEST, Baker's Plays, 100 Chauncy St., Boston, MA 02111. Annual contest open to any high school student.

General Info: Plays should be about "the high school experience," but can also be about any subject so long as the play can be reasonably produced on the high school stage. Plays may be any length. Multiple submissions or collaborative efforts accepted. Scripts must be accompanied by the signature of a sponsoring high school drama or English teacher, and *it is recommended that the script be given a public stage reading or production prior to the submission.* The manuscript *must* be typed and *firmly bound*, and must come with SASE. Please include enough postage. All plays must be postmarked by January 30. Playwrights will be notified in May. Send SASE for contest information.

Prizes: First place receives $500, and the play will be published under the *Best Plays From the High School* series by Baker's Plays the September of the contest year. Second place receives $250 and Honorable Mention; third place receives $100 and Honorable Mention.

Sponsor's Remarks: "The purpose of the contest is to promote play writing at the high school level, to promote the production of that work, and to encourage the next generation of playwrights."

*$ BYLINE STUDENT CONTESTS, P.O. Box 130596, Edmond, OK 73013. Special contests for students during the school year, sponsored by *Byline* magazine, which is aimed at writers of all ages.

General Info: Variety of monthly writing contests for students 18 and younger beginning with the September issue and continuing through May each year. Prefers typed entries on white bond paper 8½" × 11". Most contests have small entry fee, which provides cash awards to winners. Others have no entry fee and are often used as class assignments by writing and English teachers. Send SASE for details of upcoming contests. Sample copy $3.50.

Prizes: Cash prizes and possible publication.

Sponsor's Remarks: "We do not print student work except as winners of our monthly student writing contests."

Subscription Rates: One year (11 issues) $20.

[**Author's note:** Good contest for eager young writers.]

✔* CALIFORNIA YOUNG PLAYWRIGHTS CONTEST, P.O. Box 2068, San Diego, CA 92112. Statewide program sponsored by the Playwrights Project for California residents under age 19.

General Info: Accepts play scripts by California residents under age 19. Collaborations and group scripts are eligible; adaptations are not. Scripts that have been produced professionally or submitted previously to the contest will not be considered. Eligible writers may submit more than one script. Choice of subject, style and language is up to the writer. Submissions should be typed, bound, and at least ten pages long. Title page should include playwright's name, address, phone and birthdate. Writers should also include a brief cover letter. All submissions will receive a detailed professional evaluation. Scripts will not be returned. Write for additional information or contest posters, or call (619) 232-6188. Entries should be postmarked no later than April 1.

Prizes: Winning writers receive professional production of their script at The Old Globe Theatre, San Diego, in the 235-seat Cassius Carter Centre Stage. Writers participate in entire production process, and receive a $100 award plus help with transportation expenses. Four to six writers selected annually.

Sponsor's Remarks: "The mission of the Playwrights Project is two-fold: to stimulate young people to create and perform dramatic works, and to engage the minds and imaginations of senior citizens. Our goals are to nurture promising young writers; to develop future artists and audiences for theater of quality; to provide seniors with creative opportunities to express themselves; and to help all students strengthen their communication skills."

[**Author's note:** Notice that scripts should be bound before submitting, and that the contest is limited to California residents.]

✔* CANADIAN AUTHOR ANNUAL STUDENT CREATIVE WRITING CONTEST, 275 Slater St., Suite 500, Ottawa, ON K1P 5H9, CANADA. Sponsored by *Canadian Author*, a quarterly magazine dedicated to bringing news of Canadian writers, editors and publishers to developing freelance writers. Open to Canadian students only.

General Info: Canadian students in high schools, colleges and universities are eligible to enter. Separate categories for fiction, nonfiction and poetry. Details available in the October and January issues of *Canadian Author*; entry form on back page. Copies available in bookstores or send SASE for an entry form and full details. *No photocopies* of entry forms are permitted.

Prizes: Prize of $100 awarded to best entry in each category. Sponsoring instructors of winning entrants receive matching awards. A $500 scholarship, in association with the Canadian Authors Association, is offered to the writer who the judges think shows the most promise, regardless of the writer's final standing in the contest.

Sponsor's Remarks: "*Canadian Author* sponsored its 10th annual creative writing contest for students in 1993."

✔* CHICKADEE COVER CONTEST, 56 The Esplanade, Suite 306, Toronto, ON M5E 1A7 CANADA. Annual contest sponsored in *Chickadee*, a science and nature magazine for children between 3-9, published ten times per year.

General Info: Create a cover for *Chickadee* magazine by drawing an animal you'd like to be for a day. Use markers, crayons, paints, or make a collage (if you don't use tape) to make your cover. Your cover must be exactly the same size as a real *Chickadee* cover. Leave room at the top for the word *Chickadee. Don't* print the word yourself. Include another piece of paper with your name, age, address and postal code. Don't write on your picture. Mail your entry flat with a piece of cardboard. Entries must be received by October 30 each year.

Prizes: Winner is published on the cover of the January issue. Runners-up are published in the February issue.

Subscription Rates: In the U.S., one year (ten issues) $14.95. Mail subscription requests to 255 Great Arrow Ave., Buffalo, NY 14207-3082. In Canada, call (416) 946-0406.

✔* CHICKADEE'S GARDEN EVENT, 56 The Esplanade, Suite 306, Toronto, ON M5E 1A7, CANADA. Annual contest sponsored in *Chickadee*, a science and nature magazine for children between 3-9, published ten times per year.

General Info: Grow a favorite edible fruit or vegetable during summer, then take a photo or draw a picture of yourself with your plant before eating it. Write a letter explaining why you chose to grow the plant you did, and who helped you care for it. Include anything funny or unusual that happened to you or your plant over the summer, or special things you did for your plant. Send in your letter and photo or drawing by September 1. Details in magazine.

Prizes: As many submissions as possible will be published in the January issue.

Subscription Rates: In the U.S., one year (ten issues) $14.95. Mail subscription requests to 255 Great Arrow Ave., Buffalo, NY 14207-3082. In Canada, call (416) 946-0406.

‡✔$ CHRISTOPHER COLUMBUS SCREENPLAY DISCOVERY AWARDS, 433 N. Camden Dr., Suite 600, Beverly Hills, CA 90210. Sponsored by The Christopher Columbus Society for the Creative Arts, a division of the C.C.S. Entertainment Group. The Group was created in 1990 to discover new screenplays and to develop them.

General Info: Open to all writers. *Only* non-produced, non-optioned feature screenplays may be submitted. Entrant is allowed to submit more than one screenplay. Application/release form and non-refundable $45 registration fee *must* be sent with each entry. See detailed guidelines for deadlines in two categories: Discovery of the Month, Discovery of the Year. Judging criteria based on execution, originality and salability.

Prizes: See guidelines for specific details. However, awards include feedback by phone, a personal meeting with professionals in the field, and help with further development of your screenplay. Selected "Discovery of the Month" screenplays automatically qualify as finalists for "Discovery of the Year," and the writer can submit a second screenplay at no cost. Screenplay(s) are introduced to top agents, producers and studios. Award certificates are issued.

Sponsor's Remarks: "Through our monthly and yearly contests, our unique development process, and our access to major agents, producers and studios, we are able to bridge the gap between writers and the established entertainment industry."

[**Author's note:** Consider your options carefully before submitting to this competition due to the high registration fee and the tough competition.]

✔$ **COMPUSERVE MEMBER ESSAYS,** CompuServe Magazine, User ID 76004,3302. Monthly winners, no charge to submit essay.

General Info: Compete for $50 worth of connect time and free CompuServe Information Manager software. Write a 200-word essay describing an original way you've used the Information Service and send it to User ID number 76004,3302. Include your full name, address and User ID number. There is no charge to submit essay, but you must be a CompuServe member (or family member).

Prizes: Fifty dollars and software. Winning essays published in "Monitor" section of magazine.

* **CREATIVE KIDS,** Prufrock Press, P.O. Box 8813, Waco, TX 76714-8813. A full-size magazine by kids, for kids.

General Info: Various ongoing and new contests. Examples: Goofy Gadgets (Rube Goldberg-type inventions); Cover Photo

Contest (candids of kids in action); Create a New Game; Finish the Story.

Prizes: Vary. Winning cover photo entrants and Create a New Game entrants receive a one-year subscription. Goofy Gadgets winners receive a four-month subscription.

Subscription Rates: One year $24. New reader rate for one year $17.97. Schools and libraries may request a free sample copy by sending a request on school or library stationery.

* CRICKET LEAGUE CONTESTS, P.O. Box 300, Peru, IL 61354. Monthly contests for children through age 14, sponsored by *Cricket* magazine.

General Info: Contest themes vary from month to month. Refer to a current issue of the magazine. Throughout the year, contests are sponsored in four categories: art, poetry, short stories and photography. There are two age groups for each contest: 4-9 and 10-14. All contest rules must be followed. Rules are listed in each issue. You must have your parent's or guardian's permission to send your entry. Each entry must be signed by your parent or guardian saying it is your own original work and that no one helped you. Deadlines are the 25th of each month.

Prizes: Winners receive prizes or certificates and most place-winners are published in the magazine.

Sponsor's Remarks: "We have no lower age limit, but 4 is the youngest entrant to date. The *Cricket* League has sponsored contests since the magazine's inception in September, 1973. Through these contests, children have an opportunity to experience the rewards that creative writing and drawing bring."

Subscription Rates: Single copy $3.50. One year $29.97. Two years $49.97. Three years $69.97.

‡✔ DELACORTE FIRST YOUNG ADULT NOVEL CONTEST, Delacorte Press, Department BFYR, 666 Fifth Ave., New York, NY 10103. Annual book contest.

General Info: Annual contest for American and Canadian writers who have not previously published a young adult novel. Submissions should consist of a book-length manuscript (no shorter than one hundred typed pages and no more than 224 pages) with a *contemporary* setting in the U.S. or Canada that will be suitable for readers ages 12 to 18. Include a brief plot summary with cover letter. Each manuscript must be accompanied by an SASE large enough to accommodate the manuscript; otherwise the manuscript cannot be returned. Manuscripts sent to Delacorte Press may not be submitted to other publishers while under consideration for the prize. Authors may not submit more than two manuscripts to the competition; each must meet all eligibility requirements. Foreign-language manuscripts and translations are not eligible. Send an SASE anytime to receive complete guidelines. Submissions accepted between Labor Day and December 31 each year.

Prizes: Winner receives one Delacorte hardcover and Dell paperback book contract, including an advance and royalties; a $1,500 cash prize, and a $6,000 advance against royalties. All promotional costs for the winning book will be paid by the publisher.

Sponsor's Remarks: "Our YA novel contest is not primarily for *young* writers. It is for anyone who has never published a YA novel."

[**Author's note:** Suitable but tough contest for teens with novel-length manuscripts.]

*ELIAS LIEBERMAN STUDENT POETRY AWARD,

Poetry Society of America, 15 Gramercy Park, New York, NY 10003. Annual contest sponsored by PSA, the oldest poetry organization in the U.S., founded in 1910.

General Info: Prize is for best unpublished poem by a high school or preparatory school student (grades 9-12) from the United States. School attended, as well as name and address, should be noted with entry. Obtain a rules brochure by sending SASE to above address. PSA also sponsors a variety of other annual contests. No line limit; no fee to enter. Competition open to both PSA members and non-members.

Prizes: Check current brochure. Award in 1993 — $100.

Sponsor's Remarks: "The PSA's mission is to secure wide recognition for poetry as one of the important forces contributing to a higher cultural life, to kindle an appreciation of poetry in all of its forms, to develop a broader constituency for poetry, and to assist poets, especially emerging ones. The PSA was responsible for the creation of the Pulitzer Prize in Poetry."

Subscription Rates: See PSA brochure for membership information.

* ESSAY CONTEST, The Vegetarian Resource Group, P.O. Box 1463, Baltimore, MD 21203. Open to children 18 and under.

General Info: Separate contest categories for students ages 14-18; ages 9-13; and ages 8 and under. Entrants should base their 2-3 page essays on interviewing, research or personal opinion. You do not need to be a vegetarian to enter. Essays can be on any aspect of vegetarianism. All essays become the property of The Vegetarian Resource Group. Each essay needs to include the author's name, age, grade and school, and teacher's name. Entries must be postmarked by May 1 of the contest year. Send SASE for contest guidelines.

Prizes: A $50 savings bond is awarded in each category. Winning entries are also published in *The Vegetarian Journal.*

Sponsor's Remarks: "Vegetarianism means not eating meat, fish and birds (for example, chicken or duck). Among the many reasons for being a vegetarian are beliefs about ethics, culture, health, aesthetics, religion, world peace, economics, world hunger and the environment."

Subscription Rates: Membership includes subscription. Student rate for one year: $10.

*$ EXCELLENCE IN STUDENT LITERARY MAGAZINE PROGRAM, NCTE, 1111 Kenyon Rd., Urbana, IL 61801. Program to recognize excellence in student literary magazines, sponsored by the National Council of Teachers of English.

General Info: Open to all senior high, junior high and middle schools throughout the U.S. and Canada, and to American schools abroad. Only one entry may be submitted per school. In cases where a school publishes more than one magazine or more than one issue per year, a school selection committee should select the best entry. Two or more schools *may not* join to submit one entry. District-wide magazines and other kinds of publications, e.g., newspapers, yearbooks and magazines that contain faculty poetry and prose, are not eligible. Magazines submitted must have been published between September of the previous year and July of the entry year. Three copies of the entry form and three copies of the literary magazine should be received by the State Leader no later than July 1. Write for more information, official entry form, and list of State Leader addresses. Entry fee: $25.

Prizes: Initial judging will determine the entry's placement in one of five categories, the three most prominent being: Excellent, Superior and the Highest Award.

Sponsor's Remarks: "Do not send entries to NCTE. Identify your State Leader from the list. This program is intended as a means of recognition for students, teachers and schools producing excellent literary magazines; as an inducement for improving the quality of such magazines; and as encouragement for all schools to develop literary magazines, seeking excellence in writing and schoolwide participation in production."

✔* FOURTH OF JULY ESSAY CONTEST, Jon Douglas Company, 15270 Antioch, Pacific Palisades, CA 90272. Annual essay contest for Palisades elementary students in grades 3-6.

General Info: Open to children attending Palisades elementary schools in grades 3-6. Essays, of 350 words or less, must relate to each year's theme. Contestants must not copy any other written work or receive help from anyone. Entries should be printed in ink or with a typewriter or computer, and will be judged for writing style, originality and overall effect. Use the official entry form as cover page. All entries must be submitted to a Jon Douglas Company office (three locations in the Palisades area) by June 15.

Prizes: Four first-place winners (one in each grade level) receive $25 gift certificates and engraved medals; four second-place winners receive $15 gift certificate for books; 40 honorable mention winners are acknowledged from each grade level. All winners receive a red, white or blue Jon Douglas T-shirt and a Certificate of Recognition, and are asked to march in the annual Fourth of July parade under the "Jon Douglas Company Essay Contest Winners" banner. Certificates of Participation are awarded to all qualifying contestants.

[**Author's note:** Be sure to see the profile of Carole Trapani on page 139. Note that this contest is restricted to Pacific Palisades residents.]

*$ GENIE, 401 N. Washington St., Rockville, MD 20850. The General Electric Network for Information Exchange, a computer information service featuring a variety of special-interest round-tables open to member subscribers.

General Info: Many of the special interest forums periodically offer a variety of contests. Watch for announcements on the log-on banner.

Prizes: Vary, often include connect time credit

Sponsor's Remarks: "GEnie is a world of instantaneous tele-communications — across the continent or around the world; a world in which a host of electronic services put you in instant contact with thousands of other computer users."

Subscription Rates: Call (800) 638-9636.

[**Author's note:** See the separate listings for WRITERS' INK, the Electronic Writers Association.]

‡✔$ GROLIER POETRY PRIZE, 6 Plympton St., Cambridge, MA 02138. Annual competition co-sponsored by the Grolier Poetry Book Shop, Inc., and the Ellen La Forge Memorial Poetry Foundation, Inc.

General Info: Open to all poets who have not published either a vanity, small press, trade or chapbook of poetry. Entry fee $5. Each poet should submit only one manuscript of four to five poems that have never been published. Poems submitted elsewhere for publication are not eligible. Manuscript should not exceed ten double-spaced pages. Each manuscript should be accompanied by a separate page that lists the author's name, address, phone number, and the titles of submitted poems. Author's name should not be included in the body of the manuscript. Guidelines sheet available for SASE. Copyright for poems published in the annual will be re-assigned to the author on request, provided the author allows the Foundation to publish them in subsequent anthologies. Deadline in April. Winners selected and informed in mid-May. Judges remain anonymous.

Prizes: Two poets will receive an honorarium of $150. Four poems by each winner and two by each of the four runners-up will be published in the *Grolier Poetry Prize Annual*. No royalties.

Sponsor's Remarks: "The primary purpose of the award is to encourage and recognize developing writers."

Subscription Rates: Copies of 1984, 1985 and 1986 *Annual* available for $5; 1989 and 1992 for $6. Place orders with Grolier Poetry Book Shop, Inc., at the previously mentioned address. Make checks payable to the Foundation.

* GUIDEPOSTS YOUTH WRITERS CONTEST, 16 E. 34th St., New York, NY 10016. Sponsored annually by *Guideposts* magazine for high school juniors and seniors.

General Info: Open to any high school junior or senior, or students in equivalent grades in other countries. Entrants must write a true first-person story about a personal experience. All manuscripts must be the student's original work and must be written in English. Use standard format. Maximum 1,200 words. Entries must include: home address, phone number, and name and address of entrant's school. Write for rules and current deadlines. Winners will be notified by mail prior to announcement in *Guideposts*. Prize-winning manuscripts become the property of *Guideposts*. Include SASE for return of manuscripts.

Prizes: Eight cash awards totalling $20,000 in scholarships, plus seventeen honorable mentions. All winners and honorable mentions receive a portable electronic typewriter. Scholarships to the accredited colleges or schools of winners' choice will be: First prize $6,000; second $5,000; third $4,000; fourth through eighth $1,000. Prizes are not redeemable in cash, are non-transferable, and must be used within five years after high school graduation.

Sponsor's Remarks: "A winning story doesn't have to be complicated or filled with drama. It only has to come from the heart, and be an honest and straightforward account of an experience that touched you deeply or changed your ideas or outlook. Think of something that happened to you at home, at school or at a job: an exciting close call, or a tough personal decision that took moral courage. Then write about it as if you were telling a story to a friend. Don't be shy about revealing your innermost feelings."

Subscription Rates: In the United States one year $9.95. In Canada one year $10.95. Sample copy for $.52 stamp.

‡✓$ **IOWA WOMAN MAGAZINE ANNUAL WRITING CONTEST,** P.O. Box 2938, Waterloo, IA 50704. Annual contest for fiction, poetry, and essays by women.

General Info: Categories include fiction, poetry and essays by women. No residency requirement. Work must not be simultaneously submitted elsewhere, nor previously published. Send SASE for guidelines after May of each year; guidelines change each year. Nominal entry fee required from all entrants. Deadline is usually December 31.

Prizes: Awards cash and publication in the following year's Summer issue. In 1993, prizes include: first place — $300; second place — $250; a $100 bonus to the first-place prize if won by an Iowa writer. Guaranteed publication for first- and second-place winners; honorable mentions considered for publication later in the year.

Sponsor's Remarks: "The annual writing contest is quite competitive and it is judged anonymously, so no consideration for age can be granted. All writers have a much better chance of getting work published by submitting material to the magazine directly, without entering the contest. This is especially true for younger writers; we do not recommend contest entries for younger writers unless their work is truly exceptional."

Subscription Rates: One year $18. Sample copy $6.

✓* **ISLAND LITERARY AWARDS,** Prince Edward Island Council of the Arts, P.O. Box 2234, Charlottetown, PE C1A 8B9, CANADA. Includes the Cavendish Tourist Association Creative Writing Award for Children. Open to Prince Edward Island school children only.

General Info: Short story or poetry categories for elementary, junior high, and senior high school students. Competition open to individuals who have been resident on PEI at least six of the last twelve months. Students may write on topic of their choice. Maximum five pages of poetry or a five-page short story. Include a cover page showing only the title, the category, and the author's name, address and phone; second page should include title and notes (if any). The author's name or other identification mark on the entry, other than the cover page disqualifies the entry. Entries may be printed or typed, double-spaced on one side of page. Prize-winning work from any other competition not eligible for entry. All entries must include SASE. See current awards flyer for deadline and additional information.

Prizes: First place—$75; second—$50; third—$25. Awards evening, celebrating Island literary talent, occurs during National Book Festival Week in April.

[**Author's note:** Contest limited to students on Prince Edward Island, Canada. Look for similar opportunity in your own province or state.]

* KENTUCKY STATE POETRY SOCIETY CONTESTS, % Louise Logan, HC 63 P.O. Box 699, Greenup, KY 41144. Note some contest categories have modest entry fees, others have no fees. Sponsors a variety of annual poetry contests.

General Info: One category for elementary school students grades 1-3; one category for grades 4-6; and one category for high school students grades 7-12. Also category for college students, regardless of age. Other categories open to all writers. No entry fee for student categories. Fees for other categories vary according to number of manuscripts entered. Poems must be the original work of the poet. Teacher or parent may *suggest* subject matter or offer advice on poetry techniques, and may stress adherence to rules, importance of correct spelling, grammar and punctuation, neatness and legibility. Student entries may be untyped but copy must be neat and legible. No poem will be returned; keep your own copy. Do not submit poems currently submitted in another contest or for publication. Send SASE for details and list of current categories.

Prizes: Only first-place winners will be published. Varying cash awards and certificates awarded.

Sponsor's Remarks: "This contest cannot be successfully entered without a new contest sheet each year, as the contest may not always be the same! Contest chairman may change without notice and we cannot handle entries without SASE."

[**Author's note:** These contests are not restricted to residents of Kentucky. Anyone may enter.]

✔*$ **KIDS WRITE CONTEST**, *The Bonding Place*, P.O. Box 736, Dept. MG, Lake Hamilton, FL 32851. Annual writing and art contest for Christian home-schooled children up to age 18. Contest designed to encourage writing and to showcase the viability and successes of home-schooling.

General Info: Each year's contest has different themes, topics and regulations. Themes for 1991, 1992 and 1993 were: "Our Planet, His Creation," "God Bless America," "Focus on the Bible." See rules packets for guidelines, checklists, cover sheets and official entry forms. Permission statements for rights to the work must be granted by the contestant and a parent or legal guardian. Judges include many distinguished individuals who are promoters of the home education movement. Send two first-class stamps along with your name and address for rules. *Ask specifically for contest rules*. Rules are mailed out three months before contest deadline, which is usually mid-February.

Prizes: Vary from contest to contest, but are generous. Example: in 1991 more than $5,800 in cash and U.S. Savings Bonds (face value) were awarded to more than one hundred students. Bonds are awarded to winners in each age category for written work and artwork. Also pays $.02 per word for Editor's Choice selections. Winning works and Editor's Choice selections are published in a book each year. *All* contestants receive a certificate suitable for framing or for portfolio presentations.

Sponsor's Remarks: "Parent/teachers and children/students have made this contest a very enjoyable endeavor. It is an ideal adventure for home-schooling families as it gives the students an opportunity to show their work and have it seen by many people interested in home schooling. We send copies of the completed book to the White House and to key legislators. This is a chance to have your opinions heard. We are very interested in what you have to say. Previous years' books are not required reading, yet many find them very helpful in planning their entry."

Subscription Rates: Send for a free subscription to *Bonding Times* newsletter. The book *Our Planet, His Creation* sells for $6 (postage paid).

[**Author's note:** Note that only home-schooled students may enter this contest. See profile of contest coordinator Jill Bond on page 146.]

‡✓ **MARGUERITE DE ANGELI PRIZE**, Doubleday BFYR, 666 Fifth Ave., New York, NY 10103. Annual competition for books for middle-grade readers.

General Info: Open to U.S. and Canadian writers who have not published a novel for middle-grade readers. Submissions should consist of a fiction manuscript, suitable for readers ages 7-10, that concerns the diversity of the American experience, either contemporary or historical. Do *not* submit art with your manuscript unless you have illustrated the work yourself. If you do submit artwork, do not send the originals. If you submit a dummy, also submit the text separately using standard format. Manuscripts should be no shorter than forty typed pages and no more than ninety-six typed pages. Include a brief plot summary with your cover letter. Include a cover page listing the title and the author's name, address and phone. Title should also appear on each manuscript page. Authors may not submit more than two manuscripts; each must meet all eligibility requirements. Entries must be postmarked no earlier than April 1, and no later than June 30. Send SASE for rules. Contest results announced in October. Manuscripts sent to Doubleday may not be submitted to other publishers while under consideration for the prize.

Prizes: One Doubleday hardcover and Dell paperback book contract, including an advance and royalties. Award consists of a $1,500 cash prize and a $3,500 advance against royalties.

Sponsor's Remarks: "The prize is awarded annually to encourage the writing of fiction that examines the diversity of the American experience in the same spirit as the works of Marguerite de Angeli."

✓*$ **MERLYN'S PEN LITERARY MAGAZINE CONTEST AND CRITIQUE**, P.O. Box 910, East Greenwich, RI 02818. Contest for intermediate and high school literary magazines, sponsored by *Merlyn's Pen: The National Magazine of Student Writing*.

General Info: Separate divisions for high schools and middle schools compete for the Golden Pen Award, honoring the best overall entry. Three optional categories—Best Design, Best Writing, Best Art and Photography—to recognize specific outstanding aspects may also be entered. Judges evaluate the magazines with a comprehensive checklist and a 500-point rating scale. Each entry receives a personalized critique in which an experienced reviewer evaluates its strengths and weaknesses. Entry forms are included in the last two issues of *Merlyn's Pen* each school year. Note: Schools do *not* need to subscribe to enter. Entries need to be postmarked no later than June 30. Winners of awards are notified in mid-September and featured in *Merlyn's Pen* third issue of the school year. For an entry form and more information, send SASE or call (401) 885-5175. Minimum fee $50.

Prizes: Two recipients of the Golden Pen Award receive recognition in *Merlyn's Pen*, with pictures of each magazine's staff and advisor, and with selected pages from the magazine. Each of the recipients' schools also earns a Golden Pen trophy. Merlyn's Silver Award (450-500 points) and Merlyn's Bronze Award (400-449 points) also awarded. Winners of the special categories receive plaques.

Sponsor's Remarks: *"Merlyn's Pen: The National Magazine of Student Writing* is dedicated to recognizing and publishing the best in student writing and artwork. This contest is designed for school magazines that emphasize creative writing. Our judging includes a detailed critique of art and photography because they so often are a part of literary magazines. But this contest and critique is not appropriate for 'arts' magazines whose main focus is the visual arts."

Subscription Rates: For one year (four issues during school year) $18.95 each for one to ten subscriptions; $9.95 each for eleven to twenty subscriptions; $6.95 each for twenty-one or more subscriptions. Two-year individual subscriptions $29.95.

✔* MICHIGAN STUDENT FILM & VIDEO FESTIVAL, % Margaret Culver, Harrison High School, 29995 West 12

Mile Rd., Farmington Hills, MI 48334. Only event of its kind in the U.S. that showcases productions from children in grades K-12. Sponsored annually by Detroit Area Film & Television (DAFT), and funded by a number of individuals and organizations.

General Info: Festival is open to film and video work done by students who live in Michigan. Entries can be school projects or programs independently produced at home. Students compete in either the elementary, junior or senior levels, depending on their age. There is a special category for handicapped students, although they may choose to compete in their age bracket instead. Professional artists, educators, media professionals and interested community members serve as judges. Schools and other interested community organizations may borrow, free of charge, a copy of past Festival video tapes. Entries due in March.

Prizes: First Division medals and certificates are given to the best entries. In addition to "Best of Show" awards, a number of special awards and scholarships are sponsored. Clips of First Division winners are shown at the Festival, usually held in May. Selected winners appear on *WTVS Club Connect* and *WXYZ Winners Circle*. All entries receive some kind of reward. The event is juried, and students receive the judges' comments on evaluation forms that are returned with their entries.

Sponsor's Remarks: "Last year (1992), approximately three hundred entries from more than seventy sites in Michigan competed for awards, making it the biggest Festival of its twenty-three-year history. However, the Festival does not put a great emphasis on competition. Every entry is given an award. The major focus of the Festival is to positively reinforce student participation in film and video. Many Festival winners have gone on to receive great success in the film and video industry. The 1991 "Best Film" winner, ninth-grader Dan Scanlon, has been featured in *National Geographic WORLD*; "Best Video" winner in 1992, David Andora, has appeared on *America's Funniest Home Videos*. Doug Chiang, a past Festival winner, is an outstanding special effects master, whose feature film credits include *Switch, Ghost, Back to the Future 2 (and 3), Terminator 2*, and *The Doors*. Chen Rohwer was the youngest person to qualify as one of the ten finalists for the Mark Silverman/Robert Redford Sundance Institute Fellowship."

[**Author's note:** Many states offer similar contests.]

✔* **MY FAVORITE TEACHER**, 1530 7th St., Rock Island, IL 61201. Annual contest open to K-12 students, sponsored by *The Acorn* magazine.

General Info: No entry fee. Use up to 200 words to tell about your favorite teacher and what you think makes him or her special. One winner will be selected from each of the following grade categories: K-2, 3-5, 6-8, 9-12. Note your name, address and grade on the essay. Include your teacher's name and address with entry.

Prizes: Winning student and "favorite" teacher win a year's subscription to *The Acorn*. Winning entries will be published.

Subscription Rates: One year $10 (six issues: February, April, June, August, October, December).

‡✔ **NATION/I.F. STONE AWARD FOR STUDENT JOURNALISM**, % The Nation Institute, 72 Fifth Ave., New York, NY 10011. Annual award recognizes excellence in undergraduate college journalism.

General Info: Contest open to all undergraduates enrolled in any U.S. college. Articles may be submitted by the writers themselves or nominated by editors of student publications or faculty members. While entries originally published in student publications are preferred, all articles will be considered provided they were not written as part of a student's regular course work. This year, for example, all entries must have been written or published between June 30, 1992 and June 29, 1993. Each writer, editor or faculty member may submit up to three entries. A series of articles considered as a single entry. Investigative articles are particularly encouraged. No restrictions on scope, content or length. Call (212) 463-9270 for further information.

Prizes: The article that, in the opinion of the judges, represents the most outstanding example of student journalism in the tradition of I.F. Stone will be published in a fall issue of *The Nation*. Winner also receives cash award of $1,000.

Sponsor's Remarks: "Entries should exhibit the uniquely independent journalistic tradition of I.F. Stone. A self-described 'Jeffersonian Marxist,' Stone combined progressive politics, investigative zeal, and a compulsion to tell the truth with a commitment to human rights and the exposure of injustice. As Washington editor of *The Nation* magazine and founder of the legendary *I.F. Stone's Weekly*, he specialized in publishing information that was ignored by the mainstream media (which he often found in *The Congressional Record* and other public documents overlooked by the big-circulation dailies)."

✔* **NATIONAL GEOGRAPHIC WORLD**, 1145 17th and M St. NW, Washington, DC 20036-4688. Annual geography-related writing contest for students in grades K-9.

General Info: Contest details, format and deadlines are announced in *National Geographic WORLD* magazine. Contest always geography-related.

Prizes: A $5,000 college scholarship is awarded one winner in each of two age groups: K-5th grade; 6-9th grade. Each winner's current school is also awarded $5,000 worth of *National Geographic* educational products.

Sponsor's Remarks: "The mission of *National Geographic WORLD* is to inspire in young readers' curiosity about our world and beyond, and to encourage geographic awareness."

Subscription Rates: One year $12.95. Call (800) 638-4077 or (800) 548-9797 (TDD).

* **NATIONAL PEACE ESSAY CONTEST**, P.O. Box 27720, Central Station, Washington, DC 20038-7720. Sponsored by the United States Institute of Peace. Open to students in grades 9-12 in U.S., U.S. territories and U.S. overseas schools.

General Info: Students research and write a 1,500-word essay on a specified topic. New topic each year. Contest materials available free from the above address. *Do not send SASE.* Awards at both state and national level.

Prizes: National-level awards are for college scholarships in the following amounts: first place—$10,000; second place—$5,000; third place—$3,500. State-level awards are for college scholarships in the following amounts: first place—$500; second place—$250; third place—$100.

Sponsor's Remarks: "In the last five years, thousands of young people have taken part in the National Peace Essay Contest. More than six hundred of them have earned scholarship awards to college or university study. The contest challenges [young people] to learn about and express their views on some of the most important issues of our time."

* NATIONAL WRITTEN & ILLUSTRATED BY ... AWARDS CONTEST FOR STUDENTS, Landmark Editions, Inc., 1402 Kansas Ave., Kansas City, MO 64127. Annual book contest for students.

General Info: Original books may be entered in one of three age categories: 6-9, 10-13 and 14-19. Each book must be written and illustrated by the same student. Entry must be signed by parent/guardian and teacher. Home-schooled students may enter, but entry must be signed by a librarian or teacher other than a parent/guardian. Send a #10 SASE with $.58 postage for complete rules and guidelines.

Prizes: Winners receive all-expense-paid trips to Landmark's offices in Kansas City, where editors and art directors assist them in preparing their text and illustrations for the publication of their books. Winners also receive publishing contracts and are paid royalties.

Sponsor's Remarks: "Contest is sponsored to encourage and celebrate the creative efforts of students. Every year students nationwide submit more than seven thousand original book entries. Winning books are selected by a national panel of distinguished educators, editors, art directors, and noted authors and illustrators of juvenile books."

✔* NEW ERA WRITING, ART, PHOTOGRAPHY AND MUSIC CONTEST, 50 East North Temple St., Salt Lake City, UT 84150. Sponsored annually by *New Era Magazine*. Open to all English-speaking Latter-day Saints [Mormon youth] in good standing ages 12-23.

General Info: Separate categories for various types of writing (feature articles, poetry and short story), art (original designs, illustrations, paintings, drawings, prints, sculpture or crafts), photography, hymn writing, song writing, and a special category for arts entries that don't fit within another category (plays, computer games and programs, videos, instrumental music, etc.). Entrants desiring a scholarship (rather than cash award) must be in a position to accept a scholarship in the fall of the contest year. All work must be original and not previously published. Details and entry form appear in *New Era* (see September issue). Form must be completed and signed by a local church leader.

Prizes: Cash awards or scholarships to Brigham Young University, BYU Hawaii Campus or Ricks College. Nonwinning entries suitable for publication will be paid usual rates.

Sponsor's Remarks: "The editors of *New Era* will be the judges. Entries will be judged on originality, perceptivity, overall excellence and appropriateness for publication in *New Era*. All entries should reflect LDS values."

Subscription Rates: One year $8.

‡✔$ **NICOLL FELLOWSHIPS IN SCREENWRITING**, Academy of Motion Picture Arts & Sciences, 8949 Wilshire Blvd., Beverly Hills, CA 90211. Annual international screenwriting competition, open to new writers.

General Info: Writers who have not sold or optioned a story or screenplay for film or television are eligible. Writers must submit a completed application form, an original (non-collaborative) feature-length screenplay, and a $25 entry fee. Entries must be in standard screenplay format; 100 to 130 pages. Deadline May 1. Contest rules and application form available after January 1. Judges are looking for an intriguing, original story and exceptional craft.

Prizes: Up to five fellowships of $25,000 are awarded each year. The Academy acquires no rights to the work and does not participate in the marketing nor in any other aspect of the script's commercial future.

Sponsor's Remarks: "The purpose of the program is to foster the development of the art of screenwriting by providing financial support for up to five writers for one year. This award cannot be used to begin, continue or complete a formal education program. (In other words, this is not a scholarship program.) Since the program's inception in 1986, there have been thirty fellowship recipients, ranging in age from 22-61. Entrants' ages have ranged from 14-85. In 1992, there were 3,514 entrants."

[**Author's note:** Suitable only for older teen writers who have studied screenwriting. Be sure to *professionally* format your entry.]

NORTH AMERICAN INTERNATIONAL AUTO SHOW SHORT STORY CONTEST, Detroit Auto Dealers Association, 1800 W. Big Beaver Rd., Troy, MI 48084. Contest open to all Michigan residents.

General Info: All stories must be fictional and original, and may not have appeared in any publication prior to the annual NAI Auto Show held in January. There is no "theme" requirement. However, stories must be in good taste. Stories with a pornographic theme or obscene language will be immediately disqualified. Entries must be typed, double-spaced on 8½″ × 11″ paper. Length must not exceed 2,500 words. All stories must be in English. Each entry must be attached to a cover sheet containing the author's name, address and phone number. Author's name must appear on each page of the entry. Entry limit: two per person. Send SASE to above address to receive current competition rules and deadline (usually in November).

Prizes: Winners are announced during NAI Auto Show in January. Awards: first place — $1,000; second place — $500; third place — $250. Winning stories may be published in the Auto Show Program at the discretion of the Detroit Auto Dealers Association. All authors retain all rights to their work.

Sponsor's Remarks: "The contest is not open to Detroit Auto Dealers Association members, their families or family members of the judges. Entries will be judged by an independent panel of knowledgeable persons engaged in the literary field in some capacity."

[**Author's note:** In the past, this contest sponsored a separate category for high school students, but dropped it because so few entries were received. Students may still enter contest but compete on equal terms with other entrants who are likely to be older and more experienced. However, that doesn't automatically mean that they will also be more talented writers. So go ahead and enter if you think you've written a good story.]

✓$ NWC ARTICLES & ESSAYS CONTEST, National Writer's Club, 1450 S. Havana, Suite 620, Aurora, CO 80012. Annual contest open to all writers.

General Info: Any nonfiction article or essay is eligible provided it does not exceed 5,000 words. Submissions must be in standard typed format. You may enter as many manuscripts as you wish, but each must be accompanied by an entry form, $12 entry fee, and SASE with sufficient return postage. Note: Entries 5,000 to 10,000 words may be entered, however entry fee is $24. Judging will be based on originality, freshness of style, significance and marketability. Send SASE for details and entry form. Critique available for additional fee. Deadline January 31.

Prizes: First place—$200; second place—$100, third place—$50; fourth through tenth place—choice of books; eleventh through twentieth place—honorable mention certificate.

Sponsor's Remarks: "The purpose of this contest is to encourage writers in this creative form and to recognize those who excel in nonfiction writing."

[**Author's note:** Note that NWC contests *allow* writers to submit their manuscript entries to a publisher. If you do, you should tell the publisher so in a cover letter.]

✓$ NWC NOVEL CONTEST, National Writer's Club, 1450 S. Havana, Suite 620, Aurora, CO 80012. Annual contest open to all writers.

General Info: Any genre or category of novel manuscript may be entered. Only *unpublished, unbound* manuscripts eligible. Use standard typed format. English only. Maximum length 90,000 words; longer manuscripts may be submitted upon payment of an additional entry fee. Send appropriate SASE if you wish your manuscript returned. Entry fee for each novel $25. Contest opens February 1. All materials, complete with entry form and fees, must be postmarked no later than April 30. Entries may be submitted to publishers while contest is in progress. Top three entries offered to NWC's literary agents for consideration. Send SASE for complete details and entry form. Critiques are available for additional fee.

Prizes: First place—$500; second place—$250; third place—

$150; plus other awards for fourth through twentieth places.

Sponsor's Remarks: "Our purpose is to help develop creative skills, to recognize and reward outstanding ability, and to increase the opportunity for the marketing and subsequent publication of novel manuscripts."

✔$ NWC POETRY CONTEST, National Writer's Club, 1450 S. Havana, Suite 620, Aurora, CO 80012. Annual contest open to all writers.

General Info: All poems are eligible: lyric, ballad, free verse, experimental and traditional. Entry must be accompanied by entry fee, entry form and SASE. Your name and address must appear on the first page of your poems. Only unpublished poems are eligible. Authors retain all rights and may submit their entries to publishers while contest is in progress. Judging based on originality, technique, significance and emotional value. Entry fee for poems forty lines or less $8; see details regarding longer poems. Awards given in October. Send SASE for details and entry form. Critiques available for additional fee.

Prizes: First place—$100; second place—$50; third place—$25; fourth place—$15; other prizes awarded through twentieth place.

Sponsor's Remarks: "Our purpose is to encourage the writing of poetry, an important form of individual expression but with a limited commercial market."

✔$ NWC SHORT STORY CONTEST, National Writer's Club, 1450 S. Havana, Suite 620, Aurora, CO 80012. Annual contest open to all writers.

General Info: Any type of fiction is eligible provided it does not exceed 5,000 words. Enter as many manuscripts as you wish, but each must be accompanied by an entry form, $12 entry fee and SASE. Although only unpublished short stories are eligible, authors retain all rights and may submit their entries to publishers while contest is in progress. Short stories between 5,000 and 10,000 words may be entered for $24 fee. Judging based on originality, imagination, freshness of style, significance, emotional value and marketability. Send SASE for details and entry form. Critiques available for additional fee.

Prizes: First place—$200; second place—$100; third place—$50; plus other awards through twentieth place.

Sponsor's Remarks: "Our purpose is to encourage writers in this creative form and to recognize those who excel in short story writing."

* OPTIMIST INTERNATIONAL ESSAY CONTEST, 4494 Lindell Blvd., St. Louis, MO 63108. Annual contest sponsored by the Activities Department at Optimist International.

General Info: Essay contest is divided into three levels of competition: club, district and international. Contestants must prepare their own essay without assistance. Open to all sophomores, juniors and seniors during the academic year. A contestant is eligible for only one club contest during any given year. Previous district and international winners not eligible. Contact a local club or write to above address with SASE for annual topics and contest rules. Essays must be between 400 and 500 words. You must enter at club level; winners will automatically advance to next level.

Prizes: District winner will be given a first-place award and an expense-paid trip to a four-day seminar at the Freedoms Foundation in Pennsylvania. International winner receives a plaque along with an expense-paid trip for entrant and parents to the Optimist International Convention for an official reading of the winning essay. In addition, first-, second-, and third-place international winners receive $5,000, $3,000 and $2,000 scholarships.

[**Author's note:** Notice that you need to enter this contest *first* at the local level.]

* PAUL A. WITTY OUTSTANDING LITERATURE AWARD, % Cathy Collins, Ph.D., Professor of Education, Texas Christian University, P.O. Box 32925, Fort Worth, TX 76129. Sponsored by Special Interest Group, Reading for Gifted and Creative Students, International Reading Association.

General Info: Entries from elementary, junior high and high school are judged separately. Two categories: prose and poetry. Elementary prose limited to 1,000 words. Entries from secondary students must be typed and may exceed 1,000 words, if necessary. Set of five poems required. Entries judged on creativity, originality and beauty of expression. Entry blanks and more information sent to teachers for SASE.

Prizes: National awards, $25 and plaques; also certificates of merit.

Sponsor's Remarks: "Begun in 1979 to honor Dr. Paul Witty, between 500 and 1,000 entries are received yearly. Our goal is to encourage gifted writers and their teachers by recognizing and rewarding their achievements. We grant awards as deserved, from one to six in past years, although in two different years, no entry was deemed award-quality. From contact with winners, I learn that most of them write continuously and go to their portfolios to select entries."

✓*$ **THE PRISM AWARDS,** 390 Edgeley Blvd., Unit 16, Concord, ON L4K 3Z6, CANADA. Contest sponsored jointly by The Kids Netword, Scotiabank and Air Canada. The Kids Netword works directly with winners to produce professionally written and published books.

General Info: Restricted to Canadian children ages 7-14. Entry fee of $2 required. Stories must be between four and eighteen pages, and in one of the story categories listed on the official entry form. Entry form must be signed by the child and parent, attesting that the story is the original work of the child. The same story may not be submitted to The Prism Awards more than once. Children may submit one manuscript each year. Manuscripts cannot be co-authored but must be the original work of one child and not edited or changed by an adult. More than forty judges review manuscripts according to criteria that emphasize conceptual thinking. Judges appreciate manuscripts that are double-spaced. Official entry form is required; available in October. Strict January deadline. No late entries accepted.

Prizes: There is one winner in the 7-10 age group and one in the 11-14 age group for *each* story category. Winners receive a $500 cash award and an engraved crystal prism trophy. They also join The Kids Netword Training program, where they work with a team of professional editors and have the possibility of being published as part of The Kids Netword series of books. Child authors whose books are published receive royalties.

Sponsor's Remarks: "The best way to look at The Prism Awards program is to say it opens the door for 'original thoughts from enterprising young Canadian minds.' If you think you have something you'd like to write about, and you love to write, we encourage you to enter the program. Very few of The Prism Award winners ever thought they would win! We see it as a way for kids to share with other kids their talents, interests, wildest imaginings and innermost feelings."

Subscription Rates: Write to above address for the official entry form or fax your request to (416) 881-8703. Be sure to include your complete address.

[**Author's note:** Be sure to see the profile of Prism founder Lucy LaGrassa on page 157, and recent winners Duncan MacKay (page 115) and Natalka Roshak (page 118).]

* **PUBLISH-A-BOOK CONTEST,** Raintree/Steck-Vaughn, P.O. Box 27010, Austin, TX 78755. Yearly contest for children in grades 4-6 in the United States and Canada.

General Info: New contest theme announced each fall. Stories, 700-800 words in length, must relate to year's theme and be written by children in grades four, five or six. Each student must be sponsored by a teacher or a school or public librarian. Home-schooled children may enter but must be sponsored by a librarian or teacher other than a parent. All entries become the property of the publisher and will not be returned. Sponsors should submit children's stories in typed, double-spaced format. Illustrations not required. Cover sheet should include all information (name, address, grade level, school and telephone number) for both young author and sponsor. Judging criteria includes adherence to theme, potential for illustration, use of language. Rules (poster format) available free by mail, or call (800) 531-5015. Submission deadline January 31.

Prizes: Four grand-prize entries will be published in professionally illustrated, hardcover book form and become part of the current series bearing the contest name. Winners also receive a $500 advance against royalties, as well as ten copies of the book.

The sponsor named on each of the winning entries receives twenty free books from the Raintree/Steck-Vaughn Library catalog. Twenty honorable-mention young authors each receive $25; their sponsors receive ten free books.

Sponsor's Remarks: "Teachers and librarians may sponsor as many children as they wish in the PAB contest. We encourage teachers and librarians to use the contest as a classroom activity, or to encourage a young writer. A photo and biography of the author is given in the back of each of the winning entries. Authors are invited to dedicate their book to a special person in their life."

*$ QUILL AND SCROLL INTERNATIONAL WRITING/PHOTOGRAPHY CONTEST, Quill and Scroll, School of Journalism, University of Iowa, Iowa City, IA 52242-1528. Contest open to grades 7-12.

General Info: Competition open to all high school and junior high students. Each school may submit two entries in ten categories: editorial, editorial cartoon, investigative reporting (individual and team), news story, feature story, sports story, advertisement and photography (news feature and sports). Entries must have been published in school or professional paper. Entries must be tearsheet form. Two-dollar entry fee must accompany each entry. Contest rules are sent, in late December, to all schools on mailing list. Guidelines and entry form also appear in the December/January issue of *Quill and Scroll* magazine. If your school does not receive information about this contest, request information from the above address. Materials will be sent to the journalism advisor, principal or counselors at your school. See contest guidelines sheet for format and information for each category. Deadline February 5. Note: Senior national winners are automatically eligible for the Edward J. Nell Memorial Scholarship in Journalism.

Prizes: National winners will be notified by mail through their advisors and receive the Gold Key Award, and will be listed in April/May issue of *Quill and Scroll*. Senior winners intending to major in journalism at a college or university that offers a major in journalism are eligible for $500 scholarships. All winners are published in *Quill and Scroll*.

Sponsor's Remarks: "Currently enrolled high school and junior high students are invited to enter the National Writing/Photo Contest. Awards are made in each of the ten divisions."

Subscription Rates: One year $12.

*$ QUILL AND SCROLL YEARBOOK EXCELLENCE CONTEST, Quill and Scroll Society, School of Journalism, University of Iowa, Iowa City, IA 52242-1528.

General Info: Contest evaluates yearbook spreads in ten different categories and overall theme development. Photo categories must include original photo as well as yearbook spread. Contest open to students in grades 9-12. Students must attend a high school that is chartered by Quill and Scroll (more than 13,000 schools are chartered). Each school may submit two spreadsheet entries in each of the categories. These are: student life, academics, sports action photo, academic photo, feature photo, graphic and index. Only one entry may be submitted for the theme development division (twelve themes). Submit $2 entry fee for each division. Entry applications will be sent to each member school in late August. Request applications or membership information from the above address. Deadlines November 1.

Prizes: Winners receive a Gold Key Award and are eligible to apply for the Edward J. Nell scholarship during their senior year. Winners are published in *Quill and Scroll* magazine.

Subscription Rates: One year $12.

✔* READ, 245 Long Hill Rd., Middletown, CT 06457. Educational magazine that co-sponsors a variety of reading, writing and video-making contests throughout the year.

General Info: These contests upcoming for 1993-1994. Similar contests every year. See magazine issue indicated for details. Announced in issue #2, *LetterWriters Ink* pen-pal exchange program; deadline October 22, 1993. Students write letters, submit them to editorial office and, within two months, receive responses from students in a class somewhere in the U.S. Issue #3, *Ann Arlys Bowler Poetry Prize*; deadline December 10, 1993. Issue #3, *Annual Writing and Art Awards*; writing categories include short fiction, nonfiction and dramatic parody; art limited to black-and-white illustrations, paintings and photos; deadline January 7, 1994. Issue

#5, *Books Change Lives*; students write letters to the authors of a book that changed their way of thinking about some issue; co-sponsored by the Center for the Book at the Library of Congress; deadline January 21, 1994. Issue #7, *Video Voyages*; students get their chance to write, direct and produce their own class videos; co-sponsored by The Panasonic Company; deadline March 25, 1994.

Prizes: Not indicated.

[**Author's note:** Entry in these contests may be limited to *READ* readers.]

✓* **SPARK!**, 1507 Dana Ave., Cincinnati, OH 45207. Full-color magazine devoted to nurturing creativity, literary and artistic growth in children ages 6-12.

General Info: Sponsors periodic art and writing contests for children. Check each issue for possibilities.

Subscription Rates: One year (nine issues) $21.95. Send check or money order to *SPARK!*, P.O. Box 5028, Harlan, IA 51593-4528.

*$ **TAWC SPRING WRITING CONTEST**, P.O. Box 27, Sandusky, MI 48471. Sponsored by the Thumb Area Writer's Club, for amateur writers in Michigan.

General Info: You must be an amateur writer residing in Michigan to enter. For this contest, amateur means (1) one who is not currently employed as a writer in the category that he/she enters; and (2) one who has not sold a book or published more than three articles, poems or short stories in a paying market in the category entered. Each entrant may submit work in all three categories: short stories (1,500 words maximum), nonfiction (1,000 words maximum), poetry (32 lines maximum). You may submit up to three manuscripts in each category. Cost is $2 per each manuscript entered. Entries must be typed and follow standard format. Rules and deadlines available for SASE. Include SASE with entry for return of manuscript.

Prizes: The number of entries will determine the amount of the awards. Typical prizes are: $15 first-place, $10 second-place, $5 third-place, plus several honorable mentions. Winning entries may be published in TAWC newsletter, *Thumbprints*.

Sponsor's Remarks: "In the past, several of our place winners and honorable mention winners have been teens."

Subscription Rates: One year for nonmember $9. Single issue of *Thumbprints* $.75.

[**Author's note:** You *must* be a resident of Michigan to enter this contest.]

* TEEN POWER STORY AND POETRY CONTESTS, P.O. Box 632, Glen Ellyn, IL 60138. Sponsored by *Teen Power*, a Sunday School take-home paper published quarterly. Open to 12-16-year-olds.

General Info: True stories and poems must have a clear, evangelical Christian theme. Stories should be between 600 and 1,000 words. Send SASE for contest guidelines. Annual deadlines: True Story—May 31; Poetry—first Friday in January.

Prizes: True story winners receive: first-place—$100; second-place—$75; third-place—$50. Winning entries published in September quarter. Poetry winners receive: first-place—$50; second-place—$40; third-place—$30. Winning entries published in March quarter.

Sponsor's Remarks: "We are looking for personal experience stories of how teens have seen God work in their own lives. Poems should reflect a teen's relationship with God."

Subscription Rates: One year $7.50. Slightly higher in Canada.

[**Author's note:** Good opportunity for Christian teens who enjoy writing.]

* TIME EDUCATION PROGRAM—STUDENT WRITING COMPETITION FOR COLLEGE STUDENTS, P.O. Box 1000, Mount Kisco, NY 10549. Open to all college students in the U.S. and Canada.

General Info: Annual essay competition, theme changes yearly. For current rules and an entry form, see your teacher or send SASE.

Prizes: Grand prize a $5,000 college scholarship.

Sponsor's Remarks: "The aims of this competition are reflective of *Time* magazine's basic mission—to communicate ideas and information with intelligence, style and meaning. Express yourself in writing, relying on creativity, reason, observation, research, originality and style."

* TIME EDUCATION PROGRAM—WRITING & ART COMPETITION FOR HIGH SCHOOL STUDENTS, P.O. Box 1000, Mount Kisco, NY 10549. Open to all high school students in the U.S. and Canada.

General Info: Annual writing and art contest with prizes ranging from $500 to $5,000. For current rules and entry form, send an SASE.

Prizes: In 1993, prize monies awarded as college scholarships.

Sponsor's Remarks: "In sponsoring this contest, the *Time* Education Program seeks to (1) encourage students to take an interest in written and visual expression, (2) motivate student interest in contemporary issues and current events, (3) provide an opportunity for students to apply their writing and art skills, and (4) give recognition to students who demonstrate skills in written and visual expression."

✔* VI OLSEN—IF I RAN THE WORLD CONTEST, 1530 7th St., Rock Island, IL 61201. Sponsored annually by *The Acorn* magazine.

General Info: Winners in each of four grade categories: K-2, 3-5, 6-8 and 9-12. Word limit 200. Entries must include student's name, address and grade, plus teacher's name and school address. Always include SASE with entry. Deadline February 1 each year.

Prizes: One winner selected and published from each grade category. Winners receive a free one-year subscription to *The Acorn* for themselves and their classroom.

Sponsor's Remarks: "The contests are a chance to express just how young authors feel about world situations, and how they would improve conditions. [It's] also a chance to say thank-you to that special teacher. As always, just be yourself when writing."

Subscription Rates: One year $10 (six issues: February, April, June, August, October, December).

✔* **"WE ARE WRITERS, TOO!"** Brigitta Geltrich, CWW Publications, P.O. Box 223226, Carmel, CA 93922. Annual contest for young writers sponsored by *Creative With Words*.

General Info: Entries must be original writing and cannot have been edited by someone else. Child must include age and SASE with entry.

Prizes: Best one hundred manuscripts will be published. Best three manuscripts will be nominated to "Pushcart."

Sponsor's Remarks: "Know your topic, proofread your writing. Experiment meaningfully with the English language and tell your story in poetry form or prose from a new perspective. Most of all, have fun!"

Subscription Rates: No longer takes subscriptions.

‡✔$ **WELLSPRING SHORT FICTION CONTEST,** 770g Tonkawa Rd., Long Lake, MN 55356.

General Info: Submit one double-spaced typed entry, 2,000 words maximum. No limit on entries but *each* story must be accompanied by a $5 entry fee. Entries judged on intriguing, well-crafted work. Do not staple or fold entries. Annual deadlines: January 1 and July 1. Entries received after deadline will be judged for subsequent issue. Sample copies of *Wellspring Magazine* available for $5.50. Manuscripts are not returned.

Prizes: Awards of $100, $75, $25, plus publication in *Wellspring Magazine*.

Sponsor's Remarks: "Nominee for Writer's Digest's Fiction Fifty List."

Subscription Rates: For two issues $8. For four issues $15.

[**Author's note:** Suitable for mature teens. It would be best to study past issues.]

✔*$ **WRITER'S EXCHANGE POETRY CONTEST,** P.O. Box 394, Society Hill, SC 29593. Ongoing contest sponsored throughout the year by the *Writer's Exchange* newsletter.

General Info: Poems of all styles (traditional, free verse, rhyme, haiku and other forms) may be entered. All subjects and themes (family relationships, friendship, nature, inspirational, thought-provoking issues, humor, etc.) are welcome. Poems are judged by the editor (Gene Boone) on originality and presentation of idea, as well as on technique and overall effect. Poems must not be longer than 24 lines. Entries must be in standard manuscript format with poet's name and address in upper left-hand corner. Entries will not be returned. Entry fee $1. Enclose SASE for guidelines and with entry to receive winners' list. Deadline is open; poems are gathered and winners published in the issue that goes to press at the date closest to which poems were received. Late entries are not disqualified. All entrants receive a complimentary copy of the *Writer's Exchange* newsletter.

Prizes: Poet whose poem is judged best overall will receive 50 percent of contest proceeds (the amount is usually $25 or more). Second and third place, as well as five honorable mentions, receive surprise gifts — usually a book or other award of interest to poets. Winning poem and two runners-up published in *Writer's Exchange*.

Sponsor's Remarks: "Our mission is to encourage new poets, with an emphasis on poets who are just beginning and those who are seeking publication. Poets of all ages may enter poems in our contests."

Subscription Rates: One year (four issues) $8. Sample copy $2.

✔*$ WRITERS' INK ROUNDTABLE, GEnie page 440.

An electronic association of writers. No extra charge to join or take part in WINK, just basic GEnie subscriber fee.

General Info: Sponsors frequent online writing contests. Information available online.

Prizes: Includes free flagging, books and other prizes.

Sponsor's Remarks: "Writers' Ink RoundTable is *the* place for online writers to be!"

Subscription Rates: Call (800) 638-9636.

✔ WRITERS' OPEN FORUM ANNUAL CONTEST,

P.O. Box 516, Tracyton, WA 98393. Publication bringing writers together to exchange ideas and improve their skills and marketability as writers.

General Info: Send SASE after March 1 to receive annual contest information.

Subscription Rates: One year (six issues) $14; $24 in U.S. funds for foreign destinations.

✔* **WRITING CONTESTS**, The Writing Conference, Inc., P.O. Box 664, Ottawa, KS 66067. Contests sponsored by The Writing Conference, a nonprofit organization that provides services to any children, young adults and teachers interested in reading and writing.

General Info: Students in grades 3-12 are invited to submit poetry, narration or exposition on selected topics each year. Send SASE in August for yearly topics and guidelines. Deadline in January. Sample copy available upon request.

Prizes: Winners in each category receive plaques. In addition, winning entries are published in *The Writers' Slate*. First-place winners, their parents and their teachers are guests at the Saturday luncheon of the Annual Conference on Writing and Literature, held every spring in Kansas City.

Sponsor's Remarks: "The goal is the improvement of writing and reading skills of young people."

Subscription Rates: One year (three issues) for students $6; for teachers and other adults $8.95.

* **WYOMING VALLEY POETRY SOCIETY**, % Beatrice Romanowski, 62 Longdale Ave., Shavertown, PA 18707. Contest sponsored by WVPS for students grades 1-12.

General Info: Held annually in conjunction with the Fine Arts Fiesta in Wilkes-Barre, Pennsylvania, in May. Open to students in local area (northeastern Pennsylvania, primarily in Luzerne County). Contest details, including deadlines, listed in local newspapers each year, and are available at local libraries and from English teachers. Students participate with others in their grade range: Grades 1-3; 4-6; 7-9; or 10-12.

Prizes: Certificates presented for first-place, second-place, third-place and honorable mentions in each of the grade ranges. Students read their winning entries on the stage in the public square, Wilkes-Barre, on the last day of the Fiesta.

Sponsor's Remarks: "Some of the children have participated in the contest on a yearly basis. A number of English teachers are also involved in the contest by having their students write poems, and these in turn are submitted to the contest judge."

Subscription Rates: There is no Wyoming Valley Poetry Society publication.

[**Author's note:** This contest is for Wyoming Valley, Pennsylvania, students.]

* **YOUNG PLAYWRIGHTS PROGRAM,** Very Special Arts, Education Office, The John F. Kennedy Center for the Performing Arts, Washington, DC 20566. International organization dedicated to enriching the lives of children, youth and adults with disabilities; creates opportunities for disabled and non-disabled people to celebrate and share accomplishments in drama, dance, music, literature and visual arts.

General Info: Seeks plays, written by students between the ages of 12-18, featuring some aspect of disability. Students may write from their own experience or about other people's experiences. Students are encouraged to investigate the topic. Send three typed copies of the script. Also include author's name, date of birth, telephone number, and a 250-word biographical description. If there is more than one author per script, include full information for each. Write for detailed brochure and current deadline.

Prizes: The winning young playwright and a chaperone will travel to Washington, DC, at the expense of Very Special Arts to participate in rehearsals and be an honored guest at the premiere production. If the winning script is written by multiple authors, VSA will assist with financial support for the trip.

Sponsor's Remarks: "Although the play must address or otherwise incorporate some aspect of disability, the choice of theme, setting and style is up to you. Sometimes people who aren't familiar with the theater want to first try play writing with friends. If working in a group would help you, that's fine with us, as long as all the playwrights are between the ages of 12-18."

[**Author's note:** Be sure to see the profile of 1992 winner Beth Lewis on page 124 and more information about VSA on page 164.]

* **YOUNG PUBLISH-A-BOOK CONTEST,** Raintree/ Steck-Vaughn, P.O. Box 27010, Austin, TX 78755. Yearly contest for children in grades 2-3 in the United States and Canada.

General Info: New theme announced each fall. Stories, 300-500 words in length, must relate to year's theme and be written by children in grades 2-3. Each student must be sponsored by a teacher or school or public librarian. Home-schooled children may enter but must be sponsored by a librarian or teacher other than a parent. All entries become the property of the publisher and will not be returned. Sponsors should submit children's stories in typed, double-spaced format. Illustrations not required. Cover sheet should include all information (name, address, grade level, school and telephone number) for both young author and sponsor. Judging criteria include adherence to theme, potential for illustration, use of language, etc. Write or call (800) 531-5015 for rules (poster format). Deadline January 31.

Prizes: One grand prize-winning entry will be published in professionally illustrated, hardcover book form and become part of the current series bearing the contest name. Winners also receive a $500 advance against royalties, as well as ten copies of their published book. The sponsor named on each of the winning entries receives twenty free books from the Raintree/Steck-Vaughn Library catalog. Ten honorable mention young authors each receive $25; their sponsors receive ten free books.

Sponsor's Remarks: "Teachers and librarians may sponsor as many children as they wish in the PAB contest. We encourage teachers and librarians to use the contest as a classroom activity, or to encourage a young writer. A photo and biography of the author is given in the back of each of the winning entries. Authors are invited to dedicate their book to a special person in their life."

✓*$ YOUNG SALVATIONIST MAGAZINE – CONTEST, % Captain Lesa Salyer, P.O. Box 269, Alexandria, VA 22313. Published monthly except summer for high school/early college-aged youth by The Salvation Army.

General Info: Open only to young members of The Salvation Army under the age of 23. Send SASE to above address for details.

Subscription Rates: One year $4 (U.S. currency).

Sandy Asher Talks About Writing Plays

Because I know next to nothing about play and script writing, I have asked Sandy Asher, writer-in-residence at Drury College, in Springfield, Missouri, and an award-winning children's book writer and playwright, to share some tips and resources. Here are her comments:

First and foremost, young playwrights should get involved with theater groups at school and in the community. The theater presents challenges and limitations that you simply have to experience to understand! It's not necessary to perform. Playwrights need to know how things work backstage, too! Any job that allows you to watch and become involved in rehearsals and performances will give you a feel for what does and doesn't work well in the theater.

Second, attend plays and read plays as often as you can. For junior and senior high students, I especially recommend the Dell series of plays from the Young Playwrights Festival sponsored by the Dramatists Guild. Two titles I have on hand are *Sparks in the Park* and *Hey Little Walker.* Third, read Carol Korty's excellent book *Writing Your Own Plays: Creating, Adapting, Improvising.* Another good sourcebook is *Putting on a Play: A Guide to Writing and Producing Neighborhood Drama* by Susan and Stephen Judy (sometimes spelled Tchudi).

The Playwright's Companion (updated each year) is the best marketing guide I've found and lists many contests, workshops, and other opportunities for young playwrights, but you have to read all the entries carefully to ferret out those meant for young people. It's worth the trouble, though, because competing with adults in contests such as the one we sponsor at Drury College will generally result in disappointment. We received more than five hundred submissions this year [1993]! The competition is very stiff, so increase your odds by sticking with programs meant for your age group.

The Playwright's Companion also lists publishers from whom you can order catalogues and plays to read. I particularly recommend a look at Anchorage Press; Baker's Plays (which sponsors a high school playwriting contest); Dramatists Publishing Company; New Plays, Inc.; Pioneer Drama Service and Samuel French. *The Playwright's Companion* is available from Feedback Theatrebooks, 305 Madison Ave., Suite 1146, New York, NY 10165.

Many of the play publishers' catalogues also contain books of interest to teachers working with young playwrights, as does the Heinemann/Boynton-Cook catalogue. Organizations of interest to teachers include International Association of Theater for Children and Young People, or ASSITEJ/USA (contact Amie Brockway, The Open Eye: New Stagings, 270 West 89th St., New York, NY 10024) and the American Alliance for Theater and Education (Theater Department, Arizona State University, Temple, AZ 85287-3411.)

Plays need to be read aloud by actors and produced in informal workshop situations — often several times — before they're ready to win contests or be published. There's only so much you can do on your own. Those special problems and possibilities of the stage need to be dealt with "on the hoof" — with live actors and an audience interested in helping to develop works-in-progress. Again, school and community theater groups provide the best opportunities for getting your plays read aloud by actors, gathering reactions from supportive audiences, learning, experimenting and polishing your work. Many theaters, especially family theaters such as The Coterie in Kansas City and The Kennedy Center in Washington, D.C., conduct play writing workshops for young people. Ask around! If your local theater group doesn't have a play writing workshop, maybe you can help start one!

Hope I've been helpful.

Sandy Asher
Writer-in Residence
Drury College
February 1, 1992

Ms. Asher's latest plays are *A Woman Called Truth* and *The Wise Men of Chelm* (both published by Dramatic Publishing Company), and her next book-to-be is *Out Of Here: A Senior Class Yearbook* (Dutton/Lodestar, July 1993).

Real-Time Conference With Michael Crichton

The transcript that follows is part of a real-time conference (RTC) hosted by the Writers' Ink RoundTable on GEnie[1] in 1992. It is reprinted here by permission of Jack D. Smith, head SYSOP of the Writers' Ink RoundTable. A copy of the complete transcript, plus others of interest to writers, are available in the Writers' Ink RoundTable library. You may download the full transcript plus any other library files and read them for your own enjoyment. However, you may not make copies (on paper or computer disk form) to give to other people, nor reprint it in other publications without written permission from Jack D. Smith.

One of the biggest advantages of having access to a bulletin board service (BBS) or computer information service is that you can attend online conferences and workshops on practically every topic imaginable for a fraction of what it would cost to attend a similar conference in person. This is an especially good benefit for young people who normally could not attend conferences held in or outside their area.

If you've never been online or dropped in on an RTC, the format will seem strange at first. This is because you are seeing people "talk" online using a computer and modem. Each person who enters the conference sees the same information on their own monitor. During a live conference, messages would appear one at a time in the order the host computer (at GEnie in this case) receives them. As the monitor screen fills up, messages scroll up and new

---

[1]GEnie is an online information service accessed via personal computer and a modem. GEnie is a registered trademark that stands for: General Electric Network for Information Exchange.

ones appear at the bottom. Using their software's "chat" mode, members compose their messages (normally displayed on the bottom three lines of their own screen), but they do not appear on other people's screens until the member presses the ENTER key. Private messages between members, similar to friends whispering at a real conference, may also be sent.

In this transcript, the GEnie mail address of the person speaking appears in capital letters between the arrows ‹ › at the start of each message. If they use an online nickname, it also appears. During the formal portion of the conference, members type "ga" or "GA" when they have finished speaking so the moderator or guest speaker can answer. If they need to ENTER a message in two or more parts, they will often end a line with three dots (. . .) to indicate they have more to say.

As each person enters the conference area, the system automatically announces them. For example, see line 10, which shows that the guest speaker, author Michael Crichton has arrived for the conference.

A couple last notes: A full line of dots indicates that I have edited out a large portion of the text. These were either redundant remarks (how many people do you need to see welcome Mr. Crichton to the roundtable?), or of little interest to readers of this book. A series of three dots indicates where only a few messages were cut. Otherwise, it appears exactly as it would on your screen— complete with misspelling, improper punctuation, etc.

‹JESSIEBELLE› was the moderator for this conference. When a member sends the command /RAI (the electronic equivalent of raising a hand to ask a question) it appears on Jessiebelle's screen, where she will keep track of who is waiting in line to ask a question. The address ‹[Jack] WRITERS.INK› is that of Jack D. Smith, head SYSOP. Altogether more than twenty people attended this conference. The message "Room is now listen only," on line 25, tells members that the conference is about to start, and that they should only "talk" when Jessiebelle calls on them. (You'll see what I mean in a moment).

One of the strangest things to get used to during an RTC is that everything is so *quiet*. It's sort of like watching television with the sound off. But at least during the conference everyone can hear the speaker, no matter where they're sitting! And once you start reading a transcript, it's not hard to visualize a roomful of people.

It's about time for the conference to start. But first, let's listen in on the folks who arrived early:

<[Alyssa] A.MONDELLI1> Okay folks, informal poll before we have to shut up.What's your favorite Crichton book?
<[UCSD alum] BARB.DENZ> Andromeda
<[Jonathan] J.FRIEMAN> Travels
<[Alyssa] A.MONDELLI1> Mine's "The Terminal Man".
<DIANNE.SMITH> Jurassic Park
<[Patt] RSINCLAIR> Andromida
<[Ed] E.WILLIAMS24] Eater's of the Dead
<[Tony] THE.ZIPPER> Jurrasic Park   Train Robbery
....
**<CRICHTON> is here.
<[Tony] A.ROSARIO4> yeah!
<[Alyssa] A.MONDELLI1> Hello, Mr. Crichton!
<[Jack] WRITERS.INK> Right on time! Greetings Michael
<JESSIEBELLE> We'll be starting in about three minutes.
<CRICHTON> I'm delighted and looking forward to this.
<[Jack] WRITERS.INK> Michael . . . we just had a discussion about which book of yours was the favorite . . . I think Jurassic Park won . . . though they all seemed to get votes.
<CRICHTON> People seem to like the more recent books. Fact of technological life I guess
....
<JESSIEBELLE> Okay, everyone just about ready? :)
<[Jack] WRITERS.INK> All set here!
<R.GURGANIOUS> Ready !
<JESSIEBELLE> Here we go . . .
Room is now listen-only.

Please welcome MICHAEL CRICHTON, author of _The Andromeda Strain_, _The Great Train Robbery_, _Congo_, _Jurassic Park_, and the newly released novel about the United States and Japan, _Rising Sun._

1. Type /RAI to get in line to ask a question. You'll be called on

in turn.

2. You're allowed one question with a follow-up.

3. You can get back in line, but folks who have not asked a question go first

4. To save time, you can type your question after raising your hand, and simply hit return when you see the message that you can talk.

5. Type (GA) at the end of your question, so that Mr. Crichton will know that you have finished, and he may begin his answer.

You may /RAIse your hand now to get in line.

We will begin the RTC momentarily!
....

‹JESSIEBELLE› Barb, you're first!

‹BARB.DENZ› Michael—I met you when you were at Salk. Do you regret leaving medicine to write?

‹CRICHTON› Hi Barbara. Nice to hear from you. No, actually, I don't regret leaving medicine, although it may be just a feature of personality . . . I don't seem to regret things as a rule. ga

‹JESSIEBELLE› Follow up, Barb?

‹BARB.DENZ› not for now. I'll be back

‹[Nancy] D.SARTOR› Do you find authoring lonely? Can you stay connected to the "real" world and be an author? (ga)

‹CRICHTON› I find it very weird when I am intensively writing. It's quite like directing---sort of 'missing time' phenomenon. You lose a month, or a season, because you are working. As for staying connected to the real world, that's a problem for me in any case..ga

‹JESSIEBELLE› Follow up, Nancy?
....

‹JESSIEBELLE› I can't wait to see this! Alyssa, you're up next

. . .

‹[Alyssa] A.MONDELLI1› Michael, where did you get the idea for Terminal Man? And how much of what you wrote was based on the known facts about psychomotor epilepsy? I don't have a copy on hand, but I seem to recall that in the postscript you apologized for taking literary license with certain aspects. (ga)

‹CRICHTON› Interesting. It was based on a real case, and the ideas about psychomotor epilepsy came from some research of that

(1970s) era. It proved wrong.

‹CRICHTON› I have recently revised the book to eliminate any reference to psychomotor epilepsy, and have also removed the apology. The story doesn't need it, anyway. Ballantine will publish the new version in December. GA

···

‹[Dan] D.PEREZ1› . . . Could you tell us a little about your daily writing routine? GA

‹CRICHTON› I work early. I get up between 5 and 6, and drive to an office 2 miles away. And then I go to work. In the dark. Nothing else to do. And I work until about noon

‹CRICHTON› When I am pretty much finished for the day. I have lunch, come back and do a little fussing. But nothing serious.

‹CRICHTON› What happens is that as work continues, I get up earlier and earlier. It's 5 . . . then 4 . . . then 3 . . . Eventually I am staggering out of bed at 2 AM

‹CRICHTON› And going to work. And I can't continue that pace for long. I work 7 days a week until my family rebels. Then I take a day off.

‹CRICHTON› And in this intense way, it usually takes me about 4-6 weeks to do a draft. Then I have to stop and sleep. Preferably go away for a while.

‹CRICHTON› Interestingly (to me) all my drafts (I graph them) look pretty much the same in terms of how they go. Early false starts . . . then it catches . . . then . . . boom! To the end. GA

···

‹JESSIEBELLE› Thanks, Michael. How are your fingers holding up?:)

‹CRICHTON› I'm fine. I type for a living. GA

‹JESSIEBELLE› Great! Mike's next . . .

‹[Mike] M.LAWSON4› Michael - My fiancee, Laura, is a Geology Grad student at UCincinnati, and she wants to know how you did your research for Jurassic Park?

‹CRICHTON› My research methods are sort of odd. I track subjects of interest to me, over a period of years. I have been following ideas about genetic-engineered dinos for almost 10 years.

‹CRICHTON› And finally I got a book. What this means is that I have a mass of clippings and notes and conversations when I sit down to write, an accumulated . . . mess . . .

⟨CRICHTON⟩ So I don't do much research while I am writing. But it also means I don't know why I know things. After I finish a book, I have to check it as if somebody else wrote it . . . GA

⟨[Ryan] FORTY-TWO⟩ Who was your major influences as a director? Robert Wise? Blake Edwards? Did you get to hang around the sets of those movies? /ga/

⟨CRICHTON⟩ My major influence was Hitchcock, whom I met only once. When I was learning to direct, I went to observe Arthur Penn (good with actors) and Steven Spielberg (good with camera). That was about 1971. GA

⟨JESSIEBELLE⟩ Barb's up next!

⟨BARB.DENZ⟩ You have always been one step ahead of technology — putting "known/possible" together with "what if" [much like Jules verne, I might add ⟨g⟩]. Where do you see technology going next? And where are you TAKING technology next? GA

⟨CRICHTON⟩ What a question! Actually, I think it is getting harder to write about technology and stay ahead of it. While I was doing CONGO, research kept catching up with me.

⟨CRICHTON⟩ I had a chapter about light-computers (computers using light not electricity) and then there was an article in Sci Am when I was about to go into galleys and I had to change my MS

⟨CRICHTON⟩ because it would look like plagiarism. Nobody would ever believe I had made it up. And when the book was published, I went to a conference ofremote sensing people.

⟨CRICHTON⟩ And they showed me all these tiny navigation devices (then about the size of a backpack, now about the size of a cellular phone) and I kept saying, "Wow! It really exists!"

⟨CRICHTON⟩ The people who invited me to the conference were annoyed. They thought I had done all this reesearch. But I actually just figured it must be happening, or about to happen. I had no precise knowledge. GA

⟨JESSIEBELLE⟩ Follow up, Barb?

⟨BARB.DENZ⟩ . . . How do you decide when enough research is enough and GO. AND stay one step ahead of life. ⟨g⟩ GA

⟨CRICHTON⟩ I don't know. At some point the book "clicks" and I can do it. Sometimes, I track ideas for decades and nothing ever comes of it. (Or at least, not yet.) GA

‹[Ed W] E.WILLIAMS24› Still on the process, earlier you said you "graph them," meaning, I assume, yopur novels-in progress. Tell us something of that.

‹CRICHTON› One of the problems in a longish task is it's hard to stay oriented to the goal. If I begin on page 244 and end on page 249 on a given day, was it a good day, or not?

‹CRICHTON› Many writers are troubled by a feeling of getting lost in the process, and feeling a lack of feedback or reward during this long time. So I disocvered that I could graph my day's output (in the old days with MockChart, later with Works)

‹CRICHTON› And my reward was a dot on the graph. It had several advantages. It made the work "visible" and it allowed me to play a game with myself. I always begin by just working for a few days.

‹CRICHTON› To see how the book is going. Then after a week or so, I see I am getting a certain page count. Maybe it's 3 a day, or 5 a day. So whatever I am getting, I try to push it.

‹CRICHTON› Try to get it up from 5 to 5.5, and then to 6 . . . I find it a useful way to work, since the actual activity of writing is painful to me. So if I can get it done faster, great.

‹CRICHTON› But the result is that I have all these graphs, now. Which means I can COMPARE how I am doing now to how I did then.

‹CRICHTON› The other thing I do is I keep a diary daily. A very short entry (also on the computer.) It is very valuable for many reasons, but especially about writing.

‹CRICHTON› Sometimes when it isn't going well, I look back at JP or SPHERE, and read my diary . . . and see all these expressions of doubt, and discouragement. it isn't working.

‹CRICHTON› I will NEVER finish. All that stuff. Then I feel better about my current difficulties. GA

‹JESSIEBELLE› If you have NOT had a chance to ask a question, and would like to, please type /RAI now. R.GURGANIOUS is next . . .

‹R.GURGANIOUS› Hi Michal, Do you act out your characters dialogue verbally?

‹CRICHTON› Yes. And I physicalize. Walk around the room. All that. I am reminded that when I directed Sean Connery in THE

GREAT TRAIN ROBBERY, he used to want to go with me to some room, and he'd play all the parts in a scene.

<CRICHTON> Womens' parts, everything. (Sean is a great mimic.) And we'd lay it out. But when I am at home, I absolutely act out.

<CRICHTON> One day my secretary came in about 10 and saw me sitting at the typewriter jerking my head. She thought I was having a seizure. Actually

<CRICHTON> I was just a raptor trying to chew Lex's shoe. Snapping and snarling. I had a stiff neck for weeks on that book. GA

....

<[Ed] E.ABLON> You mentioned that you write a first draft in between 1-2 (HARD) months. I'm curious as to how much you know about your planned novel when you first start and how much you need to work out. GA.

<CRICHTON> It's interesting to me that I plan quite a lot, I have a fairly good outline, maybe some scenes written out here and there . . . I have a strong sense of how the book should be.

<CRICHTON> But ALWAYS when I start writing, two things happen. First, I never look at this outline. (So why do I make it in the first place? Beats me.)

<CRICHTON> And second, I ALWAYS hit some problem. In RIS- ING SUN, I intended for the detective to be the narrator. But when I started, it was impossible, I needed a Watson for Holmes.

<CRICHTON> I was unhappy with that, but it was necessary, so I did it. But it leaves me with a funny feeling. Despite all the planning, there is always a sense of not knowing what will happen when I start working. . . . . .

<CRICHTON> I can tell you a little of what this is like. It's like driving in a strange city and trying to find the center of town. You can see the glow of the city center above the buildings, and you can work your way there.

<CRICHTON> With a few false starts. But you don't actually ever know where you are at any particular time.

....

<[Jeff] J.GRAEBNER> I see that you have "adapted by" credit on JURASSIC PARK. How much input did you have into the screenplay and how close is it to the novel? (ga)

⟨CRICHTON⟩ I never wanted to do a script. Steven asked me to; he said they needed to get the story cut down to size fast (this was 2 years ago) so they could begin to budget.

⟨CRICHTON⟩ So I said I could cut the thing down and give him a basic shape, and then he could get somebody else to polish because I was sick of dinos. And that is what we did.

⟨CRICHTON⟩ My original structure is largely retained. He then went to another writer, who did a draft that tampered with the structure and that person was quickly in dino poop.

⟨CRICHTON⟩ A third writer kept the structure and rather beautifully worked on the characters. I think the present script is terrific. I imagine it is what I would have done, had I continued to work on it.

⟨CRICHTON⟩ So I have a very good feeling about this picture. GA

⟨J.CHIN9⟩ Any advice for a begining writer? GA yep

⟨CRICHTON⟩ Yes. I have the traditional advice. If you can do ANYTHING else, then do that. Writing can be rewarding but it is a very difficult work. (For example it is MUCH harder than directing.)

⟨CRICHTON⟩ And second, if you want to write, write. Write a LOT. I think in the end that writing is a craft, something like woodcarving. You get good at it by doing it. So you have to do it a lot.

⟨CRICHTON⟩ Also, by doing it a lot, you will find out if you have the temperament for it. Not everybody does. GA

⟨[Robin] SFRT.GUEST⟩ Fascinating stuff about graphing your progress and keeping your journal. Along those lines, could you be a little more specific about your "graph"? How's it setup? GA

⟨CRICHTON⟩ Well, it's just a spreadsheet. It's idiot simple. At one point I wanted to do something and I called Microsoft tech help for what I wanted to do, and they laughed at me.

⟨CRICHTON⟩ Because I was using the spreadsheet in Works. They wanted me on Excel, as befits my fame, I guess. But I have no interest in knowing all about spreadsheets, I just want a simple graph of days and pages each day, and then derivative data,

⟨CRICHTON⟩ like pages per day, and estimated completion.

Which you can work out from those data . . . Now I bought Excel but it is too powerful for me. I just want to do simeple things. GA

<W.POPINSKI> Earlier you mentioned that you go to the office to work . . .

<W.POPINSKI> I was wondering why you did not work at home. That may please your family. GA

<CRICHTON> I got an office about 14 years ago. Before I had a family. The real reason was that I was working myself to death. This way, I know when I'm through for the day. When I go home.

<CRICHTON> Also it makes me more like a normal person. I get up and go to the office like everybody else.

<CRICHTON> A friend of mine is an artist. Somebody asked her her working hours and she said, 9 to 5. And then she said, it took me a long time to work that out.

<CRICHTON> Anyway, normalcy is nice when what you are doing is so weird. GA

···

<JESSIEBELLE> Dan's next, and that'll have to be the last question . . . hopefully Michael will agree to come back and do this again for us!

<CRICHTON> Yes, we can do it again some time. ga

<[Dan] D.PEREZ1> Steven Spielberg has been criticized for making kid-oriented movies, and I thought of JURASSIC PARK . .

<[Dan] D.PEREZ1> . . as an adult book (which would certainly appeal to kids). So I worry that Spielberg's movie will revolve around the kids and have "cute" sidekick dinosaurs (like the Ewoks). Reassure me, if you can. And thanks for a fun RTC!

<CRICHTON> Reassurance. I took my kid (3) to see the dinos as they were being built, last March or so. They were still in clay. My kid loves dinos but they frightened her. In clay.

<[Dan] D.PEREZ1> All riiight.

<CRICHTON> There is no way I'll let her see this movie. Steven won't do gore, but the basic story is so intense, the dinosaurs are so precise and lifelike, that the fantasy is a bit too real for young children.

<CRICHTON> It's not Hook, if that's what you're thinking.

<CRICHTON> I saw dailies of the scene where the T-rex is crouched over the Land Cruiser trying to get to the kids, and Grant

and Malcolm get out of the second Land Cruiser and try to distract it.

‹CRICHTON› And the rex looks up at them with his huge head, looking somewhere between a lizard and a bird, and follows them with his yellow eyes . . . I think it'll scare the dinopoop out of people. GA

‹JESSIEBELLE› Michael, thank you so much for doing this — it's been a terrific RTC and we do hope you'll do it again!

** ‹JESSIEBELLE› Room is now in the talk mode.

‹[Jack] WRITERS.INK› Great RTC! Thanks for taking the time, Michael. We look forward to your return visit. And thanks Jessiebelle for running this. Ya'll make a good team ‹grin›.

‹[Dan] D.PEREZ1› Thanks much.

‹JESSIEBELLE› Thank you, everyone, for coming! . . .

‹[Dreamer] J.COON2› Thanks, Michael.

‹[Nancy] D.SARTOR› Jessie: Thanks to you, too, for an excellent roundtable and an expert handling thereof.

‹JESSIEBELLE› Thanks, Nancy!

‹JESSIEBELLE› It was great fun . . . both arranging it and running it. :)

‹[Jack] WRITERS.INK› Michael . . . thanks again. Hopefully your fingers and back survived. Being a guest is tough work!

....

‹[Jack] WRITERS.INK› Ha! Michael . . . you may be here forever ‹grin›. Folks you may have to save some of the questions for next time.

‹CRICHTON› You know, I have to be careful about online things. You can spend SO MUCH TIME there and never do any work.

....

‹CRICHTON› Folks, I have the feeling that this could go on for a while. I've got to get to bed. You've been terrific and I hope you will excuse me if I say goodbye for now.

** ‹CRICHTON› has left.

#　　#　　#　　#　　#　　#　　#　　#　　#

This file was downloaded from the Writers' RoundTable on GEnie, the home computing service. To join GEnie or to get more information, call 800-638-9636.

Download complete. Turn off Capture File.

INDEX

Other Books of Interest

Writing Books

Freeing Your Creativity, by Marshall Cook $17.95
Knowing Where to Look: The Ultimate Guide to Research, by Lois Horowitz (paper) $19.95
The 29 Most Common Writing Mistakes & How to Avoid Them, by Judy Delton (paper) $9.95
The Writer's Book of Checklists, by Scott Edelstein $16.95
The Writer's Essential Desk Reference, edited by Glenda Neff $19.95

To order directly from the publisher, include $3.00 postage and handling for 1 book and $1.00 for each additional book. Allow 30 days for delivery.

Writer's Digest Books
1507 Dana Avenue, Cincinnati, Ohio 45207
Credit card orders call TOLL-FREE
1-800-289-0963
Stock is limited on some titles; prices subject to change without notice.

Write to this same address for information on *Writer's Digest* magazine, *Story* magazine, Writer's Digest Book Club, Writer's Digest School, and Writer's Digest Criticism Service.

Young Readers

The Admiral and the Deck Boy: One Boy's Journey with Christopher Columbus, $5.95
Becoming a Mental Math Wizard, $8.95
Breaking the Chains: The Crusade of Dorothea Lynde Dix, $5.95
But Everyone Else Looks so Sure of Themselves: A Guide to Surviving the Teen Years, $7.95
Cadets at War: The True Story of Teenage Heroism at the Battle of New Market, $3.95
Codes & Ciphers: Hundreds of Unusual & Secret Ways to Communicate, $7.95
The Curtain Rises: A History of Theater From Its Origins in Greece and Rome Through the English Restoration, $14.95
The Curtain Rises, Volume II $12.95
Fiddler to the World: The Inspiring Life of Itzhak Perlman, $5.95
The Glory Road: The Story of Josh White, $7.95
Great Unsolved Mysteries of Science, $9.95
The Junior Tennis Handbook: A Complete Guide to Tennis for Juniors, Parents & Coaches, $12.95
The Kids' Almanac of Professional Football, $8.95
Market Guide for Young Artists and Photographers, $12.95
Medical Practices in the Civil War, $6.95
Mosby and His Rangers: Adventures of the Gray Ghost, $6.95
Music in the Civil War, $8.95
Roots for Kids: A Genealogy Guide for Young People, $7.95
Smoke on the Water: A Novel of Jamestown and the Powhatans, $6.95
Spies! Women and the Civil War, $6.95
What Would We Do Without You? A Guide to Volunteer Activities for Kids, $6.95
With Secrets to Keep, $12.95
Woman of Independence: The Life of Abigail Adams, $5.95

For a complete catalog of Betterway Books write to the address below. To order, send a check or money order for the price of the book(s). Include $3.00 postage and handling for 1 book, and $1.00 for each additional book. Allow 30 days for delivery.

Betterway Books
1507 Dana Avenue, Cincinnati, Ohio 45207
Credit card orders call TOLL-FREE
1-800-289-0963
Quantities are limited; prices subject to change without notice.